EMPLOYMENT INTERVI

1. When deciding how to dress for your job ~~interview, you~~ should:
   a. Choose conservative business attire, even if it's casual Friday
   b. Spend a lot of money on a fashionable new outfit
   c. Dress down to keep in step with the new casual corporate age
2. When meeting your interviewer, you should:
   a. Offer to shake his or her hand
   b. Wait for the interviewer to offer her or his hand
   c. Demonstrate your self-confidence with a really strong handshake
3. During the course of your job interview, you should:
   a. Maintain eye contact at all times
   b. Look at your interviewer's nose so it appears like you're looking into the eyes
   c. Act naturally and not worry about eye contact
4. If your interviewer asks an inappropriate question, you should:
   a. Swallow your pride and answer the question
   b. Stand up and stomp out of the room in a huff
   c. None of the above
5. After your job interview you should:
   a. Not write a thank-you note unless it was a luncheon interview and your interviewer paid for your meal
   b. Write a thank-you note that makes you stand out from the crowd
   c. Drop a quick e-mail just to say thanks

Don't leave your future to chance. If even one of these questions leaves you scratching your head, you need SWEATY PALMS to help you ace your next interview, negotiate the best possible salary and benefits package, and land the job of your dreams.

Correct answers: A, B, C, C, A

SWEATY PALMS

THE NEGLECTED ART OF BEING INTERVIEWED

H. ANTHONY MEDLEY

WARNER
BUSINESS
BOOKS™

New York • Boston

Although the writer is an attorney, nothing contained herein should be interpreted as giving legal advice to readers or establishing an attorney-client relationship between the writer and the reader. If the reader has any questions of a legal nature, he or she should consult a private attorney.

Warner Business Books
Warner Books

Time Warner Book Group
1271 Avenue of the Americas, New York, NY 10020
Visit our Web site at www.twbookmark.com.

Sweaty Palms is a registered trademark.

The Warner Business Books logo is a trademark of Warner Books.

Printed in the United States of America

First Warner Books Edition: May 2005
10 9 8 7 6 5 4 3 2 1

Library of Congress Cataloging-in-Publication Data

Medley, H. Anthony.
     Sweaty palms : the neglected art of being interviewed / H. Anthony Medley.—1st Warner Books ed.
          p. cm.
     Includes bibliographical references and index.
     ISBN 0-446-69383-9
  1. Employment interviewing.   I. Title.
     HF5549.5.I6M35 2005
     650.14'4—dc22   2004027774

Cover design by Rachel McClain
Cover photo by Colin Hawkins/Getty Images

For my mother, Connie,
wise, gentle, strong, tender, and loving

Contents

Preface

Which would you buy, a book on how to design a dress by Adolf Hitler or Donna Karan? Or a book on how to play basketball by Michael Jordan or Marilyn Monroe? Well, that's about the decision you must make between buying a book on how to be interviewed by me or by any of the other authors writing books on the interview.

Why? Because while I've conducted thousands of interviews, both selection and screening, most of the other writers of books on the interview don't claim to have conducted as many as one!

Why? Because *Sweaty Palms* is replete with tales of personal experiences I've had in conducting interviews along with stories by many of my readers recounting their experiences in real live interviews, whereas I've not discovered any personal tales in any of the other books. (Maybe because they don't have any personal tales because they've never conducted one?)

When I first wrote *Sweaty Palms* in 1977, it was the first book ever written on the job interview for the interviewee. The reason I wrote it was that at the time one of my activities was a videotape interview service (I invented the videotape interview after getting the idea while attending the Cannes Film Festival in the early 1970s and seeing a display of a new-fangled thing called a "video-tape recorder"), and the students who were being interviewed often asked me about their interview because I wasn't conducting a selection interview. They viewed me as a knowledgeable, impartial advisor, a person of whom they could ask questions without jeopardizing their chances for a job. Because I was an attorney and running businesses—and my videotape interview service was something I did to aid in the recruiting process for both law firms and law students, I didn't have time to counsel them (and had no interest in becoming a full-time advisor) and so looked for a book I could recommend. I was stunned to discover that, although there were many books on the interview aimed at the interviewer, there was nothing for the interviewee.

The result was *Sweaty Palms*. I wrote it so I could recommend it and get on with the other things that occupied my life. It was an instant success and spawned all the imitators you see out there today. Unfortunately, the authors of the other books apparently can't speak from experience when it comes to the interview. Much of their advice, which sounds nice when you don't know what you're talking about, is, in practice, dead wrong.

Take thank-you letters, for example. Virtually everyone writing advises writing one after the interview. For my opinion, see pages 378–386, an opinion that has been validated by research conducted by a candidate writing a master's thesis. Take eye contact, for another example. All those other writers say that it's very important to maintain eye contact. For my opinion, see pages 121–124, another position that has been validated by research. But I didn't need research or interviews to know what is correct, because I am an interviewer and I know how an interviewer feels when a thank-you letter is received or an interviewee stares you down, and I tell it like it is, not like people with no actual experience think it might be, or should be, or sounds right.

Another thing that continues to set *Sweaty Palms* apart from all the other imitators is where they get their information. Almost without exception the people they quote are consultants or people who work in the human resources industry. Well, I'm sure they're all nice people and that they all do a fine job at what they do. But what they *don't do* is hire. So this is really the pot quoting the black kettle to prove water runs downhill. They don't have the experience in conducting selection interviews, so their advice is just as ill informed as the writer's!

As I write this I'm looking at a special advertising supplement that appears every Sunday in major newspapers across the country, devoted to careers. Generally what this supplement publishes about the job interview is naïve, at best. The entire front page today is devoted to the job interview. In total, four different people are quoted giving advice. One is a "career counselor and work coach." Another is a "career counselor." A third is a "presentation consultant." The fourth, and last, is a "career and resumé" consultant. Not one is a person who actually has to conduct selection interviews! How much is their advice worth? This is consistent with every book I've looked at, other than *Sweaty Palms*. The advice they hand out comes from consultants, not people who actually have to conduct selection interviews.

Who am I? First off, I'm an attorney who practiced law for many years, both as a private attorney and as a member of a corporate law department. Second, I'm a businessman who developed a lot of real estate. In both professions I had to hire many people to work for me. I have conducted a plethora of interviews and made innumerable hiring decisions. I've been there. I don't need to ask people to find out what the interview is about. I know. But I did interview some people to get their views, because views vary. The people I interviewed by and large were not consultants or human resources people. No, the people I interviewed were managers and businesspeople and professionals, successful people with whom I had come in contact while practicing law and developing real estate, who had to interview and hire lots of people throughout their careers themselves. They know what they're talking about when they discuss hiring people.

But I've also conducted thousands of screening interviews, too, as a result of my videotape interview service. So I can speak with personal knowledge of both types of interviews, screening and selection. I can tell you, from the horse's mouth, how interviewers really react, not what might sound good but isn't in real life.

All the imitators out there proudly proclaim that they give you great answers to tough questions, or something like that. Well, I don't. They obviously assume you are an idiot and too stupid to answer a question by yourself. And here's where we're at the basis of the difference. The interview is about you. Who are they to tell you how to answer a question about you? What *Sweaty Palms* will do is prepare you to enter the interview room with the confidence that you can answer any question thrown at you, from your own experience in your own words. Unlike the other authors who insult your intelligence, I think you're smart enough to do that—or you will be after you've read *Sweaty Palms*.

Future editions of this book will be a joint venture with you, the reader. If you have had an experience in an interview that hasn't been covered in these pages, or if you've had an experience that would serve as a good example for other interviewees, or if something bothers you that hasn't been covered here, write a letter about it to H. Anthony Medley, P.O. Box 9723, Marina del Rey, California, 90295. If your letter is quoted in a future edition of this book, you'll receive a free copy of that edition.

SWEATY PALMS

It wasn't [the Beatles'] music that sold them to me; it was their charm.

—GEORGE MARTIN, producer of the Beatles' first record

1

The Interview

A candidate I once interviewed for a secretarial position could type 90 words per minute and take shorthand at 120 words per minute. She was presentable and had good references. But in addition to showing up ten minutes late, she called me "Mr. Melody" throughout the interview. The two main things I remembered about her were that she had kept me waiting and that she had constantly mispronounced my name. I finally offered the position to someone whose typing and shorthand skills were not nearly as good.

Connie Brown Glaser and Barbara Steinberg Smalley, in their book *More Power to You*, tell the story of a lady who always wanted to be a teacher. When she graduated, she went to a nearby school for an interview. She noticed she had a small run in her stocking but didn't think it important enough to change. But when she arrived at the interview, the run had become enormous, and she spent much of the time positioning herself to hide it. She didn't get the job, and the principal explained to one of her friends, "If a person doesn't take the time to present her best image at an interview, what kind of teacher is she going to be?"

More often than not, it is the small things that occur in an interview that spell the difference between getting an offer and being rejected. As you will learn as you read on, the basic objective of a candidate in an interview is to spark a positive feeling in the interviewer—something Aristotle called *pathos*. It's a purely subjective feeling, so your close attention to little things is essential.

The Basics

Be certain of the time and place of the interview and the name of the interviewer. Sometimes candidates are so excited to get an interview that they neglect to ask for this essential information. Write it down and keep it with you until after the interview. If no one tells you your interviewer's name, ask. Sometimes the situation precludes finding out, but you're ahead of the game if you know it going in.

Make certain you are clean and appropriately dressed and coiffed. I have an entire chapter on dress, but if you have spots on your clothes or food on your teeth, you're not going to make a good impression.

Arrive early for the interview. If you plan on arriving at least fifteen minutes before the appointed time, you will have a cushion against unforeseen delays, such as a traffic tie-up or an elevator breakdown or an inability to find the right building or office, any of which could cause you to be late if you depended on split-second timing. Being early can also give the interviewer a good initial impression of your reliability and interest.

Bring a pen and notebook with you. The notebook should fit in a pocket or purse so that you don't walk into the interview room with it in hand. Its purpose is twofold. First, the interviewer may give you some information to write down. If you're prepared with your own writing material, you won't have to interrupt the interview to hunt down paper and pen. Don't, however, make notes during the interview unless the interviewer asks you to write something down.

Second, immediately after the interview you should make notes on what occurred during the interview and what your reactions were to the interviewer. This information can be very important in future interviews so that your replies remain consistent. Further, if you have many different interviews with different companies or different people in the same company, your notes will help your recall of each and aid in making a choice in jobs, should that become necessary.

Remember the interviewer's name. There is possibly no sweeter sound to the human ear than the sound of one's own name. If you don't learn the interviewer's name prior to the interview, concentrate on it when you are introduced and remember it. For some people this is very difficult. They are concentrating on themselves so much and thinking about how nervous they are that they forget the name or don't pay attention when they hear it for the first time.

The best thing to do is to repeat the name immediately after the introduction by saying something on the order of, "How do you do, Mr. Smith." Then repeat the name a couple of times during the first part of the interview. This repetition will help you remember the name. It will also have a pleasing effect on the interviewer.

When Katharine Hepburn was a young actress in the late 1930s, she was invited to have tea with President Franklin Roosevelt. They had never met, but during the conversation he asked about her mother and some of her friends, even one of her friend's daughter's husband. Kate asked him how he could remember all those names. He replied: "That's my job, and I concentrate on it. I meet someone and I say, 'You are Mr. Jones. That is your wife, Mrs. Jones.' I look at them. I absorb them. I remember them. And next time I say, 'Why, hello,

Mr. Jones. How are you? And Mrs. Jones?' It makes a good impression."

Reader Joseph D. Lee of El Cerrito, California, writes about the importance of properly pronouncing an interviewer's name:

I recently had an interview for admission to a particular academic program; roughly one in three applicants met, as I did, with success. My interviewer had a Spanish surname, and I have the good fortune to have learned to speak Spanish well. I also had the good fortune to have heard the interviewer speak previously, so that I was certain that he was bilingual.

When I introduced myself to him, I pronounced his name as it would be pronounced in Spanish, rather than English (there is quite a difference!). The interviewer's response was notably positive. "You pronounce my name like you speak Spanish," he said, and immediately we were off to a friendly discussion of how I learned Spanish, how I hoped to be able to use it in the program, and the like. My pronunciation of his name not only opened the conversation on a positive note, it conveyed a sense of respect for another's language and culture. Thus I believe that this beginning was central to the success of my interview.

A similar point should be made about difficult names: Those who possess them are frequently either proud of them or mortified by them. In either case, pronouncing them correctly can only be a plus. And, of course, there are many ways to ascertain the correct pronunciation of an interviewer's name: Call his or her receptionist or secretary anonymously; check with the job placement director, if the interview has been arranged by another; or ask someone who speaks Greek, Spanish, or whatever.

One caveat: Do not call the interviewer by his or her first name unless you are invited to do so (which is unlikely). Calling people by their first names without being asked to do so is a familiarity that offends a great many people.

In one of Christ's parables he compares the guest at a wedding feast who took a seat near the head of the table and was embarrassed by being asked to move farther down while the guest who sat at the lowest place was honored by being asked to move up. You have nothing to lose by addressing your interviewer formally as "Mr." (or Ms., Miss, or Mrs.), and nothing to gain by calling your interviewer "Charlie" or "Shirley." If your interviewer is a woman, notice whether she's wearing a wedding band. If not, I recommend calling her "Ms." If she's sympathetic to the feminist ideology, it could be a plus for you, whereas calling her "Miss" may offend her. On the other hand, if she is not supportive of feminist beliefs, calling her "Ms." should not offend her as much as calling her "Miss" could offend someone who *is* supportive.

Don't offer to shake hands unless the interviewer offers a hand first. I was raised by my mother to obey the old rule of polite society that a gentleman does not offer his hand to a lady unless she offers her hand first. But as an interviewer I always offer to shake hands whether the interviewee is male or female. I am initially trying to put the interviewee at ease, and a handshake is a good way to break down some barriers. But interviewers differ, and some will not offer to shake hands.

A male interviewee should not offer to shake hands if his interviewer does not first offer. For a woman this is not so crucial. You may find a chivalrous interviewer who believes it is offensive for a man to offer his hand to a woman but would not be offended if a female interviewee initiated the handshake. The safe rule, in any event, is not to offer your hand unless the interviewer makes the first move.

If you do shake hands, make it a firm grip. A weak handshake can be a real turnoff. But don't go overboard and give your Superman grip. If you take the interviewer to the floor with your hearty handshake, you won't be remembered with good feelings.

Don't chew gum. Gum chewing can communicate a distinctly negative impression. It may not offend some interviewers, but it is better not to take the risk.

Wait for your interviewer to sit down or to invite you to sit down before seating yourself.

Most of these suggestions are items of common courtesy, but they are often overlooked in the context of an interview, when you are nervous and thinking about yourself.

It is a keystone of any effective interview for you to come across as an honest person. If the interviewer forms the impression that you are basically saying, "Here I am with all my warts," it should be positive for you. You don't want to expound on those warts, but you want to leave the impression that you accept yourself for what you are and that you want the interviewer to know you as the person you are.

That's exactly the *impression* you want to leave. You must attune yourself to the interviewer early, and this requires strict attention to him and his reaction to you. (Let's assume, for the balance of this chapter, that the interviewer is male.) You will have to make some astute judgments in the early moments of the interview, so you must concern yourself with the interviewer's problems, prejudices, desires, and feelings. If the interviewer is a dynamic, take-charge sort who wants to regale you with stories, go along with it. If he is somewhat shy and insecure, help him out. If he exhibits any prejudices that you are able to perceive, don't run afoul of them. You must try to categorize the interviewer early and then guide the interview along lines that help him arrive at the conclusion you wish.

Being interviewed and being interviewed well are two entirely different matters.

You Must Sell Yourself

As an interviewee you are primarily a seller. The product you are selling is yourself, and the assets of the product are your experience, skills, and personality. You communicate your experience and skills in your resumé, but your personality comes across in the interview.

You must recognize that you are in a selling situation and that it is your goal to arouse the interest of the interviewer in you. If you wait expectantly for questions and dutifully answer them, you have done nothing to distinguish yourself from the hundreds of others whom the interviewer will encounter.

"There is one sure-fire way of arousing their interest," says Paul Ivey, in his classic *Successful Salesmanship:* "Find out what they are already interested in and then talk about it. If you talk about what they are interested in, they will later on be willing to consider what you are interested in."

Techniques for Selling Yourself

Since a large part of the interview is selling yourself to the inter-viewer, it's well to know the techniques of selling and persuasion.

PERSUASION

Aristotle broke down a persuasive speech into three elements: ethos, pathos, and logos.

Ethos is persuasion achieved by establishing the credibility of the speaker. If your interviewer doesn't believe in you, has no confidence that you are honest and reliable, it doesn't matter what you say; you won't be persuasive.

Pathos is persuasion by the use of emotions. The neo-

Aristotelian rhetorician Chaim Perelman put it best: "To adapt an audience is, above all, to choose as premises of argumentation theses the audience already holds." Or, to put it in layman's terms, if you can say something with which your interviewer agrees, you will be on the road to creating pathos, or a positive emotion. This is where your preparation comes to the fore. If you've done enough research to know that your interviewer was a ballerina, or played minor league baseball, or whatever, you can use pathos by mentioning something positive about the ballet or baseball early on in your interview. While you must be certain to be true to yourself, and not sound fawning or like a sycophant, if you can express some genuine sentiment about something you know your interviewer has a positive feeling about, you will be using pathos to good effect. When I said earlier that your goal in the interview is to create a positive "feeling" in your interviewer, I'm talking about pathos, or the creation of a positive emotion in your interviewer. The desired motivation of the interviewee is to create pathos. Even if you're credible—if you have established ethos—you won't be persuasive unless you inspire a "feeling" or emotion in your interviewer.

I must mention here that you should not make a comment implying that you like something like ballet if you don't know anything about it. If your interviewer takes the bait and starts a conversation about it, he will quickly learn that your statement was dishonest and you will be worse off. Don't ever do anything dishonest or deceptive to try to gain an edge, because it can come back to bite you in the end. Don't make the comment about ballet or baseball unless you share your interviewer's passion, or can at least carry on a knowledgeable conversation about the subject. If you're ignorant about their passion, you should keep quiet about it; if the subject did come up, the most you should do is express an interest in learning more about it. This could be an opening to ask your interviewer about it. If you get the interviewer talking about something in which he's passionate, it can't hurt. And by making an innocent expression of interest you haven't done anything deceptive or dishonest.

Finally, *logos* relates to the logic of what you say ("thought manifested in speech," according to Aristotle). In terms of the interview, this is probably the least important of the three in achieving persuasiveness. Even if you're logical, if you haven't established ethos (credibility) or pathos (emotion), your logic alone won't win the day.

While ethos and logos are important, if you have ethos and logos without pathos, you're in a weak situation. Conversely, pathos without ethos and logos won't be enough by itself. You need all three, but of the three, pathos is the most important.

SALESMANSHIP

The basic goal of an interview for selection is to determine personality traits. As will be explained later, there are two basic types of interviews. The selection interview is the one by the person who can make a hire, no-hire decision. But there is often a screening interview, which determines if you should be interviewed by the selection interviewer. In *Successful Salesmanship* Paul Ivey breaks the personality of a good salesman into four categories. The first is enthusiasm, which is so important that all of chapter 4 is devoted to it. The other three are sincerity, tact, and courtesy.

Sincerity
Sincerity goes hand in hand with enthusiasm. If you generate a phony enthusiasm for something, such as a job about which you know nothing, two judgments may be made, both negative.

First, the interviewer may conclude that you're so hard up for a job that you'll take anything, and he may reject you on that basis. Or he may conclude that your enthusiasm is insincere, which indicates dishonesty. Dishonesty, whether it derives from lying or insincerity, can be grounds for immediate termination of consideration. For this reason you should reserve your enthusiasm for something in which you are sincerely interested.

Tact

Ivey's third facet of personality is tact. Many good interviewers will bring up a controversial subject or interject stress into an interview by saying something with which they know you'll disagree. How you handle this situation is a main test of the interview.

To disagree tactfully, you must first indicate understanding of, and respect for, your interviewer's position, then you can go on to disagree. For example, you might say, "Yes, I see what you mean, but . . . ," or "That's a good point. On the other hand . . ." If the communication of understanding and respect does not precede the disagreement, your answer will not have been tactful.

Courtesy

The fourth aspect in Ivey's analysis of the personality traits required of a good seller is courtesy. A lack of courtesy will probably be disastrous to the interview. You can be discourteous to the interviewer in many ways: in the way you dress, in the way you speak, in the way you ask questions, in the way you stand and sit, in the way you shake hands. If you arrive late for an interview dressed in a slovenly or unkempt manner, you are showing a lack of courtesy. If you slouch or are inattentive, your lack of courtesy will be noted. The use of profanity or telling of obscene jokes might also be received as a lack of courtesy.

Courtesy is consideration of the feelings of others. Unfortunately, society today seems to be moving in the direction where a lack of courtesy is the norm. "Doing your own thing" implies a disregard of one's obligations to others. If you are a truly courteous person, you will think of how your actions will affect others before you act. Displaying a lack of this consideration will not result in "admiration" for your "independence." Rather, it may result in your leaving the impression of being a boor and could terminate any chance you might have had for further consideration.

In addition to Ivey's four points, I would add a few tips of my own, all of which come under the general heading of keeping the interviewer's attention.

Keeping the Interviewer's Attention

Boredom is invariably an element of interviewing. If you add to the boredom, you're putting nails in your coffin. Shortly after John F. Kennedy was elected president, he decided upon a farm leader to be his secretary of agriculture and invited the candidate to his Georgetown apartment for an initial interview. "It was so boring," he said later, "and the living room was so warm, that I actually fell asleep." The candidate was quickly rejected.

An interviewer will ask the same questions of people with similar interests and backgrounds and receive the same answers. One of the better techniques of good interviewing is to break that boredom and routine by getting interviewers to talk about something that interests *them*.

If you talk intelligently about something in which the interviewer is concerned, he will be more interested in you. Interviewers are like everyone else: They are selfish, and their own concerns are paramount in their minds. If you show a genuine interest in these concerns and can discuss them intelligently, the interest in you will be sparked. You need to be careful, though. If you are unable to communicate your interest with sincerity, the likely consequence will be a loss of confidence in you, and you'll be worse off than when you started.

Pay strict attention to how you are being received by the interviewer. If you determine that interest is lagging, there are a few tricks you can use to bring it back around. First, you can vary the tone of your voice (for example, by lowering it or making it louder). Television advertisers often do this by making commercials louder than the show they sponsor. Theoretically, this change in tone beckons and makes viewers more attentive to something they may have little desire to hear.

You can also vary the tempo at which you speak (by speeding it up or slowing it down). Essentially, any change that you make from the manner in which you had been speaking will act as a lure to bring the interviewer's attention back from its wandering. You must capture and retain the interviewer's interest, or the remainder of the interview will be a mere formality and you'll probably be rejected.

What you do with that attention once you capture it will determine whether your interview is going to be successful. If, for example, you convince the interviewer that you don't have the experience for the job or the skills required or that your personality is abrasive or bland, you're no better off than you were before you walked in the door.

Once you have captured his attention, you must continue selling yourself and create the desire in the interviewer to have you as an employee.

Paul Ivey says:

> Desire . . . rests on conviction; and the former cannot be
> created without the latter. . . . The intelligent salesman
> adjusts his sales talk to the customer's system of beliefs;
> his ideas enter the customer's mind unpercepted because
> they are so similar to the customer's own ideas. There is
> no customer-resistance, but rather customer-assistance.
> There is agreement instead of disagreement.

Your preparation and perception thus become important. If
you have researched the interview (in ways discussed in the
next chapter), you know enough to make some initial judgments as to what kind of person you will be encountering. If
you know his background, you may be able to make some
intelligent guesses as to his interests and beliefs. But before
you act on these assumptions, you must make some evaluations
during the initial part of the interview. And if you're coming
into the interview with no advance preparation, these early
evaluations will be all that you have to go on.

If you can get the interviewer to reveal something personal
early in the interview, you can reinforce or verify some of your
assumptions before you act on them. The first part of the
interview is often a jousting period in which you feel each
other out. What you must realize is that the interviewer probably assumes that you are the typical interviewee who will
meekly sit and wait for him to conduct the interview. Therefore, he will not be prepared for subtle probes.

You must take your cue from the interviewer. If he starts
boldly by asking questions and gives you no signal that personal
queries will be entertained, you have to wait until the time is
propitious. On the other hand, if he is relaxed, self-confident,
and interested, you don't have to worry too much. And if you

can get him to talk about himself with interest, you will have several advantages. First, this will give you information you can use as the interview progresses. Second, everyone likes to talk about themselves, and if you're interested and communicate that interest, the positive feelings you're trying to create will be enhanced. Third, you'll have a better chance to find areas of common interest to pursue and areas of possible conflict to avoid.

If you get the chance, and he seems to invite it, ask a few personal questions. Is he married? Does he have children? Play tennis or golf? Listen to Bach, oldies, Eminem, or Celine Dion? Ever been to Katmandu? If you can discover something in common, you will be way ahead of the game.

Some interviewers can react negatively to such probing, so you have to do it in a natural, conversational way. But just think. How would you feel if the highlight of your life was when you ice-skated on the Bering Strait and suddenly you're interviewing someone who did the same thing? Would you be inclined to offer her a job? Is grass green?

If you are unable to penetrate the shield, you can still make some educated guesses about the interviewer's orientation and proceed on that basis. For example, if you submitted your resumé in advance and were then called in for an interview, you can safely assume that the interviewer has already determined that you are qualified for the position, based upon the data you provided. You may then verify and amplify the facts on your resumé by detailing specific experience and skills.

You can also assume that the interviewer knows what he wants out of the position, and you may ask how he views the position and what tasks it entails. After discussing this you can describe your experience and skills to exact specifications.

It's important that you get some kind of job specification from the interviewer early in the interview so that you can key what you can accomplish to what he wants accomplished. If you get into a detailed discussion of your skills and experience before you've had a chance to probe what he's looking for, you're adrift on a sea of unknowns.

Some interviewers will tell you something about the job before they start questioning you, but most won't. Most interviewers are inwardly oriented, just as are most interviewees, and they may not really focus on the interviewee. They may be thinking instead about asking the right questions in the interview. Therefore, if you can easily segue into questioning him about the position early on, you may discover some valuable keys that you can use to guide the rest of the interview and create the realization that you are the right person to fill the position.

When the Interviewer Identifies with You

If you can strike a responsive chord in the interviewer by having him conclude that the two of you think alike, you will have gone a long way toward creating the feeling in him that can result in an offer, as the following incident illustrates.

Robert A. Lovett was described by David Halberstam in *The Best and the Brightest* as "the symbolic expert, representative of the best of the breed . . . a man of impeccable credentials, indeed he passed on other people's credentials, deciding who was safe and sound, who was ready for advancement and who was not." Charles B. "Tex" Thornton was the founder, chairman of the board, and chief executive officer of Litton Industries, the pioneer conglomerate, a man of immense wealth and power and at one time the nominal chief of staff of the captains of industry in the United States.

One day in 1941 these titans met for the first time. Lovett was then assistant secretary of war and Thornton was a twenty-seven-year-old, $4,600-a-year statistician for the U.S. Housing

Authority in Washington. Young Thornton had written a report that had interested Lovett, and Lovett wanted to meet him. Thornton had telephoned for an appointment, then found himself waiting in Lovett's outer office long after the appointed time. He was finally about to leave when Lovett's secretary persuaded him to wait a few minutes longer, an act that Thornton later said changed the whole course of his life.

Lovett did arrive, and he and Thornton talked. The more the youthful Thornton spoke, the more Lovett liked him. Lovett was a banker who had a love affair with figures, and Thornton talked of numbers as if they were a language of their own. This impressed Lovett immensely. Here was a man in his own mold! Not only that, but Thornton was not intimidated by Lovett's authority. Lovett was looking for such a person.

Thornton was prepared. He spoke the technical language, and he revealed that he knew what he was talking about. He was respectful of the man and the office of Lovett but was not intimidated by them. He communicated his respect in himself so that he was not obeisant, meeting Lovett as an intellectual equal. Thornton ignited a feeling in Lovett, and Lovett hired him. From that point, Thornton was associating with the powers that ran the World War II logistical effort. He built a reputation that enabled him to negotiate a lucrative contract for himself and several colleagues with Hughes Aircraft after the war and finally left Hughes to found Litton and his own fortune. He traces his success to this interview with Lovett. Had he not impressed Lovett sufficiently, the world may never have heard of Tex Thornton.

Lovett later said that Thornton reminded him of himself in the way he spoke about figures. Thornton came across in the interview as a man of unusual intellectual capacity, but having Lovett identify so personally with Thornton was the essential element in the entire interview.

If you can make an interviewer see another him in you, you will have won him over.

Lovett saw that Thornton thought as he did and identified with him. Without question Lovett made a conclusion based upon the "halo effect" of this feeling. (The halo effect is discussed in chapter 15.) Thornton continued to perform, but this one impression that he created during the interview got him his chance.

Think about the Interviewer

We all think about ourselves, and the interviewer is no exception. Maybe he doesn't have the same insecurities that you have—you may be worrying about how you look, whether your palms are sweaty, whether your voice will crack—but he's thinking about himself all the same. He might be worried about his job or making the plane that night. Or the problem may be an ill child, an unfaithful spouse, or an argument with the boss. There may be a million things on the interviewer's mind other than you.

Whatever his thoughts, there's a good possibility that he's not thinking what you think he's thinking. He's not taking you apart piece by piece in his mind, coolly evaluating your every movement. But there you are worrying about yourself and your sweaty palms, and there he is thinking about something else. In fact, the interviewer may indeed have the same insecurities that you have. He may not have conducted many interviews and be worried that he's going to make a fool of himself. He may even be worried that *his* palms are sweaty. Or, worse, if he is really inexperienced, he may feel that he won't be able to think of anything to say and there will be gaps of silence.

So don't think about yourself so much. If, instead, you go

into the interview thinking about the interviewer, you will relieve yourself of the tremendous tension that most interviewees feel about an interview. You will feel that you have some control of the situation and a plan of attack.

Preparation of the Interviewer

Don't delude yourself into thinking that your interviewer is totally and completely prepared for this interview and knows exactly what he wants and how to get it. Far from it. You have to realize how people approach things and, especially, how people approach meetings. Generally, they don't prepare, and they hope to get out of them as quickly and easily as possible. This was true in 1978 when *Sweaty Palms* first came out, and it's true today.

You don't believe me? Listen to what William Goldman, Academy Award–winning screenwriter, has to say in his autobiography, *Adventures in the Screen Trade* (Warner Books, 1983):

> You have no idea how often I've had creative meetings about a script, only to realize half an hour in that the producer or executive hasn't read my script at all. . . . I had one meeting with the late Steve McQueen, involving a Western I'd written that, he told me over the phone, he liked a lot and could we meet?
>
> We met, and the then director of the project, Don Siegel, was also present. And this is about how it went:
>
> McQueen: I want a campfire scene where the two guys get drunk and talk about the old days.
> Siegel: He's got that—I think it's fine.
> McQueen: I don't mean that kind of campfire scene, I mean a *campfire* scene.

We met like that for several hours and I still don't know why. But it was madness. Here I was, closeted with these two men whose work I've admired for years, and McQueen kept going on and on about things that he wanted in the script that were already in the script, and Siegel tried to do his best. I just sat there, nodded, took notes, prayed for it all to end.

Steve McQueen had a meeting with two giants of the movie industry, Don Siegel and William Goldman, and he wasn't just partially prepared, he was totally unprepared. You think your interviewer is going to spend a lot of time preparing for you? Maybe, but the odds are, he won't.

Who Controls the Interview?

At the outset, interviewers can be expected to control the *flow* of the interview (although, as we will shortly see, you can take control of that, too). Some may begin by asking general questions to ease your nervousness and will then move on to more specific questions about areas in which they are interested that are not covered on your resumé. But, although the interviewer initially controls the flow of the interview, the interviewee controls the *content*. After all, an interview generally consists of an interviewer asking questions and you answering them. What you do with the questions is up to you. Thus you should go into the interview knowing the points you want to cover—for example, your achievements.

If you run into a situation where the interviewer is insecure and unsure of himself, try to make the interview go as smoothly as possible for him. If you do and you control the interview to the extent that there are no gaps and you say what you want to say, you will probably have conducted a very good interview.

As a law student I once entered an interview room at the end of a warm spring day, and the interviewer was standing with his back to me staring out the window. It was obvious that he was bored to tears. He had had twenty-five interviews with students who were carbon copies of one another, and he had a few more to go with the same monotonous questions and answers.

I had just heard some news on the radio, so before he could start his routine of questions, I asked, "Did you hear that Khrushchev was overthrown?"

His eyes lit up, and we spent several minutes talking about the Soviet Union, which we had both visited. Suddenly, his routine was broken, and right off the bat we had something in common. I was invited to see his firm, and although I didn't take a job with them, the interview was a success because I thought about breaking his boredom rather than worrying about whether my pants were pressed.

There is an ebb and flow in any conversation. The wise interviewee will take advantage of knowing this. During the interview you should be sensitive to the direction the interviewer is taking. Mao Tse-tung was one of the great military commanders. He coined four slogans, based upon the writings of Sun Tzu, and you would do well to remember them and act upon them in your interview:

1. When the enemy advances, we retreat!
2. When the enemy halts, we harass!
3. When the enemy seeks to avoid battle, we attack!
4. When the enemy retreats, we pursue!

These are rules that, if followed, allow you to take control of the interview without the interviewer's knowledge! In 1963

UCLA's basketball team took control of the world of collegiate basketball and didn't let go for twelve years, during which time it won ten NCAA championships. It won its first two national championships by employing a full-court zone press the entire game. For those of you who aren't familiar with basketball, this means that UCLA guarded their opponents over the entire court rather than just under their defensive basket, for the whole game.

Why? Most people thought it was because they were short and quick and they wanted to pressure the offense and cause turnovers. That's what it looked like. That's what the sportswriters and sportscasters thought. That's what the fans thought. But that wasn't what it was all about.

Pete Newell was a coach for the University of California in the late 1950s. He won one NCAA championship and was in the finals of another with talent that was laughable. Only one of his players, Darrell Imhoff, was good enough to play in the NBA. But Newell's teams won. Newell, probably the most important thinker ever to coach basketball, said, "The team that controls the tempo controls the game." So he slowed the tempo down, let his untalented players throw the ball around until they had the perfect shot, taught them to play exceptional defense, and they won and won and won.

John Wooden was UCLA's coach, and Jerry Norman was his assistant. They knew that their team was short, nobody taller than six-five, but very fast. They were also all very good shooters. And they could run. They wanted a fast-tempo game. Against Stanford in a play-off game in the spring of 1963 they had employed a full-court man-to-man defense that slowed down the game considerably. Norman came up with the idea of throwing a full-court *zone* defense to see if that would speed up the tempo.

Sure enough, the zone defense, which placed four men in

their offensive half of the court and only one man under their defensive basket, generally caused one of two things: A turnover would gave UCLA the ball in their offensive half of the court, or the opponents would break the zone and have an unbalanced two-on-one or three-on-one fast break, out of which they'd take a quick shot. It didn't matter much if they made it or not, because what UCLA wanted was a quick shot so they could play an up-tempo game. The opposition didn't figure this out for several years. In the meantime, UCLA won two consecutive national championships (with season records of 30–0 and 28–2) with a short, quick team that controlled the tempo.

That's what you want to do in the interview: control the tempo. If you control the tempo, you'll control the interview. Controlling the interview, however, doesn't mean that you do most of the talking. What it does mean is that you control the ebb and flow of the interview. If the interviewer wants to regale you with stories, let him (when the enemy advances, we retreat). If he pauses, seemingly out of stories, take charge of the conversation by asking a question (when the enemy halts, we harass). If the interviewer is very quiet, seemingly at a loss for words, take over and talk about why you would be good for the job (when the enemy retreats, we pursue). Different interviewers have different styles, and you must be in tune with what's going on. The point is that you allow the interviewer to proceed as he wants, but you are in control of the tempo. Even though he's talking, if you're aware of the tempo, you're still in control.

A corporate executive friend of mine describes how he took control of an interview, despite contrary advice:

I was recruited by a longtime business acquaintance, who had been newly appointed as the president of the company, to interview with the founder. The president was brought in by venture capitalists to put a professional management team in place and take the company public. Since the founder was the majority stockholder, his word was final.

The president advised me to focus on the technical and military aspects of my experience because that's what the founder looked for in the people he had hired in the past. That was troubling to me because they are my weakest areas.

As I was waiting, I decided to disregard the advice and put my best foot forward. If I tried to play to what he wanted to hear, I figured I'd run the risk of appearing weak, or, worse, if I pulled it off and got hired, I wouldn't live up to the founder's expectations.

To counter what I thought was coming and would expose my weaknesses, I decided to launch a preemptive strike in the interview. We started out with some chitchat, and I moved quicker than he did to getting to the interview. I told him I'd done some research on his company online and found it very confusing to define exactly what their business was. I took a stab, and he admitted he saw how one could be confused. He then explained the business, and I then summarized in very simple terms. I then took the discussion to strategy development and market positioning, my areas of strength.

In the course of the discussion, I mentioned the limitation of my technical and military experience but demonstrated how the level of understanding in these areas was enough to tackle the strategic issues without getting bogged down in detail.

In a nutshell I steered the interview away from what I did in the past to what I could do in the future. This strategy probably wouldn't work where there's a rigid set of requirements or a more formal interview process, but for a senior level position in an entrepreneurial setting, it did the trick.

This example illustrates many of the procedures you will learn in *Sweaty Palms*. My friend listened to the advice he was getting and analyzed it, but realized it was not the best way for him, personally, to approach the interview. He realized that he had to control the content of the interview from the get-go.

Since he had to do this before the founder started asking questions, he was the one to start the formal part of the interview, without being discourteous. In this way he steered the content of what he was saying and what the founder was learning away from his practical experience in what the company did to what he could do for the company in the future.

And how did he do this? By challenging the founder to explain exactly what it was that the company did and how it was set up. This required the founder to do a lot of the talking and allowed the candidate to ask questions and to tailor what he said, how he sold himself, to what the founder was telling him. This was nothing short of brilliant.

Checklist

- Write down the time and place of the interview and the name of the interviewer.
- Arrive early for the interview.
- Bring a pen and notebook with you so that you can (1) jot down information during the interview if you are asked to

do so and (2) write a synopsis of the interview immediately afterward.

- Remember the interviewer's name.
- Don't offer to shake hands unless the interviewer offers a hand first.
- Don't chew gum.
- Wait for the interviewer to sit down or to invite you to seat yourself before you sit down.
- Present yourself as an honest person; do not try to hide anything.
- Remember that you're selling yourself.
- Remember to combat the interviewer's boredom.
- Be outwardly oriented.
- Get the interviewer to talk about himself early in the interview.
- Remember that your goal is to strike a good feeling in him about you.
- The interviewer will initially control the flow of the interview.
- You must control the content of the interview.
- Recognize the insecurities of the interviewer.
- If you go into the interview thinking about the interviewer, rather than yourself, you will relieve yourself of the tremendous tension that most interviewees feel about an interview.
- Keep the interviewer interested:
  1. Talk intelligently about something in which he is interested.
  2. You can vary the tone of your voice (for example, by lowering it or making it louder).
  3. You can vary the tempo at which you speak (by speeding it up or slowing it down).

■ It's important that you get some kind of job specification from the interviewer early in the interview so that you can key what you can accomplish to what he wants accomplished.

■ If you can strike a responsive chord in the interviewer by having him conclude that the two of you think alike, you will have gone a long way toward creating the feeling in him that can result in an offer.

■ If you can make an interviewer see another him in you, you will have won him over.

■ If you control the tempo, you'll control the interview.

2

Preparation

A Broadway show consists of two and a half hours of entertainment, but it is the culmination of endless months of rehearsal and hard work. A ballerina started taking lessons at the age of six to accomplish that pirouette that seems so effortless when she's twenty-one. The basketball player started shooting baskets when he was nine to perfect that jump shot he nets with seeming ease when he's twenty-five.

If we want to do something well, we spend a disproportionate amount of time preparing for it compared with the time it takes to perform the actual deed. Being interviewed should be no different. But the typical interviewee will spend hours and hours to get an interview, then figure that the interview will take care of itself. Beyond dressing a little more carefully than usual, the interviewee won't spend any further time or effort preparing for it.

The reason interviewees act this way is based upon the misperception that the interviewer will know exactly what she wants to get out of that interview (for this chapter let's assume the interviewer is a woman) and will ask the questions she needs to in order to arrive at the answers she seeks. Thus the interviewer thinks, "What can I do to prepare? I don't know what she is looking for. I'll just go to the interview and answer her questions."

Unfortunately, the vast majority of interviewees don't realize that it is up to them to control the content of the interview. Remember that you are the seller and the product you are selling is yourself. You should not leave it up to the interviewer to probe wildly for areas of concern. If you are savvy, you'll gently lead the interviewer to your strengths. The primary element in controlling the interview is to be prepared, and the most important part of preparing is getting to know yourself.

Other books that have come along after *Sweaty Palms* pioneered the field of commentary on how to be interviewed concentrate on telling you how to answer specific questions. In my initial writing of *Sweaty Palms* I rejected this idea as being not helpful. What I wanted to accomplish in *Sweaty Palms* was to prepare you so that you could answer any question on your own.

Who am I, or who is anyone, to tell you how to answer a question? That's condescension at its worst. It's the writer telling you that you are too stupid and/or unworthy to be able to answer a question yourself, so you have to go into the interview with canned answers. What could be more absurd? What could be more insulting?

Sweaty Palms recognizes that there's more to preparing for an interview than just going down a list of questions and preparing answers for them. What I want to accomplish in *Sweaty Palms* is to help you get to know yourself so well that you go into the interview confident that you can answer any question thrown at you and that you can handle any interview regardless of its content.

In order to do this, however, we must delve into psychology, however daunting that may seem. I hope that when you finish this chapter, you will have a much better understanding of yourself and your motivations. This is going to be a trip, so, as Bette Davis said in *All About Eve*, "Buckle up your seat belts. It's going to be a bumpy ride!"

Psychologist Abraham Maslow listed four basic needs whose nonfulfillment leads to illness. These are:

1. Physiological needs (food, water, oxygen)
2. Safety (shelter, security, protection, freedom from fear)
3. Belongingness and love (companionship, affiliation, intimacy)
4. Self-esteem and esteem from others (recognition, appreciation, status)

Think about these. Deprivation of any can lead to calamity. If you are deprived of your physiological needs, you will die. If you are deprived of your safety needs, you will be bereft. If you are deprived of belongingness and love, you will be lonely and apart. If you are deprived of your self-esteem and the esteem of others, you will not value your self-worth and will be depressed and lack confidence in anything you try to do.

Preparing for an interview requires that you take care of yourself. Taking care of yourself requires that you take care of these four basic needs, so that your psychological state is serene.

If you do take care of these needs, and I'm not about to tell you how to do that, you're ready for the important part of preparing for the interview: coming to grips with who you are. Jim McMartin, in his textbook *Personality Psychology*, says, "Growth motivation, also called the *need for self-actualization*, refers to a person's desire to do those activities that he or she is individually suited for: 'What a man *can* be, he *must* be. He must be true to his own nature.'" McMartin says that "for one person, self-actualization may take the form of being the best father he can be to his children; to another person, self-actualization means providing the best possible service to those who are sick; to a third person it means creating the best

product she can, whether it is in art, architecture, or anima-
tion." Maslow notes that individual differences are at their
maximum when it comes to the specific ways we express our
need for self-actualization.

Maslow says there are eight characteristics of self-actualization. I'm only going to deal here with the two that affect your
preparation for the interview:

1. Paying respectful attention to our inner selves to determine whether or not we really like something rather
   than responding automatically in terms of how we think
   we should respond
2. Being honest rather than not.

Boy, are these important! Put them in terms of the interview.
So many interviewees think that they have to go into the interview and answer the question the way that they think the interviewer wants it answered. Nothing could be further from the
truth. There's no way for you to know how an interviewer
"wants" a question to be answered. Let me give you a specific
example.

One question that is often asked is whether or not you have
any student loans (or any debt). You might think that saying
you don't have any student loans or are debt-free would be a
good answer, showing that you are economically wise, and that
saying you do have substantial student loans that you have to
pay off or some other kind of debt would be a bad answer. You
might be tempted to lie, secure in the belief that there's no way
an interviewer could find out about your debt situation. So
maybe you have debt, but you say that you don't. Then you sit
back smugly thinking that you've really aced that question!
You've let your interviewer know that your financial situation
is sound. You think that that's what she wants to hear.

Well, this is the real world. The question of student loans is one that shows how the motivation behind the question might be completely different than what you imagine. In fact, many employers like to have an employee who has obligations to pay off substantial student loans or other debt. Conversely, they shy away from people who are debt-free.

Why? Simple. They want employees who are going to be captive to their job. This means that they won't be so independent that they can say, "Take this job and shove it," anytime something happens that they don't like or when they're told to do something they don't want to do.

If someone has a big debt they're servicing, they need the income from their job to service that debt. As a result, they will be far more compliant and more willing to go along than someone who has no debt and has more financial security.

Santa Monica, California, attorney Rae Lamothe says that she was asked this question more than any other when she was interviewing for a job as an attorney. "Every firm I interviewed asked this question. When I told them that I didn't have any loans, they almost immediately lost interest."

So if you answer this question the way you think the interviewer wants to hear it answered, you might be 100 percent wrong! Don't ever respond the way you think the interviewer wants you to respond unless your answer is honest. Don't lie!

Are you self-actualized? Do you need to work on yourself? Here's a test developed by A. Jones and Roderick P. Crandall who published *Validation of a Short Index of Self-Actualization* in 1986. Rate each of the following fifteen statements on a four-point scale, where 4 means agree, 3 means somewhat agree, 2 means somewhat disagree, and 1 means disagree. If there's an R after the statement, the numbers you assign as your answers should be reversed, with 4 meaning disagree and 1 meaning agree:

1. I do not feel ashamed of any of my emotions.
2. I feel I must do what others expect of me (R).
3. I believe that people are essentially good and can be trusted.
4. I feel free to be angry to those I love.
5. It is always necessary that others approve of what I do (R).
6. I don't accept my own weaknesses (R).
7. I can like people without having to approve of them.
8. I fear failure (R).
9. I avoid attempts to analyze and simplify complex domains (R).
10. It is better to be yourself than to be popular.
11. I have no mission in life to which I feel especially dedicated (R).
12. I can express my feelings even when they result in undesirable consequences.
13. I do not feel responsibility to help anybody (R).
14. I am bothered by fears of being inadequate (R).
15. I am loved because I give love.

The higher your score, the more self-actualized you are. The purpose of being self-actualized in terms of the interview is that if you are self-actualized, you are probably in tune with your feelings and are comfortable with yourself. As such, you are less apt to answer a question the way you think an interviewer wants to hear the answer and are probably confident enough to answer a question honestly from your heart.

Put another way, if you can achieve a high level of self-actualization, you will have the confidence to go into the interview relying on your ability to answer any question from within, rather than thinking that you have to rely on people who think that they can give you canned answers to use instead of answering questions yourself.

Your Past Is Prologue

The older you are and the more you've been around, the more you are inescapably wedded to your past. "What's past is prologue" is a rule that most selection interviewers follow. If you have a history of personality conflicts with supervisors, the conclusion will be that this problem will not change. If you have a history of missing a lot of work because of sickness, this will be considered in evaluating your future performance. If you are late often, this will be considered. You should be aware of any of these traits you possess. One of your objectives will be to establish a rapport with the interviewer so that she can accept these defects, either with a plausible explanation as to why they are not your norm or by convincing her that your assets—be they motivation, ambition, intelligence, personality, or leadership—far outweigh your track record of defects.

This is where your preparation will be most important. If you know yourself and you know that your defects will be revealed, you must prepare the interview so that you know how to downplay your defects and sell your assets. The more defects you have that are revealed in your record, the more important it is that you control the interview so that the discussion is geared toward your strengths and away from your weaknesses.

How well do you know yourself? Do you remember what you've done in the past? That sounds pretty easy, doesn't it? Of course, you remember what you've done. Think so? How many times have you seen a long-lost friend and been reminded of an episode in your past that you hadn't thought about in years? Do you think you would have thought of that episode had your friend not jarred your memory?

Being interviewed consists in part of being deft in the conversational art. You are what you have done. In order to realize what you are, you must remember what you have done and be able to relate it. If you don't remember it, you won't be able to relate it. Further, you might misconstrue what you are.

Write a Diary

The best way to begin to get to know yourself is to write the story of your life, your autobiography. It requires dedication and a great deal of time, but it can help you gain insights into yourself.

Write it chronologically. Start at the beginning of your life and go through each year, setting down incidents as they occurred. Don't be afraid to get help. If you remember someone from your past who participated in something with you but your memory of it is a little fuzzy, contact that person to get his or her recollections. This will not only help you in remembering what happened, it may trigger other memories.

Your autobiography can run into hundreds of pages and tens of thousands of words, but when you're done, you'll have a compendium of your experiences. You can use it to make a good assessment of who you are and what you have to offer, and it will be a ready reference of things about which you may wish to speak to an interviewer. Additionally, and maybe even more important, it may trigger clues about things you wish to avoid discussing with an interviewer.

Once you have your story down on paper, you have to come to grips with two things: what you want and what you have to offer. What you want can be subdivided into how much money you want and what kind of work you want.

What Will Make You Happy?

What kind of job will make you happy? Only you can answer this. Some people are happy if they spend the entire day typing. That would drive others up a wall. Some are happy selling used cars. Others would sink to the depths of depression if they had to do that. Some are happy if they have a lot of responsibility. Others want to avoid responsibility.

One of the best ways to determine the elements of a job you want is to write two lists, one consisting of the things you enjoy in a job and the other consisting of the things you don't enjoy. Make these lists as complete as possible. You won't be able to do this in one sitting. You may remember something while you're doing your marketing or watching a ball game. Whenever you think of a new element for one of the lists, write it down immediately; otherwise you may forget it. Then it'll not only be gone, but it can drive you crazy trying to remember it.

Once you think your lists are fairly complete, you should have a good job specification in terms of salary and function. You will then be able to draw up a list of questions you will want to ask your interviewer. This will also give you the confidence that the interview is a two-way street, where you and the interviewer are interviewing each other.

Desires Versus Requirements

Divide the list containing the elements you enjoy in a job into two categories, one containing the items you *must* have and the other containing the items you like but don't need. This is essential, because the odds are that you're not going to find a job that contains everything you want.

You may find a good position, but it's on the fortieth floor and you hate elevators, or it's located in Kansas and you love the ocean. Before you go into your interview, know the things that you must have and those that you can do without if you must. Maybe you can forgo seeing the ocean or can overcome your fear of elevators. Maybe you can't. If you can't, know it going in. But don't get yourself in a position of turning down the job in Kansas and later regretting it, realizing that the job was more important to you than the ocean.

Your list of requirements should be short. If it's not, you are going to find yourself in the job market for a long, long time, because most jobs fall short of being ideal.

I had a personal experience that shows the value of knowing what you want and being honest and confident enough to express it in an interview. When I was an assistant division counsel at the Guidance and Control Systems Division of Litton Industries, Wally Lukens, the defense group counsel called me and asked if I wanted to interview for the position of division counsel of Litton's shipbuilding division. Naturally, I said yes, so Wally arranged for us to meet with the division president in his office in El Segundo, California.

During the interview I made it very clear that I was not interested in the position if the division president did not consider his attorney to be on the president's staff, reporting directly to him. He agreed to this, so I accepted the position.

When I reported for work, I was ushered into the division president's carpeted, posh executive suite. He said, "I'll show you your office."

We walked out of his office and out of the carpeted, posh executive suite. We went down the stairs and walked for what seemed like a half mile through the huge open-bay office building. Finally, we turned down a hallway and entered a small, uncarpeted suite of three offices and a secretarial bay. The first office was occupied by the director of contracts for the construction of the LHA ship that was being designed and built for the U.S. Navy. It was fairly large. The next office was occupied by the head of procurement for the LHA program. It was smaller. The empty office was tiny. The division president walked into it and said, "This is your office."

I took one look at it and said, "This isn't a division counsel's office." He was stunned. At the time I was only twenty-nine years old and he was around fifty years old, and an esteemed executive who had worked for Hughes Aircraft for many years and had been recruited by Litton to run their new shipbuilding program. He said, "What do you want?"

I replied, "When we interviewed I told you I wasn't interested in the position if it wasn't on the president's staff reporting directly to you. Litton Industries division counsel's offices are all in the executive suites. If my office isn't there, I'm not interested in the job."

You might think that I was being a little aggressive, but I had reasons. One of the main reasons was that I was substantially younger than everyone with whom I would be working. Exacerbating that, I looked even younger. If I took this demeaning office, smaller than the offices in the suite of people who were not on the president's staff, it would be telegraphing the message, "This guy is not someone with influence or power, so don't pay any attention to him." I needed an office that showed the power I had. Had I accepted anything less, I would have been starting out with three strikes against me. As division counsel I would have the legal responsibility for the entire division. There were several other programs upon which the division was working; one was the competition for the design and construction for the Spruance Class Destroyer, a program valued in excess of $2 billion. He was intentionally trying to diminish my influence and power at the outset by sticking me in a small, demeaning office, one that showed me to be subservient to two people who were just working on one of the many programs for which I was supposed to have legal responsibility. These were people who would have to get my approval on any contract they negotiated, two people who should have been below me on the organizational chart.

I told him to let me know what he decided and left the building. That afternoon he called me and told me he had arranged for an office in the executive suite, so I returned to my new job the following morning. Eventually, when we moved from El Segundo to Marina del Rey, I had established good relationships with executives throughout the division and proven that I was an essential member of the team. As a result I was assigned the second largest office in the new executive suite. Had I not raised the issue in my initial interview with him, my position would have been much weaker. Since I did raise it, and since he agreed in front of the group counsel, who was at least as powerful and influential a person in the Litton corporate hierarchy as he, he would have been in a difficult position to deny me what I wanted, and he knew it.

Research Yourself

Here is an excellent treatise on preparing for an interview put together by OPEN, or, Outstanding Professionals Employment Network, the Simi Valley chapter of Experience Unlimited, a job search association sponsored by the California Employment Development Department. OPEN consists of formerly high-salaried people who are helping others to get jobs. Because this material was prepared by people who have interviewed to hire people as well as interviewed to be hired, rather than consultants, this is advice from the horse's mouth.

Time to Regroup

You have been given a great opportunity! Up to now, you have spent all of your time doing your job, learning and applying new skills, and generally focusing on what you do that they pay you for. Now you have the chance to look closely at what you have been doing and decide if that is what you want to do.

Self-Discovery

The exercises in appendix E will show you where you think your skills are and what you enjoy doing. When you have completed them, sit back and look at the results as honestly and critically as you can. It is a good idea to look at them on your own, but even better to do it with your spouse, who probably knows you as well as anyone and can help cut through your biases about yourself.

Self-Assessment

Look at your skills:

- Were these skills used in your last job?
- Are they the things that you like to do? If not—ask yourself why. Is it because you chose that job without considering your skill set?
- Did you choose your last job for the right reason? Your job should contain the elements that you like to do.

Look at the things you like to do:

- What type of job contains the elements that you best like to do?
- Do you need special training to qualify for the job?

- Do you have enough time to get qualified? If so, consider a part-time job until you have gained the qualification.

Be honest with yourself:

- Was your last job merely a way of getting paid while you pursued your passion?
- Did your job offer security without challenging your intellect? Was that your wish?
- Did your job offer a lack of professional risk for you?
- Did you think that you had security in your old job (wrong!!)?
- Were you trying to work beneath the radar?

Is it time for a change?

- Would you rather do a different type of job you enjoyed more?
- Do you want to take a job that offers you more (or less) personal risk?
- Will you take less money for a job you like to do more?
- Can you work for a supervisor again?
- Would you rather not have the responsibility of a manager?
- Does your job offer you personal growth?
- Do you want a more flexible time schedule?
- Would a different job meet your long-term goals?

RESEARCH YOUR OPTIONS

- What types of jobs match your skills?
- What types of jobs match your wants?
- What types of jobs match your needs?

Make a list of jobs that you feel would be the type of work you want to do. Investigate whether you are qualified to do the job, or if you need to gain new skills to perform well.

Discuss your goals with your network to see if they agree that you are suited for a change in your focus.

Be honest with yourself throughout this process. *Keep your attitude positive!!*

> *Life presents two kinds of problems: things you can't change and things you can. Forget the ones you can't change and change the ones you can. In either case, don't worry—life's too short.*
>
> —MICKEY RIVERS, New York Yankees

ORGANIZE FOR SUCCESS

- Establish a daily routine.
  - Get up at the regular time (same time as when you worked).
  - Keep your old work routine as much as possible.
  - When you go out, dress appropriately.
  - Set aside one hour a day for exercise, to relieve stress.
- Set up a work space away from normal family activities.
- Teach family members how to answer the telephone professionally.
- Get an answering machine and fax (make your greeting professional, upbeat).

Assessing Your Personal Status

- Be sure you understand the provisions of your severance agreement.
  - Do you need continuing health benefits? COBRA?
  - Do you need continuing life insurance or other benefits?
  - Are you eligible for unemployment benefits?
- Get your family involved immediately. They are your biggest support group. Talk out your feelings as well as theirs.
- Find a friend who will just listen; use this friend as a sounding board.
- Don't be afraid to ask for help or advice.
- Get involved in projects you enjoy. Don't forget to take time for yourself.
- Set aside specific family time for enjoyable activities.
- Set aside a day to spend with just your spouse, periodically. Rejuvenate your relationship. This is extremely important for your emotional stability. You must be a team during this job search.
- You must have a positive attitude to reflect a positive attitude. Your frame of mind comes through in the way you walk, talk, and live your life. Nobody wants to be around a Gloomy Gus. Nobody wants to hire one, either. The glass is either half empty or half full—it's your choice. Practice positive thinking. A positive attitude and healthy frame of mind are essential to finding new employment.

Don't Give Up

> *Never Give Up—Never Surrender.*
> —Tim Allen, *Galaxy Quest*

- Use support groups.
- Be enthusiastic.
- Laugh at yourself.
  - They laughed at Columbus.
  - They laughed at Ford.
  - They laughed at the Wright brothers.
  - They'll laugh at you.

Universal hiring rule: Any employer will hire any applicant as long as the employer is convinced that the hiring will bring more value than it costs.

$$
\begin{array}{r}
\text{Determination} \\
+ \quad \text{Goal setting} \\
+ \quad \text{Concentration} \\
+ \quad \text{Positive attitude} \\
\hline
= \quad \text{Success}
\end{array}
$$

If you think you can't, or you think you can—either way you're right.

Self-Discovery—the Emotional Process

We have to know where we're coming from emotionally to formulate a plan to get to where we want to be. The emotional response to sudden unemployment is very similar to that of losing a loved one or experiencing some other traumatic episode in our lives. The information on the emotional process is taken from *On Death and Dying*, by Elizabeth Kübler-Ross.

Shock
Shock is often the first thing we feel when we find ourselves unemployed. We simply can't believe it has happened.

Denial
This next step is a refusal to accept the reality of the situation. There's a mistake. This simply can't be happening.

Anger
Anger is a *secondary* emotion. Feelings and emotions that are not acknowledged and are not dealt with lead to anger. If kept hidden, suppressed, or denied, anger can lead to inappropriate behavior.

Suppose you are still angry with your boss for being laid off, and this anger hasn't been dealt with. Now imagine that you are in an interview, and the interviewer asks you how you feel about the company you just left. This question just might be the last straw that results in a suppressed emotion surfacing at an inappropriate time and, quite possibly, might lead us to make an unflattering comment about our previous place of employment, or our boss, or our coworkers.

That's the last thing we want to do in an interview. Negative comments during a job interview will absolutely sabotage any possibility of making a good first impression. Remember, we want to always project a positive attitude.

Depression
Depression can be cyclic. Anger, caused by unresolved feelings or emotions, leads to procrastination or inappropriate action, which leads to negative thoughts ("I'm not good enough"; "I can't deal with this"). This leads to inaction, which increases our depression. And the beat goes on . . .

How do we break that cycle?

- We change negative thinking by looking at old performance evaluations, job descriptions.
- We change negative belief systems.
- We focus on our accomplishments.

If I want to change my belief system from "I can't" to "I can," I simply have to act. My thoughts and belief system will adapt to my behavior (action), and vice versa. So, to break the cycle of depression, all we have to do is change our thoughts, our actions, or our belief system. The best way is a combination of all three.

But, in order to do this, we have to know what those thoughts, beliefs, and actions are. The best way to start to understand this is to allow our emotions to surface.

Understanding

Understanding where we are in the process is critical to accepting where we are and improving our situation. Once we understand that we're in shock or angry or depressed and accept that we need to change, we can start to take steps in the right direction.

Acceptance

What happened, happened.

It doesn't matter why.

I know I can find a better job.

I know I can do what I want to do.

The emotional process is dynamic. Shock, denial, anger, and depression will come and go during our search for employment, especially as we get into such issues as writing a resumé, interviewing with prospective employers, and negotiating salary, to name a few. And this emotional process will recur; it's just a matter of when. The secret to success is recognizing these emotions and dealing with them appropriately before they become major issues and possibly surface at the wrong time (as in an interview).

Self-Discovery—Instructions

You have a unique opportunity at this time in your career. Up to now, you have concentrated on doing your job and improving yourself so that you can contribute to your company's goals. What about *your* needs? What do *you* like to do? Is there something *you* would rather do than the same old . . . stuff?

Sit back, relax, and clear your mind. Forget what your last job required you to do. Think more about what you like to do, what your skills are, and what your dream job would be.

Do the exercises in appendix E in sequence. Do not read ahead. You will get more out of the exercises by taking them in sequence.

Research the Company

Learn as much as you can about the company you will be interviewing. If you were in sales, you wouldn't dream of going into a presentation without knowing something about the business of the potential customer. You would tailor your sales pitch to the needs of that business. If you were going to make a speech, you would want to know as much about the audience as you could so that you could direct your speech to the areas of the audience's interests. Similarly, when you go into an interview, you should know as much about the company as possible so that you can tailor your approach to making the interviewer feel that you fit the requirements of the job.

The impression left by your preparation is sometimes

subtle, but it is invariably positive. If, for example, you are interviewing a bank and have a working knowledge of what the bank does, this knowledge will come across to the interviewer as a positive. Conversely, ignorance of the bank's business will register as a negative.

Interviewers are looking to determine not only your interest in obtaining a job but your interest in working for their company as well, rather than some other company. Taking the initiative to find out what the company does indicates that you have done some homework. If you don't have the interest to find out prior to the interview what kind of work the company does, that lack of interest may be quickly discovered by the interviewer. Not only can you expect to be thrown for a loss by some questions asked by the interviewer, but she may draw a distinctly negative impression from your apparent lack of interest.

Interviewers will invariably ask you what you think you can add to the company as an employee. How can you answer if you don't even know what the company does? Whether you have done this basic amount of research will come out in other ways. For example, most interviewers will reach a point where they ask you if you have any questions about the company or its operations. This may seem to be a maneuver to turn the interview over to you, but in fact it's a very potent tactic. From the questions you ask, the interviewer can determine how much you know of the company and for what reasons, if any, you would like to work for it.

How to Research the Company

How do you research the company? The first place to visit is the company's Web site. I don't know of any business today that doesn't have a presence on the Internet. Generally, you just type in "www.[company name].com" on your browser's search page. If that doesn't work, go to a search engine like Google.com and type in the name of the company. That will generally direct you to the home page. From there you can do a lot of research on the company, its employees, and its products.

College placement offices are excellent sources of information. They are generally responsive to requests for information, whether or not you're a student or alumnus, although their policies differ in accordance with the personality of the person running the office. They are good places to start, and if the inquiry does result in rejection, you haven't lost anything.

There is a myriad of publications to which you may refer. Some of these are:

Better Business Bureau reports
Chamber of Commerce publications
Dun & Bradstreet Reference Book
Fitch corporations manuals
MacRae's Bluebook
Moody's manuals
Standard & Poor's Register of Corporations, Directors, and Executives
Thomas' Register of American Manufacturers
Annual reports
For public companies, documents required to be filed with the Securities and Exchange Commission (SEC), such as registration statements and 10-Ks.

Many of the above can be found at your local public library. Placement offices should also have other printed material on companies that recruit at their school.

Probably the best way to do inexpensive research is the Internet. There are a lot of services, so I'll just name a few. First, there are a couple of fee-based services that can give you access to abundant information. Hoovers.com has a service called Hooverslite that gives access to information on nineteen thousand companies, half of them private. The service costs $400 per year, or $50 per month. You can get in-depth company profiles which include history, subsidiaries, affiliates, and more. You can also get names of key people and biographies of them.

Another site is knowx.com, which gives access to business records. Again, this is a fee-based service that charges for each document you request.

You can also do free searches on many of the search engines, such as www.google.com, www.alltheweb.com, www.yahoo.com, www.search.msn.com, www.askjeeves.com, www.hotbot.com, www.lycos.com, www.teoma.com, www.inktomi.com, www.looksmart.com. One of the best sites is http://answers.google.com. Here you can post a question and the price you're willing to pay for the answer and just wait for people to respond. Even better, maybe someone's already asked the question; there are postings of questions and answers. It's incredible the amount of information you can get here if you're willing to spend a few bucks. These are just a few of the search engines that can give you a start on finding information.

OPEN provides the following material on Internet sources as they relate to job and information searches. When reading these references, remember that OPEN is a Southern Californian organization, and sponsored by the State of California. If you don't live in Southern California, use these references as a starting point for your research for similar sites in your geographical area.

The Internet—a Valuable Tool

Include the Internet as one of your job search tools. It can be used for:

- Searching jobs
- Posting resumés
- Online networking
- Corresponding by e-mail
- Conducting company research

Keep in mind, however, that the Internet should not be your primary tool. Your most important resource is your personal network.

Internet Features
- Many job search sites have the capability of defining agents that run automatically and e-mail you the results of your search criteria.
- Usenet Newsgroups are available, primarily for technical positions. However, these postings have a tendency to get overloaded with spam and are laborious to peruse.
- Beware of online scams.

Types of Job Search Sites
- Company Web sites can often be found by plugging the company's name into an Internet address, such as www.ford.com, or by a Google search using the company name.
- Newspapers throughout the country have online job ad access. For example, in Southern California there are:
  - *Ventura County Star* at http://www.insidevcjobs.com
  - *Los Angeles Times* at www.careerbuilder.com

- Become familiar with each site's search engine capability as they differ from site to site. Some allow Boolean expressions (e.g., "software AND manager" OR "software AND supervisor").
- Be leery of resumé-only sites that claim to broadcast your resumé to hiring companies. These often charge a fee or sell your personal information to telemarketers and multilevel marketers.
- Industry sites abound (e.g., IEEE, APICS, PMI, QA).
- Trade organizations provide company information such as financials, new product announcements, press releases, and SEC filings.
- Popular job sites such as www.monster.com may or may not be the most useful for you. Visit as many sites as possible and home in on the ones that seem to be oriented toward your skills. For example, www.dice.com focuses primarily on technical fields.

Online Networking

- In addition to job search and information search sites, networking groups enable "birds of a feather" communications. Some are:
  - www.ryze.com
  - http://groups.yahoo.com/group/OPENMembers
  - http://geocities.com/venturahighwaygroup
  - http://groups.yahoo.com/group/KITlist
- Your best job search weapon is your network: professional organizations, church groups, OPEN, friends, neighbors, family, headhunters, former business associates, etc.
- Take advantage of OPEN resumé scrubs and mock interviews.
- Know your strengths and weaknesses and how to make a weakness sound positive.

- Know your resumé inside out and have stories to back up your accomplishments.
- Personal business cards are a must! You can get them for free at www.vistaprint.com.

Conducting Research

- You need to be prepared to know everything you can about the company with whom you are interviewing or applying. Often the first question from the interviewer is, "What do you know about our company?" This is an ideal opportunity for you to show that you have done your homework and to exhibit a keen interest in them.
- Company research can help you make a decision: Is this a company you want to work for? What are their ethics? Are they in trouble?
- Hard information (press releases, product information, company locations, size, benefits, etc.) can be determined from the company's site.
- Soft information (financial condition, pending litigation, opinions, market outlook, etc.) can be determined from information sites.

Do your homework! There is a wealth of information available on the Internet. Visit as many sites as possible and become adept at weeding out good and bad information. If you find a discrepancy in information between www.SEC.gov (the Securities and Exchange Commission site) and www.yahoo.com (a public access site), you might lend more credibility to the government site.

Job Search and Information Web Sites

JOB BOARDS — GENERAL

http://www.6figurejobs.com/
http://www.insidevcjobs.com/
http://www.ajb.org/ca/
http://www.jobsearch.about.com/
http://www.craigslist.com
http://www.monster.com/
http://www.caljobs.ca.gov/
http://www.net-temps.com/
http://www.careerbuilder.com/
http://www.nationjob.com/
http://www.dice.com/
http://www.usajobs.opm.gov/
http://www.flipdog.com/
http://www.wetfeet.com/
http://www.geocities.com/jobsnation/

JOB BOARDS — INDUSTRY/JOB SPECIFIC

http://www.agaveblue.com
http://www.jobsearchtech.about.com/mbody.htm
http://www.asq706.com/job.htm
http://www.justengineeringjobs.com/
http://www.computerwork.com/
http://www.justinjobs.com/
http://www.engineeringjobs.com/
http://www.justmyjobs.com
http://www.engineerjobs.com/
http://www.techiegold.com
http://www.itmoonlighter.com/
http://www.thinkjobs.com/

Resumé Posting Sites

http://groups.yahoo.com/group/venturahighwaygroup/
http://www.ventura.org/earn/open/
http://www.vantug.net/

Company/Industry Research Sites

http://www.bls.gov/
http://www.vault.com/
http://www.kornferry.com
http://www.wetfeet.com/
http://www.socaltech.com/Companies/Freeway/
http://www.betterwhois.com

Job Search Help Sites

http://www.100.com/Top/Career
http://www.jobscams.com/
http://www.bls.gov/
http://www.ventura.org/earn/open/
http://www.job-hunt.org/
http://www.vistaprint.com/
http://www.jobhunters.com/
http://www.wetfeet.com/
http://www.jobhuntersbible.com/
http://www.quintcareers.com/

Recruiters/Headhunters

http://www.asktheheadhunter.com
http://www.recruitersonline.com/
http://www.nationalrecruiting.com/
http://www.zimcousa.com

Networking

http://groups.yahoo.com/group/venturahighwaygroup/
http://www.ventura.org/earn/open/
http://www.vantug.net/

Other Information Sources

Stockbrokers may know something about the company and its personnel. College professors who teach subjects in the field of the company's line of work may be helpful. You can contact the company's public relations department and get quite a bit of information about the company. If you know someone who works there, or know someone who can introduce to you someone who works there, you can get firsthand insider information.

Reader Walter S. Keller Jr. suggests another way to get information:

> Instead of anonymously contacting the company's public relations department, I have stated to them I'm expecting to be interviewed shortly. This allows them to be more specific in selecting literature to give me. I've done this by phone and in person, walking in and being directed to public relations by the receptionist.
>
> Perhaps the biggest bonus of this approach is that they usually give me copies of the company's house organ. From these I have gleaned such nuggets as the fact that my interviewer had recently received his Ph.D., that another interviewer was a new father of twins, and in one case that the department I was interested in was initiating several major programs.

A less traditional avenue is to find the cocktail lounge near the company's offices where workers go after work. If you drop in for a drink at quitting time and strike up a conversation with one of the company's employees, you can gather data in preparation for your interview. It can help you make a judgment on the company and its morale and determine how happy you would be working in such an environment.

If your interview has been arranged by an executive search firm or a placement agency, you can probe the search consultant for information. The consultant will have already done a preliminary check on you and will probably have held an interview to prescreen you. She is placing her reputation on the line by recommending you for an interview, so she wants you to look as good as possible. Ask her as many questions as you want about the company and the person who will be interviewing you. The consultant should brief you thoroughly. You are money to her. If her client offers you a job and you accept it, she gets a big fee, so she's trying her best to make a marriage.

What information do you want on the company? First, of course, you want to know what it does. Is it a conglomerate? What areas is it in? What does it manufacture? What does it sell? If it performs services, what services? Is its profit trend up or down? Is it expanding or contracting? What are its prospects?

You will also want to know about the area where the open job is. The same questions you ask about the company can be asked about the division in which you may be working.

Learn About the Product

If there's a product involved, learn about it. When I first took a job as a young attorney for Litton Industries, I was interviewing for the position as an assistant division counsel for their Guidance and Control Systems Division. That name alone was enough to boggle my mind. A scientist I was not. After a little research I found that they made something called an inertial navigation system. That was worse than the name of the division. What was an inertial navigation system?

I went to a fraternity brother who had majored in engineering and asked him if he knew what it was all about. He explained to me that inertial navigation was a method of navigating whereby if you know your starting point, the system allows you to measure speed and distance and therefore know where you are at all times. He also explained the components of the system.

When I went into my interview with the division counsel, I astounded him by my ability to speak the jargon of inertial navigation. Of course, I didn't completely understand it then, nor do I now, but I exhibited at least a modicum of intelligence about the subject.

He later told me that I was the first person he had interviewed for the job who knew anything about inertial navigation. Since he didn't understand it any better than I did, his being relieved of this obligation to explain it was a big plus in my favor. My initiative in going to this extent to prepare for the interview impressed him.

Few people have the interest or drive to do this amount of work preparing for an interview. If you do, you should have a big advantage over your competition.

Everything has its pitfalls, however, even good, diligent research and good intentions. Here's a story told to me by Michael Freeman, an executive who was out of work and looking for a job:

I was contacted by an executive recruiter from a national recruiting firm asking if I would consider a position as CEO for a company doing approximately $16 million in yearly sales. The products this company produced were sold through distributors in twenty-seven states. The owner was selling the company to a group of investors and they were conducting a search for a new CEO. My response was that I would be interested in pursuing this opportunity.

I was then given the Web address and name for this firm and told that the investors would be with the owner for the rest of the week finalizing the transaction. The sale would be completed by the end of the week and I was asked what my availability would be for the early part of the next week. No later than the following Monday afternoon, I would be contacted with a definite interview time with the new owners.

Because I had previously been the CEO of two companies for over twelve years, I knew that the competition would be great. How could I stand out from the other CEO candidates? My decision was that once the sale had been completed, I would contact several of the distributors and gather some information and insight into how well the firm was doing from their perspective.

The following Monday at noon (remember, I was told that the sale would be completed by the preceding Friday), I began contacting one of the distributors in my geographical area. I spoke with the owner of that distributor, stating that I was going to be interviewing at the company for a high level position. "Oh, really, what position are you going to be interviewing for?", was the response.

"CEO," was my answer.

"Oh, really," he replied. "Why do they need a new CEO?"

I thought, "Uh-oh. It sounds as if this guy doesn't know about what is happening." So I said, "I believe they are receiving some sort of cash infusion or maybe the company is being sold."

The voice on the other end of the line just said, "Oh, that's very interesting. So what information do you want from me?" I was glad he said that.

For the next fifteen minutes I was able to get much more information than I had expected. As a matter of fact, this guy really knew quite a bit about the company at which I was going to be interviewing. It turns out that he had been a distributor for sixteen years and had helped set up a number of the other distributors as well. I could not have picked a better person from which to gather my information. I now had enough information to go into my interview from a position of strength as I knew all about the company's history and how well they were doing and what new markets could be entered with success. I felt very confident that this would definitely set me apart from the rest of the candidates.

Later that afternoon, I received a call from the executive recruiter. "What have you been doing?" bellowed the voice on the phone. "I just got a nasty call from both the investors and the owner of this company. Did you call any distributors and tell them the company was going to be sold?"

Uh-oh! "Yes," I replied. I explained that I had only called one distributor and gave the reasoning for why I did this and also explained that I had waited until I knew the sale was complete before starting my research.

"Do you know who that distributor was that you contacted?" the recruiter asked.

"No," I replied. "Who was it?"

"That was the owner's son," I was told. "Right after he spoke with you he called his dad and asked him why was he selling the company. Right now both you and I are dead meat," said the recruiter.

The recruiter also said that what I had done was very commendable; it certainly set me apart from the crowd. The recruiter, however, should have let me know that the sale of this company was HIGHLY confidential and that I should not talk to anyone about it. This recruiter said that in his fifteen years in the recruiting business, he had only come across a handful of candidates that would have done what I did and normally it produces a highly positive reaction in the minds of the hiring managers. However, I had not been given critical information.

The net result is that I will never get a chance to interview for this position. At this point, the status of the sale of the company is in question. Reload and fire again is all that is left for me.

The moral of this story is to be certain that you get all the information you can. The one essential fact that was missing here was the confidentiality of the sale of the business. Freeman thought he was being prudent by waiting until the week after he had been told the sale would close. He made a bad assumption. Don't leave assumptions unsaid. If you have a consultant soliciting you or working to get you a position, ask the consultant if there is any reason why you should not make inquiries about the company or the people working for the company. Get your ground rules from him and be as specific as possible. Don't assume if you don't have to. I'll discuss assumptions in more detail in chapter 6.

Find Out About the Interviewer

You should discover as much as you can about the person who will be conducting the interview. Where was she born? Where was she educated? What's she done that's unusual? What's her area of expertise?

If you know the name of your interviewer, you can make discreet inquiries about her by dropping her name. This can be a dangerous tactic, however, because it could get back to her. If you ask someone, "Do you know Jackie Spratt?" and you get an affirmative response, you don't want the person with whom you're speaking to go to Spratt and mention that you were asking about her—so make it clear that you don't know her personally.

This technique is offered with the warning that if the interviewer discovers that you were doing a background check on her, she may be offended. No one likes to have someone probing about them, even if your intentions are good. So if you are inclined to go to this much trouble, be aware that it could backfire and ruin your interview before you walk in the door. If you're not excited by James Bond snooping in someone's file drawers in the dim of night by flashlight with footsteps coming down the hall, this may not be for you. On the other hand (there's always a flip side!), maybe she will be impressed that you went to the trouble to find out something about her. You never know. I just want you to be aware that you're taking a risk in doing this kind of "up close and personal" research.

An interviewer might try to get inside you, perhaps by asking you questions involving some controversy. While most often these questions are asked to determine your thought patterns rather than your positions on issues, if you have a general feel for the interviewer, it can save you from voicing a dogmatic opinion that would offend her and result in your rejection. If the interviewer is Jewish, you may decide to play down your admiration for the fatwa urging jihad against the Jews. If she is an active member of the local American Civil Liberties Union, you may not want to emphasize your support of preventive detention.

If you can learn something about the person who is going to interview you, you can steer clear of sensitive areas and concentrate on discussing things that you may have in common.

If you know something about the interviewer, you are better able to affect the flow of the interview and keep on topics where you won't offend. You may even get her to depart from the relatively impersonal format of a selection interview and discuss more personal matters. In order to receive an offer, an interviewee wants to have the interviewer come out of the interview with the feeling that "I really liked that person."

Beware of the generation gap. If there's a big difference between your age and the age of your interviewer, you can leave an extremely negative impression if you use words with which she is unfamiliar or that emphasize the disparity in your eras. This is especially true if you are much younger than your interviewer. While an older interviewee might not turn a younger interviewer off by using "23 skiddoo" or "bad trip," a young interviewee risks instant oblivion by the use of jargon like "yo, chill" or "sweet" that might be sweeping the campuses and clubs but hasn't reached the ears of an interviewer who goes home from work each night to dinner and something other than MTV. For example, if your interviewer makes a good point, you'd do well to stifle your impulse to compliment her by saying, "Sweet, girl!" Your contemporaries might appreciate such a comment. Your interviewer probably won't.

Reader Jennifer Ruggaber of Syracuse, New York, advises care in the use of vernacular:

If you're just out of college, beware of the slang words you use when conversing. Often you don't even realize you're using them, but they won't be overlooked by older people who are unfamiliar with current slang. They may even conclude that you are immature and inarticulate.

First, pinpoint these words, then think of (or make a list of) synonymous and more descriptive words that could be substituted. Next, *practice* using them *before* the interview. You'll feel more relaxed during the interview if these words come naturally.

There is one colloquialism (and I used the term advisedly) that is almost certain to turn off any interviewer with even a passing allegiance to proper grammar. While most idiomatic language is fairly harmless, sometimes something sneaks into usage through the back door that is horribly offensive to anyone not familiar with it. If you want to get off on the wrong foot in an interview quickly, use "I go" or "I'm like" or "I'm all" in lieu of "I said." Maybe on the campus or in your dorm you can get away with substituting "go," "like," or "all" for "said," but definitely not in the interview. This has become so commonplace among young adults that many use it as a matter of course. If you do, you should adopt Jennifer Ruggaber's advice and work diligently to erase it from your involuntary memory, at least while you're going through interviews.

However, there is a caveat here, as there is with most rules. If you're interviewing for a job with an employer who is dealing with people who speak like this, then the use of vernacular that's au courant is not only okay, it's probably something that will endear you to your interviewer. If, for example, you're going for a job with MTV, I'm sure that using "wack" and "I go" and "sweet, dawg!" would be fine.

Often it's the small things like the use of an offensive idiom that can spell the difference between success and failure in an interview. Maybe your interviewer never misses *Saturday Night*

Live and will take an immediate liking to you if you use "no way, yes way." But you take a big risk in pinning your hopes on this happening. Unless the employer is one who is in the style of the vernacular, like MTV, it's better to play it safe and avoid current slang.

There is a flip side to this advice, however. If you use current slang among your contemporaries just to fit in and can live happily without ever speaking it again, then you should eschew it in the interview. If, on the other hand, slang is part of your personality, then avoiding it might not be the wise thing to do. If you speak like Henry Higgins in the interview, only to revert to your idiomatic Eliza Doolittle language when you start working, they'll realize they didn't hire the person they thought they hired and the job might not last very long. Further, if you are comfortable with the way you speak but the people for and with whom you work find it offensive, you might not be very happy in the job yourself. So if speaking slang is part of you, then using it in the interview is okay. If the interviewer doesn't like it, you've still done a good interview because you won't get an offer for a job in which you wouldn't have been content anyway.

Finally, and I don't want you to get dizzy with what appears to be flip-flopping, if you don't generally use current slang and you find yourself interviewing with someone like MTV, don't try to start talking like a teenager. Nothing sounds worse than someone trying to appear hip when they're not.

Don't Flaunt Your Preparation

Many interviewees make the mistake of flaunting their preparation in the interview. They want to make sure the interviewer knows they had so much interest in the job that they devoted a lot of time to researching the company and otherwise preparing for the interview. This can come across as insincere. The reason that you do the preparation is to make yourself ready for the interview by learning about the company and the person conducting the interview. But you want this information so that you can make an intelligent decision. If you did the preparation only to impress the interviewer with your knowledge and she perceives this, it will be a negative factor.

Interviewers can spot interviewees who are acting in a "programmed" manner rather than naturally. If the interviewer feels that the interviewee is playing a game with the interview, it will rapidly turn from a selection interview to a rejection interview.

If you've done your research and preparation, it'll come across to the interviewer in the natural course of the interview. You will convey possession of knowledge and information through your demeanor and reactions to questions. If it comes across naturally, the reaction will be positive.

Determining the Interviewer's Needs

You should not go into the interview as a victim, just waiting for the interviewer to pull your strings. You've got some work to do. A good interviewee is an active interviewee. You must be mentally acute.

One of the most important things you will be doing throughout the interview is obtaining information about the interviewer. There are several methods you can use during the interview to gain such information.

One of these is by asking questions. But it's not that easy. Gerard I. Nierenberg, in *The Art of Negotiating*, points out that there are three decisions you must make about your questions.

First, what questions should you ask? Second, how should you ask the questions? Third, when should you ask the questions? Let's take them one at a time.

First, what questions should you ask? This isn't as easy at it might look at first glance. The first rule is that you shouldn't ask a question for the sake of asking a question. Some people ask them so that, they think, the interviewer will think they are smart. Well, forget that. While interviewers do take clues from questions asked, any question asked for the sake of the question itself and not for the answer it might elicit can be as obvious and phony as a three-dollar bill. If you ask a question you don't really want or need to know the answer to, you might be embarrassed.

Before you ask a question, ask yourself why you're asking it. Then be able to answer the question that you might get from your interviewer: Why do you want to know that? If you can't answer that, then don't ask the question!

If you've prepared in accordance with the advice here in *Sweaty Palms*, you should know yourself well enough to know what your needs and desires are. And it's those needs and desires that need to be satisfied. They should raise questions in your mind about the job, the company, and your potential boss that you need answers to before you can decide that you want to accept a position.

Most questions, according to Nierenberg, fall into one of five categories:

1. General questions. This is a question the answer to which has no limits, like "What do you think?" and "Why did you do that?" You have no control over the answer.

2. Direct questions. This is a question that contains limits. A lawyer asks direct questions when questioning witnesses. Generally, a lawyer in a trial won't ask a question

(or shouldn't) unless the answer is limited to a known response. This type of question usually gives the questioner control.

3. Leading questions. This is a question that suggests the answer, like, "Isn't it true that most people in my position make at least $50,000 a year?" You suggest the answer by the way you pose the question.

4. Fact-finding questions. These are the Ws: who, what, when, where. The answers are controllable because you are limiting the answer to a specific.

5. Opinion-seeking questions. If you ask "how" or "why," you are allowing the person you're questioning more control, because you're not asking so much for a fact as for an opinion.

What you ask and how you ask it can control the interview. If you want to limit discussion and give-and-take, you ask questions that give you some control over the answer. So you would ask questions of the types listed in 2, 3, and 4: direct questions, leading questions, and fact-finding questions. If, on the other hand, you want the interviewer to have some control over the answer, you ask general questions or opinion-seeking questions (numbers 1 and 5).

As you should have realized by now, most of what you learn here is a double-edged sword. This is the same with the knowledge you have of the types of questions you ask. The rules are the same for your interviewer as they are for you. So you can make some judgments on the interviewer by recognizing the types of questions being used to elicit information or discussion from you.

As you participate in the interview, be aware of the types of questions being asked, make judgments thereon, and proceed according to what you want to get out of the interview. If your interviewer is asking questions that control your answers, she might not be confident enough to surrender control of the interview to you. Or she might be unsophisticated and is just trying to get through the interview. You will find this more often than you might think. So the judgment you make if the interviewer is asking questions that control your answers might not be that she is sophisticated and looking for specific answers. Instead, it might be that she is unsophisticated and unaware of how to proceed. If you make the latter determination, then you can try to take over the interview and help the interviewer out. You can do this by occasionally asking if you can ask a question, then see how she responds.

A third possibility is that the interviewer does, in fact, know what she wants and where the interview is going. If this is the case, you should just go along with it. Eventually, you have the right to take some control of the interview and get the interviewer to talk. Don't ever just let the interviewer get out of the interview her own agenda without using the interview yourself to get some information. You should never be a victim in an interview. Or maybe it's better for you to remember this: Don't be a wimp!

More on Preparing Your Own Questions

Sometime in the course of your interview, you will almost surely be asked if you have any questions of your own, and it pays to prepare ahead of time for this. Reader Lisa F. Dawkings of Englewood, Colorado, describes the consequences of failing to do so:

> I know it's a good idea to ask questions, but what does one ask when the interviewer has answered all possible ques-

tions before she asks if I have any? Often those interviews are more of a monologue (on the interviewer's part) than a dialogue, and I feel I come off as something short of bright when I have nothing to ask.

Here are some suggestions from John Meyers of Richmond, Virginia:

1. Whom would I be working for?
2. May I have a company organization chart?
3. Tell me about your company.
4. What do you look for in a candidate for this position?
5. How many candidates are you interviewing for this position?
6. How would you describe this position?
7. Where would I be working?
8. Does your company have other locations?
9. How is the work divided between locations?
10. How many hours per week do you expect me to work?
11. What do you pay for overtime?
12. Do you reimburse employees for moving expenses?

If your interviewer has answered all of the questions you have plus all of these, and your interviewer is as talkative as Ms. Dawkings's interviewer, something will probably have occurred to you that you'd like to know about her. If not, and if she has answered all your questions about the job, ask the interviewer how *she* likes working for the company and if there's anything she doesn't like about it. That's a good question any interviewee should be prepared to ask because it can elicit information about the company you won't be able to get elsewhere and it might catch your interviewer by surprise.

If you have done the preparation of looking into yourself that I recommend in this book, you should have developed enough insight into yourself to have many questions about what you want in a company for which you work. The questions I list here are merely the tip of the iceberg to get you started. For further help, see appendix D.

There is a lot of terrible advice out there, as exemplified in an article by John Kador in the *Los Angeles Times* titled "The Right Questions Can Help Secure Job." In the first place the headline is quixotic. It's unlikely you will be able to get a job by asking a question. But then I looked at the questions. They were truly unbelievable! Here are a few:

1. What exactly does this company value the most and how do you think my work for you will further these values?
2. What kind of processes are in place to help me work collaboratively?
3. In what areas could your team use a little polishing?
4. What's the most important thing I can do to help in the first ninety days of my employment?
5. What are my strongest assets and possible weaknesses?

If anybody ever asked me one of these questions, I'd have a hard time not falling down laughing. Many selection interviewers are people who are used to performing a function, and interviewing someone to work for them is a pain in the neck. Can you imagine yourself in the place of someone who has to go through this and who is asked by some interviewee, "What exactly does this company value the most and how do you think my work for you will further these values?" That question alone would probably end the interviewee's chance if it were asked of me.

These questions are obviously nothing that any normal person would think of. So they aren't honest. They stand out as being something you've read that sounds good. But anyone who thinks these questions sound good would automatically be disqualified for lack of judgment. Do you really think that a selection interviewer wants to answer a question like, "What kind of processes are in place to help me work collaboratively?" What does that mean? I'm interviewing for a salesperson or a bookkeeper or a secretary or anything else and someone asks me a question like this? What are you going to say if the response is what I would ask: "What does that mean?" How are you going to explain what you mean? This question is nonsense.

Let's say you're the interviewer and you're interviewing your twelfth person for this position you have open and the person says, "In what areas could your team use a little polishing?" Are you kidding me? In fact, that might be what I'd ask if someone had the chutzpah to ask a question like that. I'd be so stunned I'd say, "Are you kidding me?" One thing for sure: If you ask an imbecilic question like this, you will be remembered. After work, while having a drink with her compatriots, your interviewer is going to say, "You won't believe what this jerk asked me today in an interview. 'In what areas could your team use a little polishing?'" And the crowd will erupt in laughter.

Probably the funniest one of these five is the fifth: "What are my strongest assets and possible weaknesses?" That sounds like a question that an interviewer might ask an interviewee. How is the interviewer going to know? If you asked me that, my response would be, "Why don't you tell me?"

Well, the point is that anybody who tries to tell you exactly what to say, what questions to ask or specific answers to specific questions, is somebody to be ignored. These people are telling you that you're too stupid to figure out what you want to know or how to answer questions about yourself. How can they know how to answer an interviewer's questions? Do they know you? Do they know your interviewer?

Appendix D in this book lists questions you might want to ask when on an interview. The point of this list is to raise questions in your mind about things you might want to find out about a job. Remember these four rules:

1. Don't ever ask a question because you saw it in my book, or anybody else's book.
2. Don't ever ask a question for the sake of asking a question.
3. Don't ever ask a question just because you think it sounds intelligent.
4. Don't ever ask a question because you think asking it will get you a job.

The only reason to ask a question is to get an answer to something you genuinely want to know. Is there anybody out there who genuinely wants to know the answers to any of Mr. Kador's five questions? I doubt it. And if there is, that person can work for someone other than me.

Obviously, such stuff isn't worth the paper it's printed on. My position on helping you to prepare for an interview is the same as it was when I wrote the first edition of *Sweaty Palms* in 1978: to help you to get to know yourself so that you will be prepared and confident that you can answer any question from your own experience by using your own knowledge and words.

Don't just take my word for the fact that asking questions for the sake of the question itself is a mistake. Joseph Alibrandi, former president, chairman, and CEO of Whittaker Corporation, a NYSE-listed company, told me:

Many times guys will ask questions because they think it's intelligent and it satisfies some requirement that somebody set up for the kinds of things you should know about a company. When somebody asks a question like that, I think that he's asking for my benefit. If that was really important to him, he could have found out by looking at the annual report. It gives you a feel for the kind of person he is. You feel that he can't separate the cosmetics from the fundamentals. I'm amazed that he's sitting with me and really believes that cosmetic is going to help him. It would be a real negative because what you're really looking for are the basic traits: honesty, ability to work with people, and ability to relate to people.

Joe told me this in the mid-1970s. When it comes to the art of the interview, things just don't change much.

Ernest Hemingway developed a way of writing in which he would write a story and then omit several pages at the beginning, theorizing that something omitted can affect the reader as if it were there. He used this method in several short stories and in his first novel, *The Sun Also Rises*. This same theory applies to an interviewee's preparation. Even though you do not discuss all you know about the company and the person conducting the interview, you will convey a sense of knowledge during the interview. Knowledge obtained through preparation, even though unstated, will have a presence and will affect the interview and the feeling developed by the interviewer.

Just as a person with power doesn't have to say, "I am powerful," you don't have to say, "I know a lot about you and your company." The powerful person radiates power. The knowledgeable person radiates knowledge. To discuss it, to bring it out in the open for no reason, is to diminish it and to turn a plus to a negative.

Checklist

- Preparation is the key to achievement.
- Don't go into the interview thinking that the interviewer knows exactly what she wants out of the interview and will ask the appropriate questions.
- Write your autobiography.
- Make a list of what things in a job will make you happy.
- Make a list of the things in a job that you don't like.
- Separate the list of what you like into requirements versus desires.
- Ensure that your thinking is logical when you deal with your requirements.
- Learn as much as you can about the company you're interviewing.
- Interviewers want to know specifically why you are interested in their company.
- One question to expect is, "What can you add to our company as an employee?"
- Learn about the product or service the company manufactures, sells, or performs.
- Learn about the interviewer.
- Prepare your own list of questions to ask.
- Don't ask questions for the sake of impressing your interviewer with the question itself.
- Don't flaunt your preparation.

3
Types of Interviews

The word "interview" is derived from the French *entrevoir* ("to see another, meet"). Although the term generally applies to job applicants (for instance, Webster's defines it as "a formal consultation usually to evaluate qualifications [as of a prospective student or employee]"), it should not be so limited. An interview includes any confrontation between two people when the understood purpose is for at least one of the two to make an evaluation of the other *for any reason*.

There are two basic types of interview—the screening interview and the selection interview, or interview for hire. Screening interviews are generally conducted by a staff member in the personnel, or human resources, department who may have had formal training in interview methodology. Selection interviews are conducted by the supervisor or manager to whom the open position reports. In large organizations you may have to go through both a screening interview and a selection interview. For very high-level jobs, applicants often go through a series of both.

Screening Interviews

The screening interviewer's goal is very simple: to send a qualified candidate to the supervisor who is requesting an employee. Therefore, he is looking for a candidate with a solid background and will ask questions relating to work experience. (In this chapter we'll assume the interviewer is a man.) He will probe for areas of inconsistency in your resumé or in your responses. What kind of personality you have will be of little importance.

The screening interviewer has generally been trained in interview methodology. He follows the rules and formats in which he has been trained and has probably digested most of the theories set forth in books on how to interview.

Sharyn Cole, who was director of placement and in charge of hiring the entire staff of the giant Los Angeles Bonaventure Hotel when it first opened, says, "The screening interview is a process of elimination. You try to weed out unacceptable candidates."

John Munro Fraser, in *The Handbook of Employment Interviewing*, sets forth the function of the personnel department in conducting a screening interview: "We must get at the facts of a candidate's previous history; and we must go into it as thoroughly and in as great detail as possible in the time available. . . . It is upon facts alone that a sound assessment can be established."

For the interviewer the purpose of a good screening interview is to get facts. Since your purpose is to get past the screener to the selection interviewer, it is to your benefit to provide the interviewer with the facts he so fervently desires.

In the screening interview there is very little personal involvement on the part of the screener, who will probably never see the candidate again after the interview. He needn't worry about how you will get along with other people, because he will not have to work with you. Further, he will not be subject to criticism on the point of personality, because a candidate's personality is not part of what he's looking for. His motivation is a relatively negative one: not to make a mistake in evaluating the facts, for which he can be criticized. For example, if a candidate for executive secretary was sent to an executive and it was discovered that the candidate didn't know how to type, the screener would be vulnerable to reproach. If it was found that the candidate typed 100 words per minute but had a terrible personality and alienated the executive, the screener would not be subject to criticism at all. His responsibility was not to make personality assessments, but to analyze the factual data and determine whether the candidate had the skills and experience to qualify for the position. Therefore, the screener is very careful that his judgments are backed up by cold, hard facts. Since he does not have the power to make the hire/no hire decisions, his intuitive feeling about the candidate is irrelevant.

The screening interviewer may know very little about the job for which the candidate is interviewing or about the supervisor to whom the candidate will report if hired. He works in a vacuum. He receives a requisition for a position with bare-outline requirements. What does he do? He matches facts with facts. The purpose of this interview is to verify facts on the resumé and to elicit more facts.

Uppermost in the screener's mind is not to find the best person for the position, not to make a judgment on the candidate's personality, not to determine the candidate's thought processes; it is to ensure that the person interviewed has the qualifications in terms of education and experience for the position.

What is written here is not intended to be critical of the screening function. The job is a difficult one. But you must recognize that a screener is just that, a screener. The function a screener performs is valuable because it saves the supervisor precious time in interviewing and rejecting obviously unqualified candidates.

If you survive the screening interview, it is generally an indication that your qualifications for the position are acceptable as far as the facts are concerned; you have enough experience and there is nothing on your resumé or in your background to disqualify you (such as a record of convictions of crime or unexplained terminations from prior employment).

A serious personality conflict that emerges during a screening interview could result in rejection at this stage, but it is something that would occur only if *you* brought about the problem, since the interviewer is not probing in this area.

The screening interview is mostly a clerical function, consisting of checking the facts on the resumé and filling in gaps in time that may appear on it. Knowing this when you go into the interview, you should conduct yourself accordingly. You should give the interviewer the facts for which he is searching. You should be pleasant and avoid controversy. Above all, avoid volunteering facts for which the interviewer is not searching.

The screening interviewer is an expert at discovering reasons not to send you on to the next stage, the selection interview. *The screener may not have the power to hire you, but does have the power to reject you, and will do so if you appear unqualified in any way.* Therefore, in the screening interview the key is to follow the interviewer's lead. Do not try to exert any control over the interview. Answer any questions in a simple, straightforward manner and leave it at that. Since you have nothing to gain, don't put yourself in a position from which you can only maintain the status quo or lose.

The Telephone

One type of screening interview for which you should be prepared is a telephone interview. While it's rare that an offer would be extended after conducting only a telephone interview, they are, nonetheless, important. Three reasons why a telephone interview might be legitimate: First, sometimes screeners and administrators are so inundated with resumés that in order to weed them out, they resort to telephone interviews. Additionally, a candidate may be perceived as an "on the fence" candidate, meaning he or she might not fit the right niche off the bat, but there is something there that requires a second look. Third, how one comports oneself over the telephone could be an important part of the job. The job may require heavy client contact, and the candidate may be the first person a client speaks with. If so, a phone interview is a legitimate part of the interview process. What better way to determine how one comes across on the telephone than to conduct a telephone interview?

Amy Goldware is a partner and director of business development for Rhumbline Legal Solutions in Los Angeles. She has definite ideas on the telephone interview and how one should act:

I discourage my clients from participating in telephone interviews, if I can. My feeling is that a major component of the interview process is the chemistry, personality, and demeanor of the interviewee and how that person is going to "click" with the person he/she will end up supporting. Additionally, body language is a big part of that, and you just can't get those initial impressions over the telephone. Tone and inflection, too, are important and are highly effective in having a strong telephone interview.

That being said, I would not suggest an interviewee to refuse to participate in a telephone interview. Many of my clients are interviewing for secretarial positions or positions that require good phone etiquette, so a refusal could be a turnoff, or worse, an end to possibly getting a position altogether.

I counsel my candidates to be aware of their "phone voice." Often, when speaking on the phone, one can come across flat or monotone, and this needs to be acknowledged and accounted for prior to giving a telephone interview. One thing a candidate can do is to smile while they're speaking on the phone. This might sound like an odd practice and you might feel strange when you first try it, but it actually works. If you're smiling when you are speaking, it's often reflected in the tone of your voice.

However, you might initiate a telephone contact. As I said at the opening of this chapter, any communication between two people can satisfy the requirements for an interview. I got my first gig as a movie critic through a telephone contact. I called an editor of a local paper. We had never met and she didn't know who I was when I called, so I had to be concise. When she answered the phone, I said, "My name is Tony Medley and I'm calling about writing movie reviews for you."

She responded, "We already have a movie critic."

I said, "I know. That's why I'm calling."

She had a good sense of humor and liked that response. She asked me to send her some samples of my work, she liked them, and I became her movie critic, just through that one telephone call. The point here is that when you're making a cold call to someone you don't know, you have to be quick and concise. You don't want to irritate her by taking up her time, but you must be prepared for an initial rejection. I hadn't planned on responding the way I did. But I was relaxed, and it was the first thing that popped into my head. I discuss trusting your creative mechanism in chapter 9. But this is an example of having the confidence in yourself to know that you will respond appropriately to things you might not have anticipated.

When you're going to make a telephone contact for an interview, either to try to get an interview or to actually have an interview, it's a good idea to write down what you want to say beforehand. Remember, the person to whom you are speaking doesn't know whether or not you're reading or referring to notes, so you are safe. No matter how good you think you are, anybody can freeze.

You can either write out exactly what you're going to say or just have notes setting forth the main points you want to make. When I'm being interviewed on the telephone for a radio show or even if it's just for a business purpose, I always write out the points I want to cover. Often I don't need them. Sometimes I do. Sometimes I'm speaking and suddenly my mind will be totally blank. This happens to everyone. When you're in a face-to-face situation, you just have to admit it. (And that's not bad, incidentally. When someone says, "I just forgot what I was talking about," your interviewer will identify because everyone has had that happen. Generally, if your interviewer was listening to you, he will remind you what it was you were saying.) But when you're on the telephone, you can have your notes, which will bring you right back on point.

However, do not try to memorize what you want to say. That can come across sounding canned and stilted. In addition, if you memorize something but forget the next line, you'll likely go blank. Regardless, there's no reason to memorize. It's going to be sitting there in front of you for reference, and the person with whom you're speaking won't know you are referring to notes.

Most helpfully, *High Impact Telephone Networking for Job Hunters*, by Howard Armstrong, gives seven questions to which you must have an answer. Answers to these questions, which really come up only in telephone interviews, should be generally prepared before you pick up the phone. They are:

1. What company shall I say you are with?
2. Is this about a job?
3. Why are you out of work?
4. Hello?
5. I really don't think I can help you right now.
6. Why is it that you lost your job while others did not?
7. Why should I meet you?

Consistent with my philosophy in this book, I'm not going to give you answers. You are smart enough to handle such questions if you are prepared for them. The times that these questions are deadly is when you are hit with them without any expectation and you have to give an answer immediately. If you're prepared, you will know what to say. The best guideline I can give you is to answer truthfully and from the heart. Don't devise an answer you think might sound good or might be what an interviewer "wants" to hear, because such answers are painfully transparent. Be honest and give an answer that reflects who you are and one with which you can live if you get the job.

Armstrong gives five suggestions that will help you come across positively:

1. Good posture. I know if I sit up straight, I am more alert than if I'm slouching, which can get me too relaxed.
2. Stand up. Armstrong feels that standing puts energy into your call. Many sports announcers, like Troy Aikman, stand while broadcasting football games.

3. Smile while speaking. We've already covered this.
4. Use a mirror. Armstrong suggests that this will remind you when you stop smiling and if a frown might begin to appear.
5. Tape your end of the conversation. Although Armstrong doesn't mention this, it's a crime in many states to record a telephone conversation without the permission of the person with whom you are speaking. But it is legal, and just as effective, to record your end of the conversation. You can listen to it and react to the sound of your voice and the way you phrased what you said. This is a very good procedure, and I recommend it for any telephone interview. It also helps you to make notes about what you said, and it will help you to remember what your interviewer said. Don't, under any circumstances, ask your interviewer for permission to record both sides of the conversation. I can't imagine any interviewer not viewing such a request negatively.

What if the person you are calling isn't in? Should you leave a callback message? My view is that if you are making a cold call to someone you don't know and not in response to a solicitation, you should not leave a callback message. That ties you in to waiting for the return call, and that can be deadly. It's better to say that you will call back later without giving your name. Sometimes the secretary will ask your name before telling you the person is unavailable. In that event I would still say that I will call back later. You can use as the reason, if you need one, that you are going to be unavailable for much of the day and it would be more efficient if you called again. But be sure to ask what a good time to call would be.

If, on the other hand, you are responding to a solicitation, there is no problem in leaving a callback message, because the person you are calling solicited the original call and presumably wants to speak with you. Even though it's all right to leave a callback message when responding instead of initiating the call, when you leave a callback message, you give the respondent the control. I prefer to keep control myself. So even when I'm responding to a solicitation, I would ask when would be a good time for me to call back. But I would still leave my name and number so the person could call me if he so desired.

Selection Interviews

The supervisor who is interviewing a potential employee has totally different motivations from the screener. As we have seen, the screener's primary concern is to avoid criticism by weeding out unacceptable candidates. The supervisor's problem is much more complex. If the supervisor hires someone who doesn't work out and has to be let go, the mistake is likely to cost the company thousands of dollars.

A new employee naturally has to go through a period of orientation before becoming fully productive. Still, the employee has to be paid, so the company is not getting its money's worth in work product during this break-in period. But it is making an investment in the future. If the employee has to be fired, the future will no longer be a factor; that investment is down the drain. It has been estimated that a bad hiring decision by a top manager costs more than $60,000, a middle manager at least $25,000, and a lower middle manager not less than $7,500. That's what companies figure it costs them to train someone. Not only is that money gone forever, but also the time lost is an additional expense to the company because the hiring procedure must begin anew.

So the supervisor isn't just worried about getting stuck with an undesirable worker. There are very real financial and organizational pressures to contend with.

Very few supervisors are experienced in conducting interviews. Most books on personnel interviewing are read only by those who conduct screening interviews. Although they are directed toward supervisors as well as personnel people, the supervisor who has read even one book of this sort is as rare as a sailboat in the Sahara. A supervisor's job is not to interview, but to perform a certain function (such as manufacturing a widget or selling that widget or keeping the books of the company). So job-related reading will deal with the manufacturing processes or the techniques of selling or how to make debits and credits. As important as interviewing technique may be to the portion of his job that pertains to hiring and managing people, the supervisor doesn't think about how to interview until he is faced with the situation. When that occurs, he simply conducts it using his intuition, hoping to get it over with in as short a time as possible.

Knowing this, you will want to approach the selection interview in a much different manner than you would the screening interview. Instead of being bland and brief and sticking to the facts, when you find yourself in the same room with the person who is going to make the hire/no hire decision, you must assume responsibility for the content of the interview, unless you run into that rare supervisor with interviewing experience, as discussed in chapter 1.

Above all, recognize that you are breaking into his routine. His normal day does not include a selection interview. He's got all the responsibilities of his job on his mind, in addition to trying to find an acceptable employee. Therefore, he is probably completely unprepared for the interview, and he's wondering what he's going to do to make a determination to fill this vacancy, how he's going to do it, and how he can do it in as short a time as possible.

Despite all the pressures that are placed on selection interviewers to make a good decision, the way they arrive at their judgment is not scientific. You must recognize that no matter what they say they are looking for, they are going to reach their conclusion based upon the feeling they have about the interviewee after the interview. The way you think, the way you express yourself, what you say, how you say it, your manner and style—all are more important to the selection interviewer than the bare facts on your resumé. It is a very *personal* assessment. Each selection interviewer is different; each makes decisions based upon his prejudices.

It is always advisable in any endeavor to approach it as if you are going to be faced with a conscientious, knowledgeable, and well-researched person. If you take this approach, you will never be unpleasantly surprised. If you enter expecting less than the best and you happen to get the best, you'll be at a disadvantage. On the other hand, if you enter expecting the best and get less than the best, you'll have the advantage.

Interview Styles

There are certain basic interviewing formats that are commonly used, and it is helpful to know about them ahead of time so that you will be well prepared under all circumstances.

DIRECTED INTERVIEW

The directed interview is used by most personnel department interviewers for screening. It follows a definite pattern. The interviewer works from an outline and asks specific questions within a certain time frame. The interviewer has a checklist and makes notations about the candidate's responses. Most professional interviewers use the directed interview. While appropriate and useful for screening, it is of the least value in a selection interview because it is too structured and impersonal to get at the personality of the candidate.

NONDIRECTIVE INTERVIEW

The nondirective interview is generally used by nonprofessionals. It has a loosely structured format, one where the interviewee is allowed to talk about any subject desired. The questions are broad and general, and they invite the interviewee to take control. The interviewer acts more like a moderator than anything else. It is an excellent format for bringing out an interviewee's personality. Most nonprofessional interviewers go into interviews with no formal preparation and are not set up to conduct a directed interview, so they try to get the interviewee to talk. The result is a semi-nondirective interview.

STRESS INTERVIEW

For the interviewer the stress interview can be a lot of fun. For the unsuspecting interviewee it can be sheer hell. The stress interview was developed by the Germans prior to World War II. Initially, and in its classic form, it consisted of taking close-up film of a candidate's face while he was being administered painful electric shocks. This crude technique has been refined over the years, and now it generally consists of subjecting you to long periods of silence, challenging your opinions, seeming to be unfriendly or brusque, and executing other techniques to make you uncomfortable.

Most interviews contain a certain amount of stress by their very nature. The introduction of intentional stress will be something that you will notice if you are alert. For example, you are answering questions and suddenly the interviewer lapses into silence and stares at you, introducing stress into the interview to see how you'll react. If you fidget or start tapping your fingers or look down at your shoes, your actions tell something—and it's not good in the eyes of the interviewer. If, on the other hand, you return the stare pleasantly and expectantly without showing signs of agitation, you've probably passed the test.

It is extremely infrequent that a selection interview is entirely a stress interview. The most effective interview is a combination of the nondirective and the stress types. In the hands of a skillful interviewer you can be led through a maze of ups and downs, and an amazingly accurate picture of your personality will emerge within thirty minutes.

There are other examples of the introduction of stress into an interview of which you should be aware. The main reason you should know about these techniques is so that you can combat them. And the best way to combat them is to recognize them for what they are. This will give you the advantage because you won't react negatively to what's being done; rather, you'll recognize it as deliberately injected stress and accept it as a normal part of the interview.

For example, one way to introduce stress into an interview is to keep you waiting long past your appointed hour. Maybe there's a business reason you're being kept waiting. Maybe your interviewer is just chronically late. But if you assume that being kept waiting is actually a ploy by the interviewer to see how you'll react, you will not feel the anger and frustration that are the normal results of being kept waiting. Instead, you'll say to yourself, "This person is applying stress!" And you'll just sit there and enjoy knowing you're handling it beautifully.

Another way for an interviewer to apply stress is to arrange the seating so that you are looking out the window into bright light coming from behind him. The result is that the pupils of your eyes contract, allowing less light into your eyes so that the interviewer may appear as a mere shadow, making it difficult for you to see any expression on his face and almost impossible to see his eyes. This can be extremely disconcerting, but if you recognize it as an intentional scheme used by your interviewer to see how you handle it, you will be able to bear up under the burden much easier than if you are just bothered by the bad lighting and grouse about it in your mind.

Anytime you recognize a level of discomfort as an intentional stratagem being used by the interviewer to test you, you will be much better able to endure whatever it is. Try to think of everything that happens to you in an interview, no matter how seemingly innocuous or happenstance, as something intentionally imposed upon you by the interviewer. It might not be the case, but this could save you from reacting in such a way as to cost you a successful interview.

Of course, stress may be applied more cruelly. An interviewer for one of the world's largest law firms once asked an African American female student at the University of Chicago Law School how she would react to being called a "black bitch" or a "nigger" by adversaries or colleagues. Later in the interview she said she enjoyed golf, and the interviewer asked her why African Americans didn't have their own country clubs, "like Jews."

When the student complained to school officials, the law firm apologized, stating that they "do not condone or tolerate that kind of statement. It was unthinking, and we do not approve of it," adding that the interviewer "is not a racist" and made the comments as a "stress test" for the applicant. (Despite the apology, the firm was banned from recruiting at the law school for one year.)

But you should be prepared for the imposition of stress like this. It's rare that it would be imposed in such an aggressive and offensive manner, but if it is and you can immediately recognize it as a test, even if you are offended, you should be able to handle it calmly. If you get angry, you lose. If you say to yourself, "This is stress, the interviewer really doesn't mean to offend," then you can react in a way that is in your best interest. While there's always the possibility that you are being interviewed by a direct descendant of Attila the Hun, it's in your interest to discard this possibility and act on the assumption that the interviewer is imposing stress on you to see how you will react.

And how to react? There are two possibilities. The first is to answer the question. "How would you react to being called a 'black bitch'?" Tell him. "Why don't blacks have their own golf courses, like Jews?" Answer the question. "I don't know" sounds like a good answer to me, although you could go into how you feel about discriminatory private clubs if you have a feeling about it.

The other possibility is to challenge the interviewer in as professional a tone as possible. You could tell him how you would react in a hypothetical situation. You could also tell him you feel that the question is out of line, if that's the way you feel. However, you should always recognize that the interviewer might feel he has a legitimate reason for asking this type of question and imposing this type of stress. If you're being considered for a position as a litigator, the question could be a legitimate attempt to determine how you would function in the real world, because litigation can be like war, and attorneys have no compunction against pulling any string they can to win. If a litigator thinks he can get you angry and if that will be to his advantage, he might do anything he can to upset you and gain an edge. So maybe the question might have been a legitimate imposition of stress to determine how you would react to an outrageous personal attack that could arise in the real world.

I'm not justifying the offensive imposition of stress here. But you must constantly keep in mind during the interview process that you are looking for a job and that it is not in your best interest to take offense. You should always try to realize that there could be an underlying reason for which a question is asked other than that which is apparent on its face.

If you feel you have been unfairly harassed or discriminated against, you may have recourse under certain federal and state laws. See chapter 14 for more on this.

GROUP INTERVIEW

In a group interview there are many interviewees and either one or several interviewers. This format was originally devised to select officer candidates for the armed forces. Normal one-on-one interviewers with resumés and reference checks had not been reliable in determining natural leadership ability. In this method a group of candidates was assembled and assigned a task to accomplish as a group. The group was then observed during its performance.

It is said that a group will always stratify and that eventually a leader will emerge. James D. Weinland and Margaret V. Gross, in their book *Personnel Interviewing*, say that "this person is apt to be what is called a 'natural leader.' Since he has no credentials, he must win the acceptance of the group and cannot be put in place merely by an external influence."

In a group interview normal rules no longer hold. Now that you know what a group interview is, and how to recognize it, you should have a big advantage over other interviewees because the real purpose of the group interview is not explained. In a business context it may be presented as a group discussion. Since you know that the purpose is not to study what is said or the opinions expressed, but to determine some characteristics of how you interact with other members of the group, you should try to determine the characteristics for which the interviewers are searching and direct your attention toward the group with this in mind.

The group interview is rarely used in the United States, but it is a method of which you should be aware in the unlikely event you are faced with it.

BOARD INTERVIEW

In a board interview there is one interviewee and many interviewers. A typical board interview is the doctoral candidate's oral examination. The federal government sometimes uses the board interview, too. It is perhaps most common in industry in interviewing for higher-level corporate positions, such as president or vice president.

How you should handle yourself in a board interview does not differ greatly from the normal interview. The only added factor is that there is more than one person, so you cannot concentrate on establishing a rapport with one person. *If you're uneasy, the best way to handle a board interview is to pretend that you are talking to only one person, the one who is questioning you.* In this way you might be able to forget the other eyes that are upon you, and you might, in your mind's eye, convince yourself that you are in a simple one-on-one interview. The two important rules are to be relaxed and maintain your confidence.

TELEPHONE INTERVIEW

Reader More Irvine, a judge on the Board of Industrial Insurance Appeals in Olympia, Washington, writes of a problem people may face when they are looking for work out of their home area:

> I decided to change positions, and I began a job search, mostly with the federal government, and mostly in the Washington, D.C., area. I was able to secure two excellent interviews, one with the U.S. Claims Court and the other with the Appeals Council for the Office of Hearings and Appeals for the Social Security Administration. Because these are federal positions, neither would pay for me to fly out for the interview. The law prohibits it. As a result, I had to make the hard decision of undertaking the expense of flying cross-country or accepting their offer of doing a telephone interview.

Judge Irvine's problem presents a basic financial decision that only the person involved can make. If you travel to a distant location for an interview, it's an indication of your enthusiasm for the job and your confidence in your ability to get the job. However, if you simply cannot afford it, you should make this fact clear to your interviewer and try for a telephone interview. A telephone interview produces less stress, but it lacks the immediacy of being there in person. If you don't have the funds to finance the trip, then you don't have a choice. If you do have the money but it would impose a hardship, you must make a decision involving several variables:

1. How much do you want the job?
2. Do you know enough about the job to be able to make that kind of decision?

3. How confident are you that, if you spend the money to go to the interview, you'll be offered the job?
4. How will you react if you spend the money to go but don't get an offer or decide you don't want the job?

This problem requires a great deal of self-knowledge and honesty, in addition to the financial aspect. Be sure you evaluate it properly and consider all the factors, not just one, because your desire for the job may outweigh the practicalities of the situation. If the interview is a screening interview, it would not seem worth such an expenditure. However, if you've passed the screening stage and the expenditure would be for a selection interview, you should ask for a telephone interview first.

In the telephone interview you should be as much interviewer as interviewee, trying to determine as much about the job and the employer as you can. If you then determine that the job's what you want and the person for whom you would be working is acceptable, then you would be in a position to make the decision of whether or not to spend the money for the second interview.

JESSE MARVIN UNRUH FELLOWSHIP PROGRAM INTERVIEW

The California State Assembly Fellowship Program is an excellent example of the combined use of group and board interviews in awarding fellowships for its ten-month program. Founded in 1957, it is one of the nation's oldest and most prestigious legislative fellowship programs. This unique program provides an opportunity for individuals of all ages, ethnic backgrounds, and experiences to directly participate in the legislative process. In 1987 the program was renamed the Jesse Marvin Unruh Assembly Fellowship Program to honor California's former Assembly Speaker and state treasurer. Each year, eighteen individuals are selected to participate in the program. The eleven-month fellowship provides an introduction to public policy formation and adoption in the California Legislature through full-time work as a professional legislative staff member. Charlotte Ashmun, who has been both an interviewee applying for a fellowship and, subsequently, an interviewer evaluating candidates for fellowships the following year, gives an insider's description of the process from both viewpoints:

It is a four-tiered interviewing system. The first three stages have to do with getting the fellowship itself, and the final stage has to do with the placement once you are a fellow.

First you fill out an application form, and there are usually about five hundred applicants for eight fellowships. That's used to screen.

The next stage is a board interview that consists of a committee of about nine academic people from throughout the state and Assembly staff who interview alone. They ask political questions and theoretical questions and quite a range of questions as to how you would deal with problems.

Then the final stage is a group interview with the last group of finalists. You go through a process which involves three rooms full of interviewers. The interviewers are divided into three groups also. You go into each of the three rooms in succession and have a discussion on a policy topic.

There's no interference by the interviewers. The entire process is done by the interviewees and their intergroup reactions and that sort of thing.

It's terribly effective, but it's frightening, too.

They're looking for how articulate you are, how well you think over a policy issue, and they're also looking for people who are going to be abrasive. They're not looking for people who are going to be all talk and no content.

I wasn't impressed with the validity of the test when I went through it. But the next year, I participated in it and saw the comparison of the notes by the interviewers and their discussion in choosing who should be selected for the program and who should not. Then I saw that as I stayed with one group all day long and followed them through their process, it became clear quickly who would make it as a fellow and who would not.

Some people were too shy and would not speak up about their thoughts. In the position that the fellowship holds with the Legislature you're in front of committees and are asked questions about the bills you write by the committee members with the press there, and you can't be so shy and retiring that you can't support the bill that you've been working on.

Additionally, a staff member has to be able to stay a staff member and not try to be too much of a star. So although it was good to be able to give some guidance to the group and keep them on track, if you were trying to make yourself look good to the disadvantage of everyone else, that was viewed quite negatively.

Know What the Interviewer Is Looking For

No matter what technique an interviewer uses, each is trying to fill a specific position. A set of specifications will have been formulated for that position, and the interviewer will be looking for certain characteristics.

When the group interview was devised by the armed forces during World War II, it was used to determine the leadership characteristics of the candidates. The interviewers were looking for the person who could take charge of the group naturally. If you knew the purpose, you could gear your performance to that objective.

The California State Assembly's goal was directly contrary. Even though the same format was used—the group interview—the Assembly was looking for opposite characteristics: people who will *not* exert their leadership characteristics, people who can function on a staff in an advisory role and leave the leadership to the Assembly for whom they will be working.

Once again preparation emerges as of prime importance in determining how to approach an interview. If you know what the interviewer is looking for, you will have a tremendous advantage over the other interviewees because you will be able to key your performance to those characteristics. This knowledge alone may not land you a job offer, but it can protect you against making a gaffe that might result in rejection.

Checklist

- A screening interviewer is looking just for the facts.
- A screening interviewer is looking for a reason to reject you rather than a reason to accept you.
- The purpose of the screening interview is to weed out unacceptable candidates.
- A screening interviewer is well trained in the art of interviewing; a selection interviewer is generally not.
- Don't volunteer anything in a screening interview.
- Let the screener control both the flow and the content of the interview.

- Avoid controversy.
- An interview is a meeting between two people for the purpose of evaluating the qualifications or capabilities of one of them.
- Always expect to meet a conscientious, knowledgeable, and well-researched person.
- A directed interview is structured, impersonal, and generally used only by screening interviewers.
- A nondirective interview is one where the interviewee is allowed to talk about that which he or she wishes.
- A stress interview is designed to make the interviewee uncomfortable and to bring out insecurities.
- Be aware of stress. If you are expecting it and recognize it when it is introduced, you will be better able to handle it well by retaining your composure.
- Most selection interviews are a combination of the nondirective and stress types.
- A group interview has many interviewees and either one or several interviewers.
- A board interview uses several interviewers.
- Try to determine before the interview what the interviewer(s) will be looking for.

4

Enthusiasm

Nothing great has ever been done without enthusiasm.
—Ralph Waldo Emerson

In his book *Successful Salesmanship* Paul Ivey defines enthusiasm as "a spirit which animates the whole body and makes an attractive and convincing salesman out of an assortment of dead flesh and bones." I'd go a bit further. *Enthusiasm is the exhibition of fervent interest.* And it is highly contagious.

When you take part in an interview, it is not enough just to say you are interested. You must show it through your actions. I've conducted many interviews in which well-qualified interviewees sit and answer questions as if they are going through some sort of initiation rite. When the interview is over, they just leave, having lost the opportunity to make some positive impression on me. Whether lack of enthusiasm like this is due to fear or nervousness, to the misconception that it is wise to play hard to get, or to just plain ignorance, it is bound to affect the interviewer negatively.

To prevent any such spiraling effect in your own interviews, it is essential that you go into them determined to project a sense of vitality. After all, the interview is an event in itself—something different from an offer or a job. You can be enthusiastic about yourself, your interests, the interests of the interviewer, or the company. The point to remember is that without enthusiasm, you'll risk coming across as a dud.

Reader Raymond L. Berry of Dunsmuir, California, writes:

About a year ago I moved from the San Francisco Bay Area, where I was a college instructor, to a small town near Mt. Shasta, to help a friend start a small business. I figured with my education and experience I would have no trouble getting a job.

Because I quit my last job, I was not entitled to unemployment benefits, so my savings started to dwindle as I applied for job after job, getting no offers. I made seven different versions of my resumé, left off my education, lowered my expectations, and started applying for minimum-wage positions.

Because there is no economic base up here except tourism, jobs are at a premium. But the most frustrating part of this experience is that I was being rejected because (1) employers didn't think I had a valid reason to be up here, and (2) the eight miles to the next town was considered "too far to go" and I was rejected there because they wouldn't hire anybody from "that town." Part of it I think is small-town rivalry, and part because in winter it snows and locals don't think that anyone else knows how to get around.

After reading *Sweaty Palms* I knew I had to change my strategy if I wanted to work, so I threw out my old resumé, got rid of my negative attitude, and just used enthusiasm and friendliness. I had three interviews and three job offers. Not career positions, but at least I broke the "no job" syndrome. First time I had an experience like this, and am finding out now that it happens to a lot of others who leave the big city for the mountains.

Treat Each Interview as an Experience

Each interview will probably present you with a different challenge. It's exciting to go into an interview knowing that you'll be presented with the challenge of interpreting the interviewer's personality (and for this chapter let's assume the interviewer is a woman). Maybe you'll need to discover her interests. Maybe you'll need to talk about yourself and your own interests to find a common ground. Even though you can expect similar things from each interview, the challenge is that each interview is an unknown in terms of the personality of the interviewer. If you view it this way, you can retain your enthusiasm for each interview.

This doesn't mean you have to prostrate yourself in front of your interviewer, begging for a job about which you know nothing in order to be enthusiastic. I've had many interviews in which I found out early that the interviewee was not appropriate for the job, but I was so interested in finding out more about him or her that my own enthusiasm was unbounded.

Once I interviewed a law student who was interested in working only where he could use his proficiency in the Mandarin dialect of the Chinese language. It was obvious to both of us that the interview would not result in a job offer for him. But he was so enthusiastic about his training in Chinese and his work in Panmunjom, Korea, that it resulted in one of the longest interviews I've ever had. He was enthusiastic about telling me about his interests, and I was enthusiastic to learn more about him. As a result, even though the goal each of us sought, a job offer, was not achieved, this interview stands out as one of the most memorable I've ever had, and it was solely because of his enthusiasm. I have recommended him to a couple of corporations that had international departments, and I still keep him in mind years later.

One of the best ways to project enthusiasm is to try to make the other person enthusiastic. Years ago I read Dale Carnegie's *How to Win Friends and Influence People.* In it he tells how to get people to like you. One of the methods he suggests is to get them to talk about themselves. He tells of picking out some small thing you notice about someone and asking about it. He gives examples, as I do here, of the way this has worked for him and others.

I read his book with a somewhat jaundiced eye, assuming that the examples were there just to fit the rule he was laying down. I didn't think much about it until one day I was sitting in a barber's chair. I had never visited this shop before, so I didn't know the barber. Worse, he was extremely taciturn. So I sat in an uncomfortable silence as he cut my hair, responding to my few attempts at conversation with grumbles.

Then I remembered Dale Carnegie. I tried to discover something about the barber and his shop upon which I could comment to see if Carnegie's method could really work. Finally, the barber lathered my neck, and, after stropping his straight razor, he started shaving. I commented, "Gee, that sure is a sharp razor."

That simple comment was akin to "Open, sesame!" He told me that his father had given him that razor, that it had come from Germany, and that he had used it for years. "There's not another razor like this in America," he said. He was as proud of that razor as a parent of a child. He talked and talked and talked about his razor. I was interested not only because his story of the razor was unique but because my innocent remark had opened a door to the man's heart.

No longer withdrawn, he was warm and friendly. I was excited because I had never dreamed that the rules I had read in Carnegie's book would work so well. I stayed after he had finished my haircut and talked with him for fifteen minutes while he worked on the next man. When I left, he said he hoped I'd be coming back because he "really enjoyed talking" to me, even though all I had done was ask a question or two while he monopolized the conversation.

I had turned a silently morose barber into a William Jennings Bryan of fire and brimstone just by asking him about his razor. This was the love of his life, apparently, and he was enthusiastic about it. His enthusiasm was contagious. It made me enthusiastic just to listen to him. Although I had little interest in his razor, his tremendous emotion conveyed itself to me and I was caught up in his enthusiasm.

My barber story is not the exception that proves a converse rule. I am constantly amazed at how often it works to bring people out of themselves. When I was practicing law in London, I used the Middle Temple law library to do my research. The American section was on the top floor, and there was rarely anyone else in there but me and the librarian, a wizened old fellow who never opened his mouth or acknowledged my presence.

One day, after months of coming and going, I noticed him reading a book on gardening. Although I'm no expert, I was raised in a house that had a large garden, and one of our flowers was hibiscus. I stopped by his desk and asked if there were hibiscus in London. He opened like a blooming flower, told me of his garden in Cornwall, the flowers in it, and the years he had devoted to it. From that point on we were bosom buddies.

When you've successfully brought someone out of himself in this way, you'll be amazed at the rewarding feeling you'll have. I doubt if there's anything I'd rather talk about less than gardening, but I was never bored by the librarian's discussions. The combination of his enthusiasm and the success of my ploy worked to keep my interest aroused.

It's not enough to simply ask a question. You have to project genuine interest. And if you get a response like I did from the barber and the librarian, you're going to be interested. It won't matter if he's talking about the time and methods he used to observe grass growing; if he's turned on about the subject, you're going to be spellbound, if not by the subject, certainly by the emotion you have sparked.

Be Willing to Take a Chance

Even if it appears that you don't have a chance in a million of landing a particular job, you should still go into the interview with a positive attitude. My files are full of stories of job seekers who did a little extra, took a chance, and accomplished the seemingly impossible. For example, reader Marylee Nurrenbern of Irvine, California, says:

> I am sixty-four years old and I was beginning to think all I could get for employment was "bagging" in a grocery store! Then I read your book and started interviewing. I tried twice and didn't get a job, but I kept remembering things you said! And I didn't give up! On the third try I landed a very nice job in a beautiful legal office. All I did was strike a wonderful rapport with the interviewer; I really "took a chance" and was just myself. I knew the job was right for me, and I told her that—*bingo!*

When I was in law school, it seemed that 90 percent of my class was interested in practicing international law. On the day when one of the largest international law firms on Wall Street visited campus to interview, the line to sign up was almost unending.

The interviewer was the senior partner in the firm. He also taught a seminar on international law at the law school. He interviewed for three days but made only one offer and that to one of the top students in the class. I was in the seminar he taught, along with another member of the class who had interviewed but been rejected and whose grades caused him to languish in the middle of the class. This student was determined that he was going to work for that firm, and so he was always well prepared for the seminar. Unfortunately, the seminar was usually conducted by associates in the firm, not the partner. Nevertheless, my classmate continued to prepare while the rest of us took it easy, knowing that our grade did not depend on performance in the seminar. One day the associate who was scheduled to appear could not make it, and the senior partner had to conduct the seminar—but he wasn't prepared at all. He was saved by my classmate, who virtually took over the class that evening. He was the only one who was prepared, and he talked for almost the entire two hours. The senior partner was so impressed that he offered the student a job, and, in storybook fashion, the student became a partner in the firm.

By showing enthusiasm and ingenuity and perseverance, he impressed the one who had to make the decision. The job was offered not so much because of the interviewee's quality, but because of the extra effort he took to figure out how to get the job after the initial rejection. This way of thinking will impress an interviewer time and again. So do something unusual to set you apart from the others. Be enthusiastic.

As a teenager, First World War flying ace Eddie Rickenbacker wanted desperately to work for the Frayer Miller automobile manufacturers, so he started hanging around the plant on his days off. Finally, Lee Frayer noticed him and asked him why he was always hanging around every Sunday. Rickenbacker told him that he wanted a job. Frayer said they didn't have anything he could do. But Rickenbacker had noticed how dirty the place was and told Frayer that there was something he could do and he'd be back the next Sunday.

He arrived at 7 a.m. "with broom and brush" and worked feverishly. When Frayer arrived at 8:30, half the work area was spotless and the other half filthy. Frayer smiled and said that Rickenbacker had his job.

Reader Margot L. Wawra of Clearbrook, British Columbia, tells of two instances in which her enthusiasm paid off:

When I came to Canada thirty-five years ago, my knowledge of English was limited. So I went to the university of our town, sitting in free lectures where I could and devouring books and magazines in the library. One day I noticed on the blackboard a job opportunity for a library helper. I applied. The interviewing woman looked at my neat portfolio and my past experience and remarked that I seemed well qualified, but she was afraid that my knowledge of English was not yet sufficient. That didn't dampen my enthusiasm: "I will work the first month without pay, then you can see what I can do." Instead, they hired me but at the lowest possible wages. I didn't mind. I worked there for a couple of years and then entered the university as an art student. I made my B.A. with great honors and did postgraduate work in Los Angeles. Then I opened an art studio in our town where I worked on my sculptures and paintings and taught art classes.

Years down the road, our local YWCA needed a program director. The salary was very tempting, and with two degrees in my pocket, I felt confident. The executive director seemed very interested, though she probed in all directions, and I sensed a hidden agenda, a hesitation in her voice in connection with certain questions. I tuned in on her wavelength and heard myself say: "I am very interested in the work, even if there is no prospect of long-range employment. If you decide to hire me, I plan to keep my art studio open. I like to spend my spare time there and then I can slip back into teaching whenever my work here ends." The director showed signs of relief. She had been afraid to carry a highly paid employee longer than needed. I got the position and worked for the Y for many happy years.

These stories point up the fact that sometimes you have to take a gamble. To do so, you must be so enthusiastic about the potential rewards that you are willing to risk what prospectively looks like certain failure. Without enthusiasm your frame of mind will tell you that your actions are illogical and a waste of time. With enthusiasm your frame of mind is such that you will not admit failure, and you will then proceed with abandon.

Sometimes you have to risk a lot of time in taking a chance. The story told me by a real estate broker, Ginger, epitomizes how taking a chance on spending a lot of time preparing for something that might just be a crapshoot can pay off. When a real estate broker goes to get a listing, this is just as much a job interview as when someone goes to interview for a secretarial position or any other position with someone else. So how this woman prepared is a very important lesson. Here's her story.

There was a very attractive property that was coming up for a listing, but it was in an area with which I wasn't that familiar. I work in the Marina del Rey, Venice, Playa del Rey areas of Los Angeles, and this was coming up in Santa Monica. That can be Afghanistan as far as "knowing the territory," as Harold Hill of *The Music Man* might say. The other agents who had "big names" in the neighborhood, or knew the people, did the minimum work and gave a personal opinion. I had two big negatives. First, I didn't know the area. Second, I was going out of town for almost three weeks and wouldn't be able to start on it until I returned. Even though I knew it was a long shot because of those two negatives, I decided to take a shot at it. I really did extensive, time-consuming research and drove by similar properties so I could talk about them. I gave my opinion—before I asked how much they wanted—but only after I had properly informed them. But that wasn't all.

My presentation consisted of:

1. My philosophy of a sane work ethic (who am I?)
   a. I do not spend money on expensive pamphlets, luxury cars, or secretaries. These savings allow me to pass the savings on to the seller in the form of a lower commission. This is important to emphasize because the standard commission is 6 percent of the sales price. If I spent a lot of money, I couldn't afford to cut the commission. But because my overhead is low, I can reasonably work for a lower commission than a Realtor who drives a big car, has a big or expensive office to maintain, and spends a lot on sales brochures to get listings. I wanted to go into this in detail to explain why I could work for a lower commission and to point out that the other Realtors have to have a higher commission just to pay for their overhead or lifestyle. I don't have to, so I wanted them to understand that I was able to work for a lower commission and that accepting a lower commission didn't mean I was desperate or trying to cut other Realtors out.
   b. In this market properties sell quickly. I spend less time and less money on advertising; therefore, to expect

even a 5 percent commission isn't being fair to the seller. This is a big selling point as to accepting a lower commission because most brokers have their standard pitches about how valuable they are and how they are worth the full commission. If I can explain to them how I can make what I consider to be adequate compensation by agreeing to a 4 or 3 percent commission, it gives me a real leg up on the Realtors who are pushing to get the full commission, which I think is insane.

   c. I have twenty-three years' experience and have owned three offices, an escrow company, and a mortgage company.

   d. I prepared plain, simple resumés and let them do any boasting.

   e. I can be reached immediately on my cell phone.

2. My cooperation ethic

   a. Other Realtors are part of my team.

   b. I cooperate to the fullest extent and treat everyone with exceptional courtesy. This offsets their irritation over my discount fees and allows my clients the greatest marketing exposure.

   c. I never cut their commissions (selling agents)—only my own.

   d. Every agent who shows or writes an offer is treated like "family" (only better).

3. The property's value

   a. A brief history of the city where they live. I had to do a lot of research on this because I just wasn't familiar with the area. But it paid off. I could tell them chapter and verse of what sold when and for how much. I could tell them the values of each area of Santa Monica by the time I made the presentation. I also xeroxed maps of their property and other similar properties from *The Thomas Guide*, which allowed me to give them a better understanding of the area where they were located and why different properties that might look comparable might sell for different prices.

b. I brought a list of properties currently in escrow and those that recently sold in their area, but I kept this very brief.

c. Finally, I went over the advantages and disadvantages of their property and was very frank.

4. A statement of understanding of the work they had put into their property. They told me that not one other agent recognized this or said anything about it. It turns out that they had spent three years rebuilding it and were extremely proud of it. So my volunteering this information was big. I told them I understood how hard it was to get permits through any municipality.

5. I expressed verbal support for them to attempt to get maximum dollar in a booming market, and I explained to them that this did not make them "greedy," just good businesspeople. But I emphasized that getting more money might take more time and that we had to work together.

6. I went over the advantages and disadvantages of "multiple offers."

7. I went over the things they must do prior to selling that expedite the offer and escrow periods.

8. I covered the things they must do to avoid future legal problems.

9. I went over the things they must do now to assist their accountant in decreasing their capital gain problem later.

10. I talked to them about the things they must do to help their buyer live in this home without future problems.

11. I briefly covered the California requirements on disclosures that must be made by any seller of residential property.

Lastly, I gave them the bad news. I would be gone for two and a half weeks. They felt I was worth waiting for. Not because I am smarter, but because I genuinely care about doing the very best job possible to get them maximum dollar, with the least aggravation and the best legal protection. I also want the buyer and other agents to be treated fairly, and they liked that.

Attitude

Because you radiate what you feel, your state of mind will be directly related to the success or failure of your interview. If your attitude is bad, there's no way that you can be enthusiastic. If you enter the interview with a chip on your shoulder, you'll be written off in a trice.

I conducted an interview at a law school several years ago that epitomizes how a bad attitude can affect an interviewee's enthusiasm. The interviewee showed up dressed as if he were going to play football in the mud. He wore a dirty sweatshirt with holes in it, dirty blue jeans, and old Adidas sneakers. Although he had an excellent scholastic record, he responded to my questions sullenly and abrasively. Finally, after the videotaping was over, I asked him if he showed up for all his interviews dressed that way.

That was what he was waiting for. All the rancor in him exploded. "If they don't like the way I look, the hell with 'em."

This fellow was so proud of his antiestablishment posture that it dominated his personality. His antagonism for the way people dressed permeated the interview. Lighted bamboo shoots under his fingernails couldn't have affected his interview worse.

His goal in the interview was to make the point that he would do, speak, and dress as he pleased and no one was going to change him. He knew in advance that his dress was atypical for an interview and that it would be noticed. He waited for me to bring it up, and when he got his chance, he exploded.

He sat through the entire interview waiting for a fight. He flaunted his sloppy attire like a flung gauntlet. The content of the interview was merely a prelude for making his point. Even had the subject not been raised, he would have blown the interview because he came across as sullen and negative.

More often, however, the problem with attitude is not a childish temperament, but a defeatist outlook. If you have been through a few interviews and have not received any offers or encouragement, it's very easy to become downcast and feel that you're a chronic failure. You must do everything in your power to overcome this mind-set because while a sense of failure or doom may not make much difference in simple social contact, in an interview it can easily cause you to fail. An interviewer is trying to get at the person beneath the surface. The worst thing that you can display is a sense of gloom or defeat. If you do not believe in yourself, why should the interviewer?

When Roger Ailes, a public relations executive who was the moving force behind the success of the Fox News network, among other things, was in college looking for a job, he had no experience. As reported by Ken Auletta in the *New Yorker*, "he had a job interview with the program manager of a Cleveland television station. The manager, Chet Collier, remembers him as a slender, self-confident young man. 'I was impressed with his enthusiasm, his willingness to think in different ways.'" Ailes's enthusiasm got him the job and he was on his way to a great career.

No matter how many rejections you receive, you must keep your outlook bright and positive.

The most an author can do is to offer his advice and ideas. It is up to the reader to decide whether to accept the advice and then to decide whether to use it. You may read this book, find it entertaining, and even believe it. But if you don't try the things outlined here, it will be to no avail. *I urge you to lose your inhibitions and give the techniques a whirl.* I'm sure you will find that you'll get far more out of an interview, are less nervous going in and more confident during it. You should find that your interviews will flow more easily and that you will establish a better rapport with your interviewer. Best of all, whether you get a job or not, you'll come out of each interview feeling that you have learned something new.

Checklist

- You must show that you are interested.
- Communicate your interest to the interviewer.
- Be interested in the interview as an event in itself.
- Lose your inhibitions and try what you've learned.
- Enthusiasm begins with a positive attitude.
- Think that you're going to win.
- Make an impression on the one who is to make the decision.
- Be willing to gamble on what may logically appear to be certain failure.
- Take as much time as needed to prepare for a good presentation.

5

Question and Answer

No matter how many questions you ask of the interviewer (for this chapter let's assume the interviewer is a man and the interviewee is a woman), and no matter how much control you are able to assert over the interview, the essence of any interview remains locked in to the format of a question-and-answer session run by the interviewer. Ultimately, whether your interview is successful or not depends on your ability to answer the interviewer's questions effectively.

To do this, you will want to prepare yourself by doing research on the interviewer, the company, and the job for which you are applying, as discussed in chapter 2. You should also review the list of typical interview questions in appendices A and C. If any of these questions give you difficulty, work out answers so that you'll be ready if you're hit with them in an interview. Remember the old saying, "To be forewarned is to be forearmed."

This book will not provide you with canned responses to these questions, however, or any other questions you might be asked in an interview. The purpose of an interview is for the interviewer and the interviewee to get to know one another, and using my words to answer questions will not accomplish that purpose.

What this book will give you is the confidence to answer any question you might be asked and to answer it yourself in your own words from your own experience. After you finish reading *Sweaty Palms*, you'll be able to enter any interview without the fear of being surprised by what's going to happen. If you take the advice to heart, you'll know yourself well enough to be able to handle anything an interviewer might throw at you. Anybody who gives you canned answers to prospective questions is doing you a disservice. Not only will it impede your growth as a person and rob you of the confidence and pride you should have in yourself, but an interviewer who hears the same answer more than once will immediately realize what has happened, and that will not result in his forming a favorable impression.

It's important to understand that in the question-and-answer session the interviewer is trying to do more than find out if you are qualified for the position. The interviewer is also trying to find out what kind of person you are, and this subjective feeling is apt to be the most important aspect of the interview.

The questions and answers of an interview are merely the tools used to make an evaluation, the trees in the forest of impression. The manner in which you answer the questions and whether or not you appear self-confident are far more important than the words you use in your answer. Your goal, then, is to use the format of the interview to establish the proper rapport with the interviewer and generate a positive feeling. How the interviewer feels about you will have greater weight than your qualifications when it comes to making final judgments.

When the Beatles were still struggling Liverpool musicians, their manager, Brian Epstein, tried for months to get them a tryout with a record company. Finally, he convinced producer George Martin to give them an audition. Martin was favorably impressed, and the rest is history. But what was it that persuaded Martin to give the greatest songsters of the generation their start? In a candid interview Martin said, "It wasn't their music that sold them to me; it was their charm. They were very charming people."

When you realize that the Beatles got their first record contract on the basis of charm rather than musical ability, you will understand the importance of making a good impression. Martin's admission should be enshrined in every interviewee's mind and should be recalled before the start of each interview.

There's a distinction to be made between preparing answers to questions and preparing to answer questions, and this distinction can mean the difference between a successful interview and an unsuccessful one. The purpose of this chapter is to give advice on how to handle questions in a manner calculated to leave a good impression on the interviewer. Remember, one of your prime goals in any interview is to enhance the feeling the interviewer develops about you. It's not only the content of your answers that contributes to this feeling. The *manner* in which you answer them is as important as what you say.

Listen to the Question

The first mistake that many interviewees make is that they don't listen to the question. In order to avoid misunderstandings, or giving answers that miss the point of the question, always listen very carefully to the question and the way it is phrased. If the interviewer asks for specific information, don't play semantic games; answer the question specifically. If you don't wish to answer, sometimes it's better to decline frankly than to beat around the bush with an evasive reply. Later we'll discuss when ignoring this rule might be in your best interest.

The Ambiguous Question

One of the reasons answers often do not address the questions is that interviewees tend to make assumptions and base their answers on these assumptions without stating them.

In their book *Pairing* George Bach and Ronald Deutsch warn never to "assume or predict that you know what your partner is thinking until you have checked out the assumption in plain language; nor assume or predict how he will react, what he will accept or reject." This is easy to say but very difficult to do, particularly in an interview. You can't state your assumptions prior to answering a question as if you were writing a legal brief. People are not machines, and they don't converse like machines.

While psychological self-help books like *Pairing* treat things on a plane where all solutions are ideal and people react consistently, in reality this is not true. Each person is different from another, and each reacts differently. So while the scenarios that are acted out in these books always work out the way the authors intend, their successful conclusions may bear little correlation to real life.

If a question could be interpreted in more than one way, and you are unsure about the point, ask for a clarification. For example, one question that is often asked in interviews is, "What are your goals?" This is ambiguous; people generally have several types of goals—personal, recreational, professional. When I ask this question, I am as interested in how the interviewee handles the inherent ambiguity of the question as I am in the content of the reply. Will the answer be, "Well, I want to be happy and raise a nice family," or "I want to be manager of the department," or "I've always wanted to break ninety on the golf course"? Or will there be a request for clarification? How the interviewee interprets the question, the assumptions she makes, tells me something as valuable about her as the actual content of the answer.

Often the answer will be a request for clarification. "What do you mean? Do you want to know what my professional goals are or what I want out of life?" There is nothing wrong with this answer. It is quite good. I then state what I want to hear, and the interviewee answers accordingly. This type of answer involves no risk. There is a question in the interviewee's mind and rather than guess at the interviewer's meaning, she clarifies the ambiguity and then answers based upon the clarification by the interviewer.

When a question is ambiguous, the ball is in your court. You can do with it what you want. If there's something you want to bring out during the interview, and the ambiguous question gives you the opportunity to say what you want, don't ask for the clarification. Interpret the question the way you wish and answer it to your best advantage. If, on the other hand, the ambiguity troubles you, ask for the clarification. There is no risk involved. You find out what the interviewer wants to know, and supply the information.

The Thinking Pause

Another technique you may use in answering questions is to think over an answer before you give it, a method that can work in your favor. Yet often interviewees, intimidated by the power of the interviewer, are overly conscious of the time they are taking, and tend to rush into their answers.

Many times a few seconds for thought will be a godsend. Asking for clarification is a good ploy to gain this thinking time. It gives you time to think about your answer while the interviewer is clearing up the ambiguity. You can also gain a little thinking time by using a bridge such as, "Let me see . . ." or "That's a good question . . ."

If you have been asked a particularly difficult or weighty question, don't be afraid to take up extra time to consider your answer. The interviewer is talking with you because he is interested. He has budgeted time to talk with you, so the few extra seconds you spend formulating your thoughts will not be resented; they will probably be noted with approval.

The story of Dwight D. Eisenhower's interview with General George C. Marshall after the bombing of Pearl Harbor is a case in point. Marshall was looking for someone to command the forces in the Philippines and the Far East theater, and he summoned Eisenhower to Washington for an interview.

When Germany invaded Poland in 1939 and World War II was finally unavoidable, Eisenhower was a lieutenant colonel and felt that even with the war and America's almost inevitable involvement, he had little prospects for advancement. Despite this feeling, two years later, on December 12, 1941, less than a week after the Japanese bombed Pearl Harbor, Eisenhower had been promoted to brigadier general and was summoned to Washington by General Marshall, the chief of staff.

Eisenhower and Marshall had talked only twice before, once in 1930 and once in 1939. Marshall greeted Eisenhower perfunctorily and then outlined the stark situation that was facing the United States in the Pacific: the devastation of the Pacific fleet at Pearl, the invasion of the Philippines, the lack of any effective air strength, the damage caused by the Japanese army and air force, the critical supply shortage, the Japanese blockade. He painted a very grim picture of the situation. After he set the facts before Eisenhower, he looked Eisenhower in the eye and asked, "What should be our general line of action?"

Eisenhower was taken aback. He had just stepped off the plane and had no real personal knowledge of the situation.

Here was the man who had to make the decision, a man who had been well briefed and was on top of the situation, asking his opinion! Eisenhower was intuitive enough to recognize the importance of the question both for the war effort and for him personally. He said later, "His tone implied that I had been given the problem as a check to an answer he had already reached."

If ever an interviewee could have been pressured into giving an immediate answer, Eisenhower at that moment in history was that man. Here was the newly appointed chief of staff asking his opinion of the situation in the Philippines where Eisenhower had served for four years. Yet he kept his composure and did not reply off the top of his head. He asked General Marshall for a few hours to consider his answer.

Eisenhower returned later that afternoon with his recommendation: Even though the situation was almost hopeless from a military point of view, he felt that the United States should do everything possible in defense of the Philippines. Marshall replied, "I agree with you. Do your best to save them."

Marshall's assessment of Eisenhower was undoubtedly based as much upon Eisenhower's method of answering the question as it was on the content of his answer. He wanted a man of judgment and depth, a man upon whom he could rely to make decisions based on analysis and cogitation. That Eisenhower displayed the confidence in himself to ask for time to formulate a reply must have impressed the chief.

This does not mean that you can ask for several hours before answering difficult questions in an interview. But it does illustrate the point that a few seconds of thoughtful silence before responding could be exactly what the interviewer is looking for.

Where to Look

Where do you look during an interview? Should you always look the interviewer straight in the eye and stare him down? Should you look away? This is one of the traumas many interviewees go through during an interview. The failure to establish any kind of eye contact during the interview is one of the reasons selection interviewers give for a no-hire decision. But this means only that you should occasionally look your interviewer in the eye. Constantly staring at your interviewer's eyes is just as negative as never looking at him. The best advice is simply to act naturally. Talk with the interviewer as though you were having a cup of coffee with a friend.

Dr. Gerhard Nielson of Copenhagen conducted a study of how and where interviewees normally looked. He filmed interviews on a fast-running camera. In replaying the films in slow motion, his results showed that there is less eye contact maintained during an interview than one might expect. The most an interviewee looked at the interviewer was 73 percent of the time, which means that there was no eye contact 27 percent of the time. One man looked away for 92 percent of the time. Nielson found that half of the interviewees looked away for 50 percent of the time.

Nielson discovered other interesting things. When people are speaking, they tend to look away; when they are listening, they tend to maintain eye contact. Thus it's normal for you not to look at the person with whom you are speaking. But I have found that interviewees worry about this and feel they should always look their interviewer in the eye. Yet, as Dr. Nielson's study found, this is abnormal. Being abnormal, it would strike the interviewer wrong and could very easily make him uncomfortable.

Nielson also discovered that interviewees tend to look away from the interviewer when they start to speak. There is a subtle timing in speaking, listening, looking, and looking away. Interviewees tend to look away just before or just after the beginning of one-quarter of their statements. Fifty percent of the interviewees look at the interviewer as they finish speaking.

Reader Jennifer Ruggaber of Syracuse, New York, quoted earlier, writes:

> As a shy person it makes me self-conscious and nervous to look the interviewer in the eyes. A trick I use that really works is to look at his nose. It is impossible to detect (except at very close range) and helps me to relax.

Forcing yourself to look the interviewer in the eye will come across unnaturally and leave a bad impression. Try instead to treat the interview as a conversation and act as you would in such a situation. The best rule is to act naturally and not to worry about eye contact.

Eye Signals

You should be aware of signals people make, often subconsciously, with their eyes. Even though neither party to a conversation may recognize the signals overtly, they may accept them as a nonverbal form of communication and act accordingly. You should be aware of these signals both as an interpretation for you to make of your interviewer and as signals you may be giving your interviewer.

Julius Fast, who has analyzed these signals in *Body Language*, postulates these meanings relating to eye signals:

1. If you look away while you speak, it means that you're explaining yourself and shouldn't be interrupted. If you

then look the other person in the eye, you are passing a signal to interrupt when you pause. But a pause without looking in the eye would mean that you aren't finished yet.

2. If you as a listener look away from a speaker, it may indicate that you are dissatisfied with what is being said or that you are trying to conceal your reaction to the speaker's words.

3. If you look away while you are speaking, it may be interpreted to mean you are uncertain of what you're saying.

4. If you as a listener look at a speaker, it may be a signal of agreement.

5. And if you as a speaker look at a listener, it may be a signal of confidence in what you say.

These are some assumptions that people may draw from your actions during conversation. Your actions may thus easily result in eliciting negative or positive reactions without your knowing exactly why. These are simply postulations based upon Fast's observations. They may be accurate in a certain situation, and, then again, they may not be. The point here is that you should be aware of the way your eye signals might be interpreted by your interviewer.

Never forget that the important thing an interviewer derives from an interview is an intuitive feeling about you. It's either positive or negative. More often than not, he will not be able to specify the exact reasons for his feeling, but he will have developed one nonetheless. It may be derived from how you have handled silence or how you've answered one question or how you've acted during conversation. Whatever it is, it's your task to enhance a positive feeling. It is therefore important to be aware of the signals you make, or might be interpreted as having made, during conversation and the typical reaction of others to these signals.

You can also use this information to make judgments on your interviewer. You can make assumptions based on where, when, and how he looks when he is speaking and listening.

The premise that a person who is uncertain of what he or she is saying will look away while saying it is probably accurate. But to conclude that all people who look away while speaking are uncertain of what they are saying is absurd. Most people look away while speaking, and it's unrealistic to think that they are all doing so because of uncertainty. They look away because that's the way most people naturally speak! So although eye signals are something of which you should be aware, I don't think they are especially important. What is important is that you act naturally and maintain a level of eye contact that is comfortable for you.

I mention Fast's ideas here simply because they add to your awareness of what's going on in an interview. If you're worried about whether you should concentrate on your eye signals or just forget them and act naturally, it's much better not to think about where you're looking and let your eyes fall where they may.

Just do what's natural to you. If it's natural to look your interviewer in the eye, do it. If it's not natural, don't do it. You shouldn't force anything, especially eye contact. You have to look at the interviewer in the eye occasionally, especially when he's speaking, but you needn't worry about doing it all the time. The key is to be natural.

Rolling Your Eyes

While it's important to relax and just do what comes naturally as regards eye contact, you do have to be concerned that you're not giving off the wrong vibrations. One woman, extremely bright and qualified, received rejection after rejection when she'd go on interviews for a high-level position. She couldn't figure out why.

Finally, she received an offer as a result of interviews on the telephone and her resumé, with no personal contact with her interviewer. Thinking about it, she realized that her mother and boyfriend had been criticizing her for rolling her eyes when they'd ask her something. "Don't go rolling your eyes at me," they'd say.

As we've seen, it's normal to look at someone when they're speaking, and normal to look away when you're speaking. She realized that when an interviewer was asking her a question, she'd look at him. But when the question was finished and it was time for her to answer, when she looked away, a natural movement, she did it by rolling her eyes. She didn't mean anything by it. It was something that had become a habit just in the past year or two. But to the interviewer it conveyed the impression that she was thinking, "What an idiotic question!" and the result was that it was taken as a personal affront.

This was a mannerism that cost this woman dearly. But it's a small thing, and if she hadn't been as smart as she is, she might never have realized what she was doing. I bring it up here so that you become aware of the way in which you look away. You might ask someone with whom you are close if they've ever noticed you rolling your eyes during conversation. If the answer is affirmative, work to develop the habit of looking away without rolling your eyes.

In his classic study of communications Professor Albert Mehrabian postulated that only 7 percent of your meaning is communicated by the words you use. Thirty-eight percent is in the way you use your words, and fully 55 percent of the meaning is communicated in your facial expression. Put another, more emphatic way, 93 percent of what you're trying to get across is communicated by your body language. Frankly, I don't buy this. Sociologists can generally put forth statistics to support anything. And, let's face it, how can this be proved? To postulate that only 7 percent of your meaning is communicated by your words is, to me, absurd. But the reason I mention this here is that you can get all sorts of crazy information when you read books written by people who have never done what they're writing about. Lots of people quote Mehrabian, and others, and just accept what he, and they, say as fact. Never having had the experience of actually conducting an interview, they don't question what people say to them. I've conducted too many interviews to buy into this stat. I know that what I get out of an interview is mostly from what people say and how they say it. Their body language is important, and it does convey something and it does contribute to the "feeling" I develop. But is 93 percent of what I receive based on nonverbal communication? No. It's important, though, and you should be aware of it and try to control it.

Treat Every Question as Important

Interviews are generally short. Therefore, you must recognize that each question has significance and that you shouldn't answer offhandedly, thinking that the interviewer is just trying to make conversation.

Act as if every question the interviewer asks has a purpose. If the interviewer is inexperienced, he may well be just trying to make conversation and keep things moving. But you can't rely on this judgment. If you assume the interviewer knows what he is doing and that there is a purpose to all the questions, you won't be harmed. If you make the contrary assumption, you can be devastated. The purpose of the question may be hidden.

A smart interviewer can determine many things from one response to one question.

Whenever you are tempted to throw away an answer, remember a story J. Paul Getty told about a test he once gave. He was concerned about cost consciousness at one of his companies and decided to test the attitude of his three top executives. He instructed the payroll clerk to make a five-dollar reduction in each of the executives' next paychecks, and told the clerk to send anyone who complained to Getty's office. Within an hour of distribution of the checks, all three executives were in Getty's office, complaining that their checks were short five dollars.

Getty pounced on them. He told them that there were so many inefficiencies in the company's operations that the company was losing tens of thousands of dollars. The executives were blind to these inefficiencies, but when the payroll department had an inefficiency that cost them five dollars, they were on it like a rabbit on a carrot. Getty reports that this test cost one of the executives his job. What seemed to be a simple thing to the executives was actually a career-testing confrontation.

Seemingly innocuous questions can have a great bearing on the judgment an interviewer makes on you. One interviewee told me of a lesson he had learned by not being attuned to the fact that every remark or question an interviewer makes may be meaningful. He was being interviewed for a position as a trainee by the buyer to whom he would report for a major toy manufacturing company. As part of their selection process he was required to take an IQ test. The interviewee had an IQ in excess of 150 and had the highest score ever achieved on the test.

The interviewer began by asking if the interviewee had been interviewing at many companies. The interviewee replied that he had been looking for a job for about a month. The interviewer offhandedly said, "I guess you're getting tired of these tests, eh?," to which the interviewee smiled and nodded in what he felt was a noncommittal way.

The interview didn't last much longer, but even before it ended, the interviewee realized that he had been tricked into indicating that he had done well on the IQ test only because he had been taking the same test over and over. In fact, it was the first IQ test he had taken since he graduated from college. He had made a noncommittal response to the buyer's friendly intimation merely to be agreeable. His failure to be alert to provide accurate information to the question had cost him.

His response should have been along the following lines: "No, this is the first such test I have taken since I was a sophomore in college, and I was somewhat surprised to find that you would require an IQ test for this position. Do you find that it adequately tests for an aptitude for being a buyer?"

This response not only gets across the fact that the test score was an accurate measure of the interviewee's IQ, but it puts the interviewer in the difficult position of defending the use of the test to a person who scored very high on it. If the interviewer does defend the accuracy of the test, how can he logically reject an applicant who scored so well, at least on that basis?

The answer, however, carries a greater risk than most, because the challenge is pretty aggressive. Basically, the interviewee is challenging not only the interviewer but the company's entire selection format. An answer like this could cause the interviewer to think, "Who is this person, a job applicant, challenging the criteria we have set for this position?" And this kind of thinking could lead to a negative response to the essential question each interviewer has: "Do I want someone like this working for me?" If your goal is to create the impression that you would be an agreeable person in the organization, this type of response could be extremely damaging. This dilemma is just an example of the many decisions with which you are faced when you are in a person-to-person interview situation. The solution lies in the personal assessment you have made of the interviewer by this stage of the interview. Since, in this instance, it was the first question asked, the interviewee was shooting from the hip, and that's probably why he reacted the way he did, and his timidity cost him the interview. At the first stage of the interview a better response would be a simple straightforward denial—"No, this is the first IQ test I've taken since I was a sophomore in college"—with no challenge.

Unfair Questions

Life, as John F. Kennedy once said, is not fair. Sometimes you'll be presented with a situation by a prospective employer that is eminently unfair. Colman Andrews, who was a restaurant writer for the *Los Angeles Times*, reported the following story about the manager of a tony private club in Los Angeles:

> One day, one of his better busboys came to him during the breakfast service and asked when he might be allowed to graduate to waiter status. "I'll get you a jacket and you can go on the floor right now," he replied, "if you can answer one question for me: What varieties of fruit are on the assorted fruit tray today?"
>
> The busboy was unprepared for the question and couldn't answer it. "When you start paying attention to details like that without anybody asking you," he told the aspiring waiter, "come ask me about being a waiter again."
>
> What the busboy replied is not on record.

When I first read this story, I was outraged, and I'm still outraged now, years later, as I write this. Here was a person starting out as the lowest employee in the restaurant hierarchy, a busboy, cleaning off tables. But he had ambition and showed it by approaching his boss and asking a simple question; he didn't need an impudent reply.

There are two conclusions the busboy could draw from the reply. One was that the reply was designed to put him in his place and keep him there instead of encouraging his ambition. As a busboy there was no requirement or need for him to know what kind of fruit was in the assorted fruit tray; his job was limited to cleaning off tables after the food had been eaten. So to ask a busboy something unrelated to his job was unfair. Besides, a wise manager wouldn't want his busboys wasting their time looking at the fruit trays every day to see what was on them. What for? That's not going to make them better busboys. Further, it's difficult to imagine that the manager of an exclusive private club would promote a busboy to waiter just because the busboy knew what was in the fruit tray that day. There's certainly more to being a waiter than that. So it's most likely that the manager was just being a wise guy and making a cruel joke at his busboy's expense, which he could later relate to a nationally prominent writer, who could then poke fun at the poor busboy.

The other conclusion the busboy could draw was that the manager was a wise person and he was answering his question honestly. And that's the initial conclusion the busboy should have drawn from the answer because, if you draw two conclusions from an answer, one of which requires no action to test the conclusion and the other allows action that could test the conclusion, you should adopt the latter. Even though the likelihood of this conclusion being accurate was slight, the busboy had little to lose by adopting and testing it and little to gain by taking offense at being made the butt of a joke.

So, taking the manager's answer literally, the busboy could make it a point to check each day on the fruit tray, then, a couple of weeks later, approach the manager with the same question about becoming a waiter. If the manager is an honest person, he will ask the same question. Upon receipt of the correct answer he would then take steps toward promoting the busboy. If he puts the busboy off once again, the busboy will know that the manager is a dishonest person and that he has no future working for him. He could start looking for another job with someone he could count on to reward his ambition and competence. Short of getting a job, what could be a better result of an interview than to discover the low character of the person for whom you would be working?

But not all restaurant managers are as arrogant and insensitive as the preceding one. Patrick Terrail, who established Ma Maison restaurant in Los Angeles, which was so successful it had an unlisted telephone number and was frequented by the Who's Who of Hollywood, developed a list of test questions applicants had to answer when applying for a job as a waiter:

1. Describe the service procedure in four or five steps for serving a bottle of red wine.
2. List four jobs a waiter should do before the restaurant opens.
3. List in order of importance to you the reasons for a successful restaurant.
4. True or false:
   a. A guest is not the person who makes it possible for us to earn our salary.
   b. A guest is dependent on us, we are not dependent on them.
   c. Waiters should chew gum while working at the restaurant.

It's no wonder that Patrick Terrail is successful. But when you're an interviewee, you must be prepared for both the good and the bad. If you discover the bad, you've done a good interview. I just hope that you have the courage and financial resources to reject the bad when you discover it. Sometimes you must take whatever is offered, but at least, if you've done a good interview, you will know the character of that person for whom you are working and will be able to act accordingly.

The Throwaway Joke

The many interviews I have conducted over the years tend to run together in my mind, but naturally, a few stand out for one reason or another. One fellow I interviewed for a position with a client gave me a classic answer when I asked him what he felt his biggest asset was. "I had my wife interview me last night," he said. "That was one of the questions she asked, and we discussed how to answer it. [Beat.] I guess my biggest asset is that I'm always on time."

I was nonplussed. Here was an entrée for him to tell of his most glowing achievement. He could have picked anything from when he won his high school debating medal to his courage on the battlefield to his industriousness, morality, candor, likability. Anything. Instead, he used this opportunity to crack a joke.

Revealing that he had gone through a mock interview was a calculated risk. Naturally, it's better to try to appear spontaneous, but to admit that you've prepared as much as this is not necessarily a negative. It shows the interviewer that you care enough to do some homework, and that's all to the good. Another point in his favor was that he was perceptive enough to anticipate a question that generally takes interviewees by surprise. Up to this point he was doing well.

But then he blew the opportunity. His answer indicated two

things to me. First, the easy judgment is to accept the answer at face value. His biggest asset is that he's on time. If that's the case, I don't want him. I want someone who has more to offer than that. The second possibility is that he's making a joke. In that case, I want him even less. Here is a man undergoing an interview that could change his life. He is asked a serious question, one that is obviously meaningful to his interviewer and begs for an intelligent response. Yet his response is a flip joke. This indicates a shallow, insensitive individual with whom I would never entrust serious problems.

I did not offer this man a job. I did interview him again to ensure that my initial judgment was correct. In this second interview he launched into a monologue that lasted an hour and fifteen minutes. My first impression was confirmed: The man had an abrasive personality and was insensitive. Even so, I checked the two references he gave me. Both were surprised that they had been given as references and, under probing questions, revealed their dissatisfaction with his personality and his ability to get along with others.

Here was a man who had three opportunities and flunked all three. Had his answer to the question he had anticipated been more mature, perhaps I would never have received the vibrations that I did. But then, that's the purpose of an interview, and it is what separates the good interviewer from the bad and the good interviewee from the bad.

Humor is not necessarily bad in an interview. The first time George Martin got the Beatles together for a recording session, Martin, trying to make them feel comfortable, explained what was going to occur and told them if they didn't like anything to let him know. George Harrison replied, "Well, for a start, I don't like your tie." This joke worked (even though it was Martin's favorite tie) and contributed to his positive feeling about their charm. Harrison's joke did not occur at the beginning of the interview, though, but after they had spent a considerable amount of time with each other. In addition, the Beatles were entertainers, and spontaneous humor was part of their job. Further, Martin's question was not a serious, probing one, but was clearly meant to put them at ease. Harrison's joke told him that he had done so without saying it in so many words.

So humor can be used if it is at an appropriate time and in good taste. Avoid poking fun at your interviewer, as it can be insulting, and the probability is that it will not inspire empathy. If you feel the need, it is better to make yourself the butt of your joke rather than taking the risk of offending your interviewer. Whether or not you use humor depends on whether or not you can recognize the right spot and are mature enough not to use a serious question as a straight line for a comedy routine.

The Blockbuster Question

Sometimes an interview will start with a real blockbuster of a question. The one that I think is the most difficult by far is, "Tell me about yourself." You think that looks easy and innocuous? Have it sprung on you at the beginning of an interview for a job you desperately want and then see if you think it's so simple.

What do you say? Do you repeat what's on the resumé? Do you tell about your love life? Talk about your outside interests? I was once doing a mock interview with a woman engineer who was applying to become an astronaut. She had already gone through the process once and been rejected. She reapplied and had been accepted for further consideration. She had read *Sweaty Palms* (I later found out that it was widely read at the Space Center in Houston) and contacted me to help her to prepare for her interview. My first question was, "Tell me about yourself." She proceeded to recite her resumé.

This surprised me. I told her that I didn't want to know what was on her resumé because I had already read it. I said that she should use this opportunity to tell something personal that wasn't on it.

If you've done your preparation, you know something about the interviewer, the company, and the job. You know what you want to say in the interview. Try to formulate an answer to this question *before* you go into the interview so that you can jump right into it. It is actually a terrific opportunity to take charge of the interview and talk about your strengths.

You can talk about accomplishments of which you're most proud. You can talk of your special qualifications that aren't on your resumé, and why you think you want the job and why you think you would do a good job. You can say anything you want.

Here's good advice from the OPEN Network on how to develop a response:

TMAY (Tell Me About Yourself)

The following is a general guideline for composing a response when you are asked to "Tell me about yourself." Remember, this is only a guideline.

Structure your TMAY in a brief, conversational way that shows you in your best light. Point out one or two of your most significant accomplishments in a way that is quantifiable (numbers, dollar figures, percentages, etc.) if possible.

I have ___ years of experience in _____ (industry or function).

Most recently (or currently), I _____

_____

_____.

Prior to that I _____

_____.

My areas of strength include _____

_____.

Particular accomplishments or distinctions relevant to the
position you have open are _____

_____

_____.

I would be interested in learning more about the qualifications and performance expectations for the position.

Example of an Answer

I have ten years of experience with increased responsibility
in sales management. As the leading salesperson for ABC
Industries nationally, I established a reputation for accoun-
tability and results with my national sales accounts. In one
particularly successful year, I expanded market share by 8
percent and generated $2 million in new revenues. As a man-
ager I have also mentored five sales leaders in the pharma-
ceutical industry and have developed expertise in selling,
marketing, and developing talented staff for the sales director
position. It would be helpful to know more about the job
qualifications and performance expectations you have for this
position.

How to Develop Your Brief (60 Seconds or Less) Speech

- Write the speech on a half page of paper.
- Read it aloud and change the words until it sounds right.
- Record it and listen to it.
- Change the speech again if necessary.
- Get another opinion (from your spouse or a friend).
- Rehearse until your speech sounds *un*rehearsed, natural.

A question of this sort also tells you that the interviewer may be fairly sophisticated. By putting you in control of the interview at the outset, he can be making judgments on you right away, not only from the content of your answer but from *how* you choose to answer.

On this subject, reader Dr. Daniel J. Fink, vice president and medical director of AmeriMed of Burbank, California, writes:

> A friend of mine was applying for a psychiatry residency, so I offered to do a practice interview with him. By the time we could set up the hour, he had already interviewed at the prestigious university teaching hospital he really wanted to attend. I began our interview by asking him how his interview had gone. "Not too well," he replied. The three interviews with faculty members had gone well—not overwhelmingly positive, but not overwhelmingly negative. The last interview, however, had been a disaster. The chief resident asked him, "Tell me about yourself," and he responded, "I'm just a plain schmuck like anyone else." The interview had gone downhill from there. I gently explained to my friend that in Yiddish "schmuck" is slang for penis—most closely translated into English as "prick." The lessons: Don't use words you don't understand, and be prepared to answer open-ended questions.
>
> Another friend was being interviewed for admission to medical school by the admissions dean, a man nationally known for intimidating applicants. The interview had gone very well until the dean asked my friend, "What field do you think you might be interested in?" My friend, who actually was and still is quite socially conscious but was trying to appear even more so, answered, "Community medicine." "That's great," the dean responded. "Tell me what you mean

by community medicine." My friend, who really did not know, was speechless. Lesson: Don't say something unless you mean it. If you are going to say it, especially when it's not entirely true, be able to answer questions about it.

Dual-Purpose Questions

Questions are often asked for reasons other than are apparent from their content. For instance, the question "What have you done of which you are most proud?" seems to ask you to tell of some outstanding accomplishment. But there is more to it. The question probes, on an unstated level, your ability to make a decision. A question such as this is calculated to flood the mind with recall of many accomplishments. An indecisive person may be unable to decide which achievement to discuss. In a situation like this you should choose one and talk of it, even though there may be many things you've done in the past of which you are proud. This will show that you are a decisive person, able to make up your mind quickly.

Questions About Your Private Life

Sometimes interviewers will ask insensitive questions about your private life, not only about marriage but also about lovers and so on. This commonly happens in interviews for real estate sales positions in which the rationale of the interviewer is that he wants to be sure that, if offered a position, you will devote sufficient time to selling real estate.

I cover unlawful pre-employment inquiries in chapters 12 and 14. While you should be familiar with what the law allows, you should also use your common sense in determining whether a personal question is appropriate or relevant.

I don't think it's ever appropriate to answer questions of this sort. Questions like, "Do you have a boyfriend/girlfriend? Do you spend weekends together?" are nobody's business but yours. They have no relation to your job, and nobody has a right to butt into your personal affairs. Interviewees are generally so docile that they will answer such questions. For one thing, going through an interview is not unlike going through a lie detector test. Furthermore, most interviewees are afraid they will blow their chances for a job offer if they do not reply.

Nonsense! When you are asked a question that is off-limits, you should have the courage to say honestly, but without rancor, that you're applying for this position because you feel it's something you want to do. If you were not planning on devoting sufficient time to performing the duties required, you wouldn't be taking the interviewer's time, and your own, to apply and go through the interview process. What you do in your private life and with your free time will have no effect on how you perform the functions of the position.

A reply like this serves notice that you know the interviewer is skating on thin ice, so he may accept a gentle rebuff. But you can't be so sensitive that you have a whole list of questions you won't answer. If it's a major point and if your objection is legitimate, it's perfectly acceptable to decline to answer. But if you do it too often, you have either had the misfortune of being interviewed by Attila the Hun, or you're too sensitive and will encounter great difficulties in getting beyond the first interview.

In any event, don't let the interviewer intimidate you and push you around. Your private life is private and is of no legitimate concern to him.

Skeletons in Your Closet

Virtually everyone has at least one skeleton in the closet that could be a source of embarrassment. If yours is job- or school-related, there is a fairly good chance that the interviewer will strike upon it. You should prepare your response carefully on this point because an unexpected thrust at a vulnerable area can be devastating.

For instance, assume that you left one of your previous jobs because you had a fight with your supervisor. Assume further that you had worked there for a considerable period of time, so you can't omit the job from your resumé. It's possible that an interviewer will ask you why you left. You must be able to respond to this question honestly but in a way that places you in a favorable light.

You should review the circumstances of the situation and come up with a truthful explanation that cannot be contradicted by a reference check. On your side is the fact that previous employers are reluctant to give out derogatory information on former employees, so the facts of the situation may be difficult for your interviewer to discover from any other source. It is helpful, however, for you to know what kind of reference you will be given. You may have a friend make a check on you with the prior employer to discover how a real reference check will be handled. Knowing this, you can face an interviewer with a fair degree of confidence in how an inquiry by him will be received, and tailor your response accordingly.

It is not a bad answer to say that you had a personality conflict with your supervisor and were unable to work it out, so you felt that it was better for both you and the company if you left. That's all right to explain one departure on your record. But if you use it more than once, the interviewer may decide that you are a difficult person to get along with—and this can be the kiss of death. Just about everyone has had one or two people with whom they have had personality conflicts and have been unable to get along. But if you've had this unfortunate circumstance more than once, you will be at a disadvantage if the subject comes up in an interview. As a result, you had better have another honest, verifiable reason for leaving more than one job. This is where preparation is most important. Your answer must be honest. If this is your skeleton, you must be prepared for it. It may not arise, but if it does and you haven't planned for it well in advance, the likelihood of your surviving the question is slim.

You must be careful about the advice you get and the advice you take. Contrary to what I write here, in an article written by *Wall Street Journal* reporter Joan E. Rigdon, Mike Leavell, a vice president of Hewlett-Packard in Cupertino, California, is quoted as saying, "I don't know why someone who wanted me to hire him would say he had a clash with a boss. That always puts up a big red flag."

Well, Mr. Leavell, what do you suggest? Lying? What if that's the truth? What, Mr. Leavell, would you think of someone who answered your question with a lie, maybe by saying something like, "Oh, I just felt as if the job didn't offer the potential I wanted. There was no place for me to grow," or something vague and ambiguous like that, and then you contacted his last boss and got a different answer? What if you got a lie and found out it was a lie?

I'm here to tell you that you should never lie. You might get a job by lying. It may never be discovered. But the problem is that any good interviewer might check with your prior employer. Maybe he won't, but the chances are, he will. And the chance always exists that he will discover the truth. Now, I ask you, what's better: for you to have revealed the problem frankly, or for you to have withheld the truth by giving an untruthful answer? Won't that be a strike against you? First, you give an untruthful answer, and then the interviewer discovers that the reason you left was that you had a clash with your prior boss. Now, instead of you having to overcome only the problem caused by the reason you left, you've compounded the problem by hiding the real reason and lying about it. Do you think you'll be hired? Not a chance, unless they are looking for someone dishonest to work for them.

No, regardless of the advice of Mr. Leavell, if you're confronted with a question such as this, it's far better to face it head-on and tell the truth. Clearly, you should try to spin it to your best advantage. But tell the truth and face the consequences. My feeling is that if they bring it up, you're much further ahead of the game by telling the truth and getting it out into the open than if you try to hide it. If you don't get the job because of this, well, you just have to conclude that if they are going to hold this against you, you probably wouldn't be happy there anyway. But if you are truthful and do bring it out into the open, and then get the job, what a wonderful feeling to be able to live your life without having to worry that some undiscovered deceit you've made will come back to haunt you! And, further, you'll start out with a clean slate, knowing that your employer knows the truth and hired you anyway!

Of course, you may have other skeletons. If there's something that you hope won't be asked, you should know exactly what you're going to say if he *does* ask you about that. This is another area where your demeanor in answering the question will be almost as important as the words you use. If it appears to the interviewer that you're equivocating or lack confidence in your response, it won't matter much what you say. The impression you leave will probably be negative. So know how you're going to respond, and respond with confidence and candor.

Admitting a weakness can be disarming. An answer along the following lines assumes responsibility and gets the point across without saying anything negative. (This is one of the few instances where I give a specific answer. I'm not recommending that you use this. I'm just setting forth this answer as an example of one that would make sense to me.) "You know, he just had the type of personality that was very difficult for me to get along with. I like to be able to admire and respect the people I work for, but there was something about him that I felt was wrong. I handled the situation very poorly because my attitude seemed to be communicated to him and it alienated him, so he treated me in a manner that I felt to be unacceptable. I blame myself for this entirely and have felt bad about it. Since I recognized that he rubbed me the wrong way, I probably should have been able to work out our differences in some manner that would have been agreeable to both of us. But it was a very difficult situation for me. I was so close to the situation, so emotionally involved, that I was unable to take an objective view of it and it just seemed to get worse. Looking back, I can see some things that I probably should have done to alleviate the situation, but the best that I can say now is that I learned from the experience and if it ever arose again, I think I'd be better able to handle it."

Answering a question in that way will show that you accept full responsibility for the situation. Even if you don't feel responsible for the problem, this type of answer will place you in the best light and will protect you against a bad reference check. Basically, you're saying, "This guy was a jerk, but I should have been able to handle that. Therefore, it's my fault and I'll know how to deal with it if there's a next time." On the other hand, if you tell the interviewer, "The guy was an absolute loser—no one could get along with him—I finally had him up to here and told him to shove it," and on a reference check, the interviewer gets a similar response about you, the interviewer, not knowing whom to believe, will probably conclude that it's not worth the risk of hiring a potentially disagreeable person and reject you.

Don't keep fighting the battle. If you accept the responsibility and say that you learned from the experience, you disarm any negative things that may be said about you and project an image of peacemaker rather than warrior.

Grievances Against Former Employers

Don't criticize a former employer. The advice many of us heard from our mothers, "If you can't say anything nice about someone, don't say anything," applies here. Even if you have a legitimate grievance against someone, don't talk about it. If you are asked, just say something that will dissuade further questions. You can turn the interviewer away from the subject with a tactful answer like, "I don't feel it's fair to them for me to discuss our disagreements with other people." This will not only turn away further inquiries; the interviewer should consider you a person of discretion.

I had an interview with a potential client once who had a great deal of lucrative legal work that she needed to have done. We discussed the details of the work and then I asked her about her prior attorney. This loosed a wave of virulence about the lawyer. She castigated him for every indiscretion of which she could think: He overcharged her; he did poor and sloppy work; he was never available to talk with her; he continually pressed her to pay his exorbitant fees. Her diatribe went on for fifteen minutes.

The impression she made upon me was completely different from that which she had intended. My conclusion was that no matter how much work she had for me, she would feel that she owned me. She would call anytime, day or night. If I happened to be working on other problems, she wouldn't understand. And eventually, she would be sitting in some other lawyer's office speaking of me as she was now speaking of her last lawyer. I declined the client mainly on the strength of the feeling I developed during her criticism of her former attorney.

An interviewer can be expected to form the same sort of judgment if you severely criticize a former employer. He will probably conclude that hiring you isn't worth the risk and reject you. He doesn't want to hire someone who will be sitting in another interviewer's office a year hence complaining about him.

If you refuse to discuss your grievances, you improve your position. Even if a check of the situation results in a negative report, it's probable that the interviewer will respect you for not talking against someone with whom you have had problems, and the empathy thus gained might be enough to overcome any negative feelings your antagonist might have aroused in the interviewer.

Of course, if the interviewer pressed you, you have no choice but to give your side of the story. A refusal on your part could leave the impression that you have something to hide. This, buttressed by a negative report from your antagonist, would probably be enough to cause a rejection.

If the interviewer refuses to allow you to drop the subject, explain the situation in as dispassionate a manner as possible. Some interviewers will probe such points, but not for the purpose of discovering the facts of the situation or to find out who was right or wrong. Rather, they may be examining your ability to maintain control in an emotional situation. If you become emotional while telling the story, it could indicate that you lack self-control, and this could result in a negative inference. Although you want to present your case in a forceful enough manner to counterbalance your antagonist's story, you want to do it as unemotionally as you can.

Questions Asked as a Test

I have found that the most successful people are the ones who possess, and use, common sense. It's fine to have complicated solutions to problems, but most problems can be resolved by simply resorting to common sense. This is especially true when applied to the job interview and answering questions. Two anecdotes amply illustrate the point.

When Scotty Connal was hired by Chet Simmons to bring top production people to ESPN when it was nothing more than a gleam in founder Bill Rasmussen's eye, he began all his interviews with the question "What section of the paper do you read first?" According to biographer Michael Freeman in *ESPN: The Uncensored History*, if the answer was anything other than the sports page, the interview was terminated.

Now, how would you react if you were interviewing at a sports network and were asked this question? This is a good example of when you should pause and not answer off the top of your head by saying, "I always open it up to the comics page." This question would undoubtedly be unexpected, so take a moment to reflect, not on what's the first page you actually read, but on why the question is being asked. If you think about that, then you should know that your answer should be the sports page.

You might accuse me of hypocrisy in that I'm a big fan of always telling the truth and here I'm counseling you that in this situation you should give an answer that is not the absolute, 100 percent truth. But you have to understand why I give this advice. I don't think that Simmons was asking this question just to find out what section the interviewee actually read first, although that might have been relatively important. I think one of the purposes of the question was to determine how perceptive the interviewee was, to see if the interviewee could determine what answer Simmons wanted in order for him to continue to consider the interviewee for a position with ESPN. So if you view this question as a test to see if you can give the answer Simmons wanted, not the absolutely 100 percent true answer, you're not lying by giving him the answer for which he's looking. He's not really looking to find out what the first section is that you read. He's really looking to find out if you're smart enough to come up with the answer he wants.

So common sense should be used in this situation in three ways. First, to determine whether the question is to discover facts or is a test. Second, to determine the answer for which the interviewer is searching. And finally, to give the right answer.

The second anecdote was told to me by my brother-in-law, Dick Olerich, about something that happened when he was a member of Phi Delta Theta fraternity at USC. During Hell Week they'd sit initiates on a large cake of ice. After a short period of time they'd ask, "What do you want most in the world?" Most answered, "To get off this cake of ice." That answer meant they had to continue sitting until they figured out the correct answer, which was, "To be a Phi Delt."

You have to use your common sense and put things together and in context. Here the appropriate answer should be obvious, but to most it wasn't. You must ask yourself, "Why am I being asked this question?" If you're a fraternity pledge and your fraternity brothers have sat you on a cake of ice and then asked you what you want most in the world, it should be clear to anyone but the most mentally deficient that the answer wanted is not, "To get off this cake of ice."

So if that's not the answer, what would the answer be? When you approach it like that, the answer should become obvious. Here again the question is not being asked to get an absolutely 100 percent true response. Like Simmons's question, it's a test. The interviewer, in this instance, knows that your answer might not be 100 percent true. What person in his right mind who's sitting on a block of ice wouldn't have as his most fervent desire in the world to get off the block of ice? But the question isn't being asked to really discover what your most fervent desire in the world is. The question is being asked to see if you're smart enough to know what answer the interviewer wants and if you're smart enough to give it.

If the question is a test, and not a question seeking to discover a fact, answer it so that you pass the test.

Unfair or Impossible-to-Answer Questions

Sometimes you will be asked a question that is just unfair or impossible to answer. There is a way to handle a question like this, and as examples I point to three celebrities. The first is Rudy Giuliani, former mayor of New York City. Rudy is controversial, to say the least. Before 9/11 his popularity was not at its zenith. But Rudy is one of the best interviewees I've ever seen. When asked the unfair/impossible-to-answer question, how does Rudy handle it? He laughs. Someone might say, "You are a dishonest, lying crook. How do you answer that?" Rudy's first reaction is to laugh like he has just heard the funniest joke of his life. His entire face lights up. It really doesn't matter what words he uses to answer the question, Rudy is clearly treating it as something not that earth-shattering.

In the quarter finals of the 2004 U.S. Open, Serena Williams received four of the worst line calls in the history of tennis in the third set and lost the match. One was particularly egregious. At the news conference afterward everyone was primed for a tirade. When asked about it, what did she do? Like Rudy, she laughed. With a big smile on her face, she said that she thought she had been cheated, that there was a conspiracy, etc., etc. But all the time she was saying this, she had a huge smile on her face and she was laughing. Regardless of what she said, she won over many who were watching.

Finally, several years ago I went to the Century City Rotary Club to hear Willie Brown speak. Willie Brown had been a powerful, allegedly corrupt, Speaker of the California Assembly and was, at the time, running for mayor of San Francisco. Most everyone there was on the other side of the political spectrum and anticipated disliking him. But you can't listen to Willie Brown speak and dislike him, even if you disagree with everything he says or believes. Why? Because he speaks with humor and apparent goodwill. When he criticizes, it's in a jocular form.

The moral is, don't take anything personally. If someone asks you a horrible, unfair question and your first reaction is to bristle in anger, try seeing the humor in the question and laugh. You'll be ahead of the game.

Checklist

- The most important aspect that an interviewer gets out of an interview is a subjective feeling about the interviewee.
- You must enhance that feeling.
- Listen to the question.
- If the question is ambiguous, you should either interpret it in your own way and say what puts you in the best light or ask for clarification.

- Use ploys to get thinking time: ask for a clarification or use a bridge.
- Don't worry about thinking for a few seconds before you answer.
- Don't worry about eye contact; just act naturally.
- Assume that every question is asked for a purpose.
- Be ready for the blockbuster question.
- Handle the offensive question firmly but tactfully.
- Recognize dual-purpose questions and answer them decisively.
- Tactfully decline to answer questions about your private life.
- Prepare good answers for questions that may probe skeletons in your closet.
- Find out how your references will respond to a check.
- Accept responsibility for personality conflicts.
- Don't put the interviewer in the middle of a battle.
- Don't talk against a former employer.
- If you must discuss a bad situation with a former employer, do so dispassionately.
- Answer specific questions specifically.
- Don't respond to a serious question with a flip joke.
- If you joke, don't make the interviewer the butt of it.

6

Assumptions

Reactions can be illogical. It is almost impossible to determine in advance how an interviewer is going to respond (and for this chapter let's assume the interviewer is a woman and the interviewee a man). An interviewee takes a particular risk when he assumes an aggressive position with someone he has known for less than ten minutes.

When a person shows up for an interview with me dressed in a slovenly manner, I generally ask about it. One time the response I received was, "I want people to judge me for the kind of person I am, not for the clothes I wear. Do you think it mattered what Clarence Darrow wore?" The interviewee sat back smugly, thinking that he had scored a tremendous point. He had assumed that my immediate reaction would be to conjure up an image of Darrow defending a great cause in his studiedly unkempt dress. Unfortunately, he was wrong.

Instead, it brought to mind images of Earl Rogers, a renowned trial lawyer of early-twentieth-century Los Angeles, called by many the father of demonstrative evidence and the witness box denouement so often seen in Perry Mason mysteries.

When Darrow was indicted for bribery in the *Los Angeles Times* bombing case, Rogers got him acquitted in a brilliant defense. Rogers's trademark was to show up in court dressed in formal evening wear, and that's what I thought of when my smug interviewee mentioned Darrow. Irrelevant? Illogical? Perhaps. But an interviewee has no way of knowing how an interviewer will react to an assertion. This particular interviewee obviously assumed I shared his belief that Clarence Darrow was the mahatma of the legal profession. Because his assumption was wrong, his thrust was not just impotent, it created a negative feeling in me.

This epitomizes the great risk we all take in the interview process. The person conducting the interview is a stranger. We cannot hope to discover much about her—her education, intelligence, and prejudices. We are at sea in a world of uncertainty. For this reason, if for no other, we must base our actions on facts as we perceive them in the short period of time at our disposal. To venture into the unknown by making rhetorical parries is to step into an abyss. You may hit the bull's-eye and score grandly. On the other hand, the odds are much in favor of missing the mark and creating a negative feeling that no amount of rehabilitation can overcome.

Observe the Interviewer

What is positive for one interviewer may be negative for another. For instance, Dr. Robert Langrod, when he was president of Bertea Corporation, said, "I'm not looking for quick, fast responses. I'm looking for responses that are logical and make sense." On the other hand, Paul Moller, who was president of USA Petroleum Corporation, had an entirely different view. "I interviewed a man I hired about two months ago. He really came across like a go-getter. Any question I asked he had a quick reply. He never had to hesitate. Some people have to hesitate on a question. He never hesitated. He knew the answer right away. That really impressed me."

So unless you have advance knowledge of your interviewer's prejudices on any point, you will have to size her up quickly during the interview. You should pay very close attention to her and be sensitive to her reactions to you.

The perceptive person can detect hints others give that subconsciously communicate their feelings. Sharyn Cole of the Los Angeles Bonaventure Hotel says, "I don't consciously use body language myself. But if an interviewee knew what he was doing, I'm sure that it would work. If I sit up straight, it means that the interviewee is getting on my nerves, or I'm getting defensive. If I sit back, it means I'm relaxed and that would be a good sign for the interviewee."

Each interviewer may be different, but they will all give clues as to how you are being received. You should be perceptive enough to observe these clues and adjust your interview accordingly.

If you notice what seems to be a negative response—the interviewer is sitting up straight, fidgeting, folding her arms, or looking away while you are talking—you should take the hint and either stop talking or change the subject. If you strongly feel that the body language of the interviewer is telling you that you are not being well received in what you are doing, don't compound the problem by continuing. When some people perceive they are not being well received, they become nervous and talk too much. If you have the insight to read body language, use it to your advantage and stop doing whatever it might be that is causing negative reactions.

You must be sensitive, however, that you do not make an assumption based upon a superficial observation of your interviewer. Many times the true situation is far different than it appears to be at first glance.

Superficial Assumptions

A few years ago when I was engaged in a negotiation with another lawyer, I instantly developed a negative attitude toward him because he wouldn't look me in the eye; he always seemed to be gazing at a spot just over my left shoulder. This grated on my nerves, and I took it for a sign of weakness and uncertainty on his part.

A few months later I was spending the weekend with a friend and her family in Old Greenwich, Connecticut. She had her college roommate over for dinner, and her roommate looked at me exactly as had the lawyer I considered weak and uncertain. My reaction was similarly negative. As the evening progressed, my friend brought up the fact that her roommate was walleyed, and it had caused her no end of self-consciousness.

I felt mortified and guilty. Clearly, my judgment on the lawyer was wrong. He had the same problem, and I had made an assumption without establishing the facts. By this injustice I had insensitively formed a negative impression of him for a reason that didn't exist. In fact, it took a great strength of character for him to persevere in a profession where eye contact is so important and, for him, virtually impossible.

It's difficult to judge things without making assumptions. But it's essential that your reactions and actions in an interview be based upon facts to the largest extent possible. In addition to their inherent inequity, erroneous assumptions acted upon can be disastrous.

But even though it's important to be sensitive to the way you're being received, it's never wise to try to role-play to something you might think the interviewer wants, because you might be wrong. A story told by Tzu-lu, a disciple of Confucius, points this out. Tzu-lu asked Confucius what sort of man he'd take with him on a dangerous task. Confucius replied,

"The man who was ready to beard a tiger or rush a river without caring whether he lived or died . . ."

I'll stop here. Is this the man you'd choose? Sounds good, doesn't it? A fearless warrior who had no thought of his life, but only for the good of the mission? A man who would sacrifice his life for success? But Confucius continued: "That sort of man I should not take. I should certainly take someone who approached difficulties with due caution and who preferred to succeed by strategy."

Surprised? Confucius wouldn't want the daredevil. He wanted someone thoughtful who would try to figure out a way to victory without sacrificing his life. This is an example of why you should not try to play a role that isn't yourself. And it's why, instead of giving you tips on how to answer questions that you might think will please your interviewer, *Sweaty Palms* concentrates on teaching you how to get to know yourself as well as you can so that you can present *yourself*, not somebody you aren't, to the interviewer.

Anybody who tries to tell you how to answer a question, what specific words to use, or what specific thought to convey, is leading you down a crooked road to perdition. You must recognize your own worth and go into the interview comfortable with yourself. You must be yourself. This isn't the first time I've said this in this book and it won't be the last. It's what will get you the job that you want, so I'm going to keep repeating it until you try it and believe it. One reader, who asks to remain anonymous, writes:

I'd never heard of a "stress interview" until I read your book. Two years ago a major corporation spent $200 to bring me up from Los Angeles to San Francisco for an interview. It was a panel interview. The three people who interviewed me were so hostile from the minute I walked into the room that I assumed that seeing a middle-aged woman arrive, they were angry at having spent $200 to bring me there. Their questions were, from the outset, designed to put me on the defensive (e.g., "What makes you think you can do such and such?"). One of the interviewers even asked me why I'd dared to send them a letter typed with dirty typewriter keys!

I was certain, afterwards, that my age was a factor in my not being offered the job. I'd never heard of a "stress interview" until reading *Sweaty Palms*. But *Sweaty Palms* has quite literally changed my life. It made me realize how I've messed up in past interviews because I'd *assumed* when I didn't get the job I interviewed for that it was because of my age (fifty-five). Realizing that in all probability it was *another* reason (my not handling some aspect of the interview as well as I should have) has lifted a burden from my shoulders. What a relief it is to forget about age in an interview and concentrate instead on what the interviewer's saying and how she's saying it—and my own responses.

When "Yes" Doesn't Mean "I Agree"

Don't delude yourself that the interviewer agrees with everything you're saying merely because she nods agreement. You can easily be led down the primrose path by your assumption that you've hit upon a common belief when in reality her reaction may not signify agreement at all. Averell Harriman had an especially close relationship with President Franklin Roosevelt during World War II, and he commented on Roosevelt's penchant for using the word "yes" when he didn't really mean "I agree."

Lack of understanding of what the President means when he nods or says "yes" has led to much bitterness on the part of . . . businessmen who assume they have the agreement of the President when all they have, really, is an indication that the President is not prepared to argue the point with them. . . . It means that he hears and understands what you are saying, but not necessarily that he agrees to it. Anyone who assumes otherwise is engaging in wishful thinking, or is not very astute.

A nod of the head or a brief "yes" may mean just the opposite of agreement: It may be a signal that the interviewer has heard all she wishes to hear of the subject and wishes you to get on to something else.

Analysis of Specific Technique

One of the most sophisticated interviewing techniques was used some years ago by the Life Sciences Division of Whittaker Corporation in performing their contract with the Saudi Arabian government to provide hospital and related services in Saudi Arabia. They needed to hire specialized individuals, such as doctors, nurses, technicians, and administrators, who were of a high caliber.

The positions in Saudi Arabia had many negative factors, the primary one being culture shock. Thus the selection process became a most important component of Whittaker's performance. Each hire cost the division approximately $10,000. Therefore, if someone was hired who did not fulfill the minimum contract time period of eighteen months in Saudi Arabia, the mistake was extremely costly to the company. Not only were they out the $10,000 it cost them to make a selection, they lost a significant period of time and performance.

Jerry Kenefick was the manager of the international recruitment office of the division. His staff consisted entirely of professionals in the fields for which they were interviewing. Doctors interviewed doctors, nurses interviewed nurses, and so on.

They received approximately sixty resumés a day from all over the United States. Ninety percent were from people who were obviously not qualified. The remaining 10 percent were prescreened by telephone; this interview eliminated 95 percent of the remaining 10 percent. So out of the resumés received, one-half of 1 percent were invited in for the second-stage interview.

Cheryl Vanos, the logistics coordinator, characterized the interview as a "negative stress" one—that is, the negative aspects of the position were stressed in order to weed out those who would not survive the tour of duty.

Kenefick said that although their interview process was designed to pick not only those who were qualified but those who would be able to adjust to the Saudi lifestyle, the final decision was based upon a "feeling" that he and the other interviewers had about the candidate. He can't define how he arrived at his feeling but stated that it was generally reliable and that he and the other interviewers usually arrived at this feeling within the first ten minutes of the interview.

Kenefick's interview consisted of two parts. Initially, he looked for qualifications, so he would go down the resumé with the interviewee item by item. If he discovered a gap or an inconsistency, he'd ask about it. Any intentional misrepresentation could seriously damage a candidate's chances.

The second phase was to determine if the interviewee was the right kind of person to go to Saudi Arabia. He asked many questions to get to the inner person: What do you do in your spare time? Do you have close friends? When was the last time you got together? What was the last movie you saw? He probed these areas because Saudi Arabian society is spartan by American standards. There are no movies, no churches, no television.

Interviewees generally tried to give answers they felt the interviewer was looking for. A typical answer was, "I read, never watch TV, don't go to movies, and like to be by myself." Kenefick would let this pass and then later in the interview (which lasted from forty-five minutes to four hours, depending on the level of the position) would gently ask if the interviewee happened to see a certain television show or movie. Normally, it turned out that the interviewee did like television or movies or American sports and answered the way he had only to get the job.

Kenefick used other ploys to get candidates to eliminate themselves. "Once," he said, "I had an interviewee who was dressed very fastidiously. Everything was perfect from his hairstyle to his shoelaces. As we talked, I dwelt on the size of the roaches over there, the fact that the flour moved constantly because of the weevils, things like that. The interviewee actually had to excuse himself as I was talking because it upset him so. He came back and said that he didn't think he was interested."

If the candidate got by Kenefick, he went to the final stage by meeting with Vanos, whose ostensible job was to brief the candidate on life in Saudi Arabia.

"The interviewee has been through an entire day of interviewing with Jerry and the others," she said. "He gets to me and thinks that it's all over. So he tends to relax and drop his pretensions. He doesn't realize that I'm assessing him, too. He may confide his trepidations to me. Or he may inadvertently let me see what he's really like. After I'm through with him, I'll get together with Jerry if I have some doubts about him, and several times a candidate has been rejected because of my input. We have to be very sure that the person we hire will stick it out and perform in an acceptable manner once he gets there.

"I remember one fellow whom we were interviewing as hospital administrator. He got to talking about his daughter and her fiancé. He exhibited a very low tolerance for her fiancé's goals and ideas. He came across as very inflexible. Well, how's he going to react when his forty-year-old head nurse comes to him and complains that she's been caught by the Saudi religious police for living with some American engineer and is going to be deported? She will be crying that she's forty years old, recently divorced, and lonely, that she needs companionship. How's he going to deal with that if he doesn't have the tolerance to cope with his daughter's fiancé and his contrary ideas and lifestyle?"

Kenefick said that he probed candidates' motivations for wanting to go to Saudi Arabia. "Invariably," he said, "they say that they want to go for three reasons. One, they want to do good for Saudi Arabia. Two, they want to travel. Three, they have an adventurous spirit.

"My job is to get beyond these three reasons to the real reason. Are they running away from a divorce or an unhappy love affair? Why do they *really* want to go? Not that their reasons that they give initially aren't what they believe. They are generally highly motivated people and these are real reasons. But we know that there quite often is some other reason, and if there is, we want to know what that is. Saudi Arabia is no place to recover from a broken heart."

Vanos wanted to hear "that they were motivated by money. Because in Saudi Arabia, when you have to be there from eighteen months to two years, money is the thing that keeps you going in the final analysis. If they admit this, we can be more confident that their motivations are such that they will last for the term of their contract."

There are several lessons to be learned from this. First, always make the assumption that you are going to be exposed to a good, sophisticated interview technique on the part of the interviewer. Even though the chances are that the interviewer won't be as competent as Kenefick and his crew, if you prepare for the best, you'll be ready for anything. "You must prepare for the enemy's capability, rather than his intentions," said Prussian military philosopher Carl von Clausewitz.

Second, assume that every question is asked for a reason connected with the job, even if it sounds like idle chatter. The man who sharply criticized his daughter's fiancé didn't realize that this was being projected by the interviewer to an actual job situation and a judgment made thereon.

Third, don't assume that just because you're talking to someone other than the person who makes the final hiring decision, the interview is over. The interview lasts until you have accepted an offer or been totally rejected. Remember, there's many a slip twixt the tongue and the lip. Even though they make up their minds on you once, they can change at any stage.

Table Manners

You are *always* evaluated when you are in the presence of the interviewer or anyone connected with the interviewer. Often an interview will include a meal. Don't be misled into believing that this is a "break," a time to relax, to let your hair down. Not only is this still a part of the interview, it might be the *most important* part. As a result, you need to develop good table manners. I recommend buying a book on etiquette, like *Miss Manners' Guide to Excruciatingly Correct Behavior* or *Amy Vanderbilt's Everyday Etiquette*. But some common rules are these:

1. Be on time. Miss Manners says there is "no excuse for being late to a business luncheon short of having been run over on the way there."

2. Don't fake pronunciation of menu items. If the menu is in a foreign language and you are unfamiliar with it and there's no English translation, ask for an explanation. Feigning knowledge makes you look ridiculous and could result in a negative inference that could cost you a job offer. If you can't pronounce something or don't know what it is, just ask. Nobody will ever forget you if you order steak tartare well done, but you'll wish they would. Showing that you are not afraid to reveal that you don't know something is an indication that you are comfortable with yourself and are not pretending to be something you are not.

3. Don't put your arms on the table.

4. Don't talk with food in your mouth.

5. Take the time to learn how to use the proper utensils. The general rule is that you work from the outside in. If there is more than one fork, for example, you use the outside fork for the first course, usually a small fork for the salad. Then after the salad and salad fork are removed, you use the next fork, the larger one, for the main course. It's easy if you know the rules.

6. Never force someone to have another drink, dessert, or whatever. Let the others make up their own minds.

7. Don't put your briefcase or carrying case on the table. Gauche floods to the mind. Not a bad idea, however, to

have your pen and notebook handy. Just don't set them on the table.

8. Don't pick up the check unless it's your obligation. The general rule is that whoever invites, pays. And this is true regardless of gender.

9. Don't complain publicly in front of your companions about the service. If there's a problem and it's your responsibility, excuse yourself from the table and, instead of confronting the miscreant privately, lodge your complaint with the maître d'.

Good manners consist of simple common courtesy. If you're thoughtful and considerate of your companions and think of their comfort before your own, you will be on the road to being well mannered.

Reader Dr. Daniel Fink, quoted earlier, tells of a case directly in point:

We just had a bizarre experience interviewing a potential vice president. First, we are a "shirtsleeves" organization, at least in the office, and the candidate declined to remove his suit coat, despite the fact that the president and I were both in our shirtsleeves. Second, the interview had been set for 11 a.m. so we could have an informal working lunch. The candidate declined to join us, stating he had eaten a big breakfast, and sat drinking a glass of water while we ate our sandwiches. Even though he is qualified in terms of experience, we wonder how he would fit in. If the host-interviewer offers food or drink, I think the interviewee should at least accept something, perhaps just a salad or a bowl of soup and a diet drink, even if he doesn't finish it.

Finally, to combine table manners with the concept that the interview isn't over until a job offer is accepted, there's this story attributed to President Woodrow Wilson, who was president of Princeton University before becoming president of the United States.

Wilson would invariably take a prospective employee to a meal and observe for one specific trait. If the interviewee salted his or her food before tasting it, rejection was inevitable. Why? Wilson concluded that anyone who would salt food before tasting it to determine whether or not the food actually needed salt was a person who made up his or her mind without knowing the facts.

So just as an opera is not over until the fat lady sings, a job interview isn't over until you've been offered and accepted the position.

Physical Impairments

Reader Thomas A. Ruhoff of Tucson, Arizona, writes:

I was scheduled for interviews on Thursday and Friday. On Wednesday I came down with a recurrence of Bell's palsy, in which one side of the face is temporarily paralyzed. The paralysis was noticeable to myself, but other people said they did not notice it at all—until I smiled. I was advised to not tell the interviewer about my condition. I did not think it wise to let him or her draw undue conclusions, for instance that I had had a stroke and would need long-term medical care. In both interviews I started off by explaining why my face did not work and emphasized that it was a transient condition. Both interviewers thanked me for telling them about the palsy, and then we went on with the rest of the interview.

Mr. Ruhoff's way of handling his impairment was perfect. Because interviewers generally form impressions based more on the way they feel about an interviewee than on the empirical data derived during the interview, it would be unwise to let the affliction pass with no comment. It's clearly not in your best interests for the interviewer to draw a negative inference that might be much worse than the actual cause. Further, even if the interviewer didn't conclude that you had a permanent affliction, the conclusion might be more vague, and that could be even worse. For the interviewer to come away thinking, "I didn't like that person," without knowing why can be worse than coming away thinking, "Maybe he's got a permanent affliction." The latter can be overcome. To combat the former is herculean.

Don't Key Your Performance to Assumptions

The Whittaker interview process described earlier illustrates two disadvantages of making assumptions not based on fact and trying to key your performance to those assumptions. If your assumptions are correct and you play the role so well that you get the job, when you return to your normal self, you won't be happy with the job and the employer won't be happy with you. You'll be worse off than if you had never gotten the job. And if your assumptions are wrong, and the company was actually looking for someone just like you, you could be role-playing yourself out of an opportunity.

Never answer a question just to please the interviewer. You must come across as yourself, an honest person who knows himself or herself, and is comfortable that way.

This doesn't mean you should ever be rude. Your honesty does not diminish if you back off from a subject or manner of acting when you observe that it is not being well received. Would you tell Julie Andrews how much you detested *The Sound of Music*? Discretion does not imply dishonesty. Rather, it is simple courtesy.

False Conclusions

Never walk out of an interview and say, "Boy, did I do lousy there! I'm sure I made a bad impression and blew my chance." How do you know how the interviewer reacted to you? You really don't know what she was looking for. You may have connected on all cylinders, yet you're projecting your standards upon her and making the assumption that you failed.

Dr. Robert H. Schuller, in his book *Move Ahead with Positive Thinking*, relates a classic story, about a Chinese man who had one horse and one son, that points out the errors of assuming. The horse ran away and the neighbors commiserated on his bad luck.

> "Why," the old Chinese said, "how do you know it's bad luck?" Sure enough, the next night the horse came back to his familiar corral . . . leading twelve wild stallions with him! . . . The neighbors heard the good news and came chattering to the farmer, "Oh, you have thirteen horses! What good luck!"
>
> And the old Chinese answered, "How do you know that's good luck?"
>
> A few days later his son broke his leg falling off one of the new horses, and once again the neighbors tried to console him on his bad luck.
>
> And the wise father answered again, "How do you know it's bad luck?"

Sure enough, a few days later a Chinese warlord came through town and conscripted every able-bodied young man, taking them off to war, never to return again. But the young man was saved because of his broken leg.

Don't make assumptions based upon your narrow frame of reference until all the facts are in. The man to whom Schuller referred was the epitome of the pragmatist: He made no judgments upon events. He accepted them and let the events move to their inevitable conclusions. To conclude that the things that happened were "good luck" or "bad luck" required him to make assumptions that he was unwilling to make. He acted and waited.

So, too, after an interview you should not make evaluative judgments because they will be based upon assumptions that will have no basis in fact. How can you know whether you had a "good" or a "bad" interview? How do you know whether you made a "good" or a "bad" impression?

You waste your time by making such judgments. You are in the worst possible position to evaluate your performance. In the first place, you certainly are not able to make an objective appraisal. Second, you don't know what the specifications for the position are. Third, you can't possibly put yourself inside the head of the interviewer to determine the feeling she got from you.

Finally, what good will it do for you to make some kind of a judgment on how the interviewer thought you did? You can't go back and redo the interview. You can't change what's happened.

I once had an interview with a man for a position with a client of mine. I came away from the interview thinking that he was probably the worst interviewee I had seen in months. The next day the executive search agent who had set up the interview

called for my response, and I told him that I wasn't interested
in pursuing the matter further. He expressed great surprise:
"When I talked with the applicant, he was jubilant. He felt that
he had come across well and that you had been very favorably
impressed!" All that applicant did was to delude himself and
to build himself up for a great letdown. He had apparently
made some very basic erroneous assumptions about me and my
reaction.

All of us wonder about how we did in an interview, but wondering serves no purpose. You waste your time, and you can
either build yourself up for a letdown or worry yourself into a
state of acute depression. Wait until you discover what the
interviewer's judgment on you has been before you evaluate
the interview. If she rejects you, then you can gain from
reviewing the interview objectively to determine what happened so that you can better prepare for the interviews in the
future. If she asks you to a follow-up interview or makes you an
offer, you can then bask in the glow of an interview well conducted, without the possibility of being cruelly let down by
believing in a false assumption.

Don't Be Intimidated by Your Competition

Inevitably, during the course of the interviewing process you
will see other candidates and they will impress you. They will
be good-looking, well dressed, charming, and sophisticated,
and you'll assume you don't have a chance. You will feel a failure immediately. You'll wonder, what's the use? This other
person has it all wrapped up.

*Don't assume yourself into a position where you are intimidated by
style rather than essence.* When I was preparing my videotape
interview service, I videotaped interviews with three people as

samples. One of the interviewees was an experienced, outgoing person who had style. Another was sort of average, and the third was a shy and retiring introvert.

In my own mind I rated them with the extrovert on top and the introvert capable of impressing no one. After I showed the interviews to prospective clients, I asked them to rate the interviewees. To my surprise the introvert was rated first by more clients than the extrovert. They felt that the introvert's personality was more amenable to their type of operation. The extrovert came on too strong, and they felt that he would be difficult to get along with.

Time and again interviewees have told me that they felt their interview was poor, yet they later received more offers than the seeming "superstars."

Interviewers are rarely misled by style as a substitute for substance. They are looking for a personality that will fit in with their operation. A hail-fellow-well-met may be a smash at a party, but as a candidate for a job he might not have the advantage that his sophistication projects.

Don't compare yourself with other candidates, because you don't know what the interviewer is looking for. Be yourself. It's just as likely that the interviewer is looking for you as it is that she's looking for someone completely different. If she is looking for someone completely different, you wouldn't be happy in the job in any event, so it's better to find that out.

Think Positively

There is one assumption that the wise interviewee should make prior to an interview. Although many selection interviewers are not knowledgeable in the art of conducting an interview, you should assume that the interview in which you are to participate is going to be professional and that the interviewer will be well prepared. Assuming this, you will take the time to prepare yourself properly in advance, using the techniques that are explained in this book. If you assume the best and get the worst, you are not going to be hurt. But if you assume something less than the best and get the best, you're going to be at a disadvantage.

Norman Vincent Peale says in *The Power of Positive Thinking* that if you expect the best, you'll get it. Of course, that is not always the case, but the point he makes is valid as much in the converse as it is in concept. *If you think you're going to fail, you undoubtedly will.*

Two things that happened to me as a young lawyer point out the importance of attitude and expectations of success. I had recently become counsel of a large division, and I was going to have to negotiate with a potential supplier. I had heard stories about the abilities of their attorney and how smart and vicious he was. I was intimidated. I went into the meeting assuming that he knew a lot more about the problem than I did and that he was more experienced. I just hoped that I would come out of the negotiation without making too much of a show of my ignorance.

The negotiation was the disaster I had anticipated. The other attorney was arrogant and intimidating. When I'd say something, he'd laugh snidely as if to say, "How can anyone be so dumb?" Afterward I was in a blue funk. Here was my first chance to leave a good impression, and I had blown it.

A few weeks later I had to fly East with another negotiating team. I was told that the people with whom I would be negotiating were very nice and easy to get along with. I had no fears.

It turned out that they were not "nice." In fact, they were tougher and more knowledgeable than those in the first negotiation. But I went in confidently and unworried. I locked horns with them on several key points and emerged unscathed and victorious on each. The word got back to management that I was a tiger, and my reputation was made.

Later I met the lawyer who had so intimidated me in my first negotiation. By this time I had built confidence in myself and didn't make any assumptions about his superiority. It turned out that he was all show and no substance. When I didn't let him intimidate me and didn't assume failure, he caused me no problems.

Bad assumptions can so intimidate you that you can be defeated before the fray begins. The only cure is to prepare as best you can and have the confidence that you can handle anything that arises.

Hidden Assumptions

A hidden assumption is one that is so subliminal one may be unaware of it. Gerard I. Nierenberg, in *The Art of Negotiating*, gives a classic example of a hidden assumption:

> A husband was watching his wife as she prepared a roast for the evening meal. After placing the roast on the cutting board, the wife cut the first slice and dropped it in the refuse can.
>
> "Why did you do that, dear?" the husband asked. "I don't know," was the answer. "My mother always did it." The next time he saw his mother-in-law, the husband asked if she always removed the first slice from the roast before cooking it. "Yes," was the reply. "My mother always did it." So the husband, intrigued, called up his wife's grandmother. That elderly lady explained, "Oh, yes, I always removed the end slice from the roast because the pan I cooked it in was too small."

So here was an assumption made by two women that they should cut the end of the roast off before they cooked it because that's what their mother did, without either of them knowing why she did it! They just assumed that because their mother did it, it was the correct way to do it.

Nierenberg gives a terrific example of how a hidden assumption can affect a negotiation, either by manipulating the person with whom you are negotiating, or by being manipulated yourself. So read the following tale and realize that it can apply both ways:

An attorney was in negotiation over a lease closing. One lawyer told his opponent, "Here is a standard lease form that's been in use for fifty years. Since you've been practicing so long, you probably know it by heart." The opponent didn't want to look as if he wasn't prepared or didn't know what was in the form, so instead of reading it, he concentrated only on what had been typed in as recent additions. He had been manipulated into accepting "standard" terms and conditions without actually knowing what they were.

You can use this technique to your advantage. For example, if you're looking for a job and you have something on your resumé that you're concerned about, you can make the resumé several pages long and put the feared item in the middle. Taking the chance that the interviewer might wait until the interview to go over your resumé, something that does happen often, you could then say something like the manipulating lawyer: "I'm sure in your preparation for the interview you've gone over my resumé like all my other interviewers have, so maybe you'd like to talk about some other things than just a review of the resumé." The interviewer might not fall for it, but, then again, she might. If what you're trying to avoid is having the interviewer learn that you left a job because of a conflict, or something else that won't look too good if it's probed, this might keep her from either finding out about it or raising it.

Similarly, if you are aware of this technique, you can recognize it if it's used against you. I've already mentioned the way one interviewer manipulated an interviewee by implying that the reason he did well on the IQ test given by the company as a screening device was the fact that he had taken a lot of tests, not because he actually had a high IQ. This was a classic example of an interviewer making the interviewee accede to a hidden assumption that wasn't true! Nierenberg says, "A negotiator who fails to understand the immediate situation because he is influenced by a hidden assumption is often stuck with the assumption as a fact throughout the negotiation." This was true in the situation of the IQ question. Although shortly after the incident the interviewee realized that he had been manipulated into a false assumption, by that time he felt it was too late to rectify it, and it affected his performance during the rest of the interview because it was gnawing at him.

Nierenberg lists three categories of hidden assumptions: those made about what he calls the extensional world, those made about what he calls your intensional world, and those made about the other person's intensional world.

Assumptions made about the extensional world are assumptions you make about the world around you. In terms of a job interview these assumptions are those about the job itself, the company, the people with whom you will be working, the things that you will be using in the job. Part of the purpose of your interview is to clarify these things. It might be difficult to refrain from doing so, but you shouldn't make any assumptions in arriving at conclusions about these things. If you have a question, ask it.

Assumptions made about your intensional world are assumptions you make about the way you feel and believe. I'm going to spend substantial time on helping you to get to know yourself. One of the main purposes of this endeavor will be to get you to realize the difference between your inner beliefs and your assumptions. I hope when you finish this book, you'll be able to tell the difference between what you believe because your mother said so or did it that way, like cutting off the end of the roast before cooking it, and what you believe because you have made a conscious, intelligent choice based on an examination of the facts.

Assumptions made about your interviewer's intensional world are assumptions you make about the way your interviewer feels and believes. This is basically what the rest of this chapter is about. Knowing some of the pitfalls and how to avoid them will help you immeasurably in going through the interview process.

As an interviewer I will generally not let the person I'm interviewing get away with answers that result in me making an assumption he wants me to make without him actually saying something. A few decades ago I wrote an article for the *Hollywood Reporter* on the relationship between television and sports. Two of the people I interviewed for it were Peter Ueberroth, then the head of the Los Angeles Olympic Organizing Committee for the 1984 Olympics, and Jerry Buss, the owner of the Los Angeles Lakers. I asked them hard questions about finances. When the interviews were over, both said that they were the best interviews anyone had ever conducted of them.

There were two ways I could take the compliments. The first was that it was true, my interview was the best. Frankly, I believed that. However, the other was that they were manipulating me, telling me that so that I'd go out of the interview feeling so good that I'd treat them well in my article. That might have been true, too. But because I was aware of the hidden assumption of their intensional world—namely, that they might be insincere and trying to manipulate me—their flattery didn't affect what I wrote.

Asking Questions

One way to make sure that there are no hidden assumptions before you answer a question is to ask the interviewer to clarify it. I recently had a great lesson in making a hidden assumption.

I was having breakfast at Joni's Coffee Roaster in Marina del Rey, where many of my friends meet every morning for coffee and conversation. Sitting next to me was a couple, Glen and Elizabeth, who often joined us, but who were not regulars. After about a half hour Elizabeth got up and came back with a new glass of coffee. She sat down and poured the entire glass into her old, empty glass of coffee, which she had left on the table. She then started drinking from the old glass. When she started pouring, I thought she was going to share the glass with Glen, but when she poured all of it into the old glass, that clearly was not the case.

I thought, "That's strange. I wonder why she did that." Glen, who was sitting across from her, also watched as she did this, but he didn't say anything. I therefore assumed that it was something she did often and that he knew why she did it, so it must be something that was not out of the ordinary.

We all sat there for a few moments as she drank. Then Glen said, "Why did you do that?" Those were the exact words that had been floating through my mind. He said, "I thought you were going to share it at first, but then you didn't, so why did you do it?"

Elizabeth then explained that the new glass of coffee was hot to her lips, whereas the old glass was cool and easier to drink out of. That was a perfectly logical explanation, but neither Glen nor I would have known had he not asked her for an explanation. I said, "That's exactly what was going through my mind, but I thought you must know why she did it when you didn't say anything!"

He then explained that he has learned that Elizabeth does things like this all the time, and if he doesn't ask why, he will never know, so now he asks at least four times a day!

The point to learn from this is to try not to assume anything. I assumed that Glen understood her actions when he didn't say anything, but because *I* didn't understand it, I should have asked the question he asked.

If you don't understand something, ask! And be sure you ask before you answer a question that you might be answering by making a hidden assumption.

Checklist

- A bold assertion you make can be met with an illogical reaction by the interviewer.
- You can't discover an interviewer's quality and makeup in a short interview.
- If you make a negative impression early with an assertion based on a false assumption, you will have a very difficult time reversing the impression.
- Closely observe the interviewer and be sensitive to her reactions.
- Observe the interviewer's body language and react accordingly.
- If you perceive hints that you aren't being well received, stop doing whatever might be causing the negative reaction.

- Don't draw conclusions after the interview ends about how well or how poorly you did.
- Don't be intimidated by your competition.
- Think positively.
- Assume that you are going to be exposed to a sophisticated, professional interview technique.
- Assume every question is asked for a reason that is job-connected.
- Assume that everyone with whom you speak before an offer or rejection is made is making a judgment of you.
- If you are unsure of something, ask for a clarification.

7

Honesty

Honesty in an interview is made up of three elements: truth, consistency, and candor.

Truth

There comes a time in every interview when you will be tempted to exaggerate your accomplishments. The interviewer (and in this chapter let's assume the interviewer is a man) may ask you how much money you're making, and you may decide to add a couple of thousand dollars a year to your actual earnings. Or he may ask you where you finished in your college class, and you may think there's little difference between the top third and the top quarter.

When you feel this temptation—and it strikes everyone, no matter how honest—remember this rule: *When in doubt, tell the truth!* Sir Walter Scott said it years ago in iambic tetrameter:

Oh, what a tangled web we weave,
When first we practice to deceive!

If you lie, and that's what an exaggeration is, it may haunt you for the rest of your days. A lie is a terrible cancer that can plague you with fear of discovery. Once discovered, it can destroy your credibility forever. If you are caught lying in an interview or on your resumé, the interviewer can logically assume that you will also lie on the job. Since no employer wants employees who cannot be trusted, you may be eliminated immediately. Even if you are not caught, what could be a worse way to start a relationship than to build it on the foundation of a lie?

It has been estimated that 22 percent of resumés contain outright lies. In one extreme case a professor at a major American university was found to have used false identities to join six other college faculties in the previous four years. Caught, he was charged with twenty-seven counts of forgery, theft by deception, false swearing, and tampering with official documents.

The Thomas Brown Affair

I am as fascinated as the next person by stories of grand deceptions and imposters who have succeeded. The reality of it, though, is that sooner or later a web of lies will almost certainly break down. Here's a classic example:

A young man to whom I shall refer as Thomas Brown (not his real name or any of his aliases) applied to Harvard Law School and was admitted. His application listed a degree from Tulane University. Three years later Harvard discovered that this was false and forced Brown to withdraw from the university.

Two years after this, Brown was admitted to Harvard Law School again, under a different name. This time he claimed to be a graduate of Louisiana State University. He obtained loans of $2,500, the maximum amount a student could borrow at the time.

Law school is a three-year program, and traditionally, students spend the summer between their second and third years as clerks in law firms. Brown, who told the interviewing firms that he had straight As, that he had been a football player at LSU, and that he had spent a year at Oxford, received offers from two of the largest firms in Los Angeles, as well as invitations for follow-up interviews from major firms in other areas of the country.

Brown knew how to play his role. He told his fellow students that he wore a beard to look older (he was thirty-one at the time, claiming twenty-four), always dressed in a suit, drove a Mercedes, and dropped names judiciously. He gave the impression of wealth and would casually mention he was flying to Brazil one weekend, another far-off place the next.

He was undone while interviewing with a major New York firm. One of the partners had attended LSU and did not remember Brown playing football. An inquiry caused his house of cards to tumble. He ended up facing civil and criminal charges. As a tagline to the tawdry story, it was later discovered that Brown's wife, who was a student in the Harvard Business School, had credentials every bit as false as her husband's.

I strongly recommend against any kind of intentional deception. Eventually, one of the threads will break and they'll find out you didn't play football at LSU or spend a year at Oxford or graduate from Tulane or get all As. Then you will have invested years for naught, in addition to having your reputation ruined.

You Don't Know How Much the Interviewer Knows

Few interviewees would consider lying on such a grand scale as Thomas Brown, but probably all of us would succumb to the temptation to do a little "puffing." And a little of this is acceptable—expected, in fact. Interviewers know that interviewees want to present themselves in the best possible light, and recognize that a certain amount of image enhancement will take place, with interviewees exaggerating their accomplishments or downplaying their failures.

There is a fine line between embellishment and misrepresentation of facts, though, and you never want to be found on the wrong side of the line. Keep in mind that the interviewer may know much more about you than you realize. To repeat the basic rule: When in doubt, tell the truth.

A colleague of mine recommended a friend for a position with a client for whom I was interviewing. He told me that his friend was dissatisfied with his present job. He was making less than $20,000 per year and was looking for a higher-paying position. I met with the friend, and after an hour's amiable conversation I gently probed areas I felt were important and casually asked how much money he was making. He told me that he was making "around $35,000." Of course, he had no way of knowing that I knew better.

Suddenly, the tenor of the interview changed. Within the space of a few moments a metamorphosis occurred in him. The cocoon fell from this fellow, and different colors shone through. Whatever subject I broached was followed by a dogmatic diatribe defending his view, which was absolute. There was no moderation in his tone, no conversational amenity. He was a completely different person.

How much of this was an attitude of his that was there but

that I didn't perceive, and how much was caused by his lie, I don't know. But my opinion of him changed instantly. Thinking of it later, I traced my change of opinion to two causes. First was the unacceptability of his lie. Second was the personality change. Did I see him with different eyes, or did his knowledge of his lie make him change? That's the danger in lying. You never know the knowledge of the person to whom you are lying; you don't know the sources available to him to check out your stories; and you are unaware of the effects that lie has on you and your subsequent performance!

A reader from New York writes about a problem of an opposite sort: how to downplay credentials without really lying:

We hear a lot about fictitious degrees and other credentials. My problem is the opposite—I want to *hide* some of my degrees and jobs and downplay my age. Let me explain. My old resumé showed three bachelor's degrees and a caseworker job. Yes, I did change my mind several times. However, I am now an accountant and sure about it. Starting with my work on my accounting degree, in one way or another I have been connected with accounting for fifteen years. My old resumé posed two problems: (1) Interviewers invariably say something like, "Why did you change fields so many times?" The answer is that I wasn't exposed to accounting and had no idea that would be my field. Also, I thought that showing my caseworker job on my resumé would *help* me—showing that I have *people* skills as well as *number* skills. However, I believe that, instead, the three degrees and the caseworker job just make me look wishy-washy. (2) I am forty-five years old but look about thirty. While I can't prove age discrimination, I strongly suspect it exists. I don't have the time, money, or inclination to fight it—I just want a job. However, I believe that I can fight it my own way—through omissions on my resumé.

My feeling is this: I am generally an honest person. I am applying for positions for which I feel I qualify. I am in excellent health and physical condition. Therefore, why should I put something on my resumé that is irrelevant and that could hurt me? After all, I could also put down grade school, high school, Girl Scouts, babysitting, and other teenage activities. Where do you draw the line?

If anybody subsequently asks me about these omissions, I am prepared to say, "I feel it was too long ago and not relevant."

I was laid off from my last paid job, where I had worked four years, due to lack of work. I was not replaced. I had always had an itch to start my own practice but had been afraid to quit my job to do it. So I figured as long as I was laid off, this was the time to try to start my own practice.

Although I have quite a few individual tax clients and have some businesses, I have to admit the business is a failure. I think the only way I could make a go of it would be to buy out or merge with another practice. I am, for the most part, being supported by my husband's salary and am now actively seeking employment.

My question is this: Should I tell interviewers I left to start my own business, or should I say I was laid off and then decided to start my own business?

If I say I left to start my own business, an interviewer might think I lacked common sense to quit a secure job for a business that didn't prove successful. He also might think I am wishy-washy, not giving myself enough time for success, as it usually takes three years to establish a practice.

If I say I was laid off, it might be more understandable why after just one year I decided to reenter the job market. On the other hand, "laid off" may have a stigma.

This reader needs to realize that the purpose of a resumé is to get an interview, not to get a job. Once the resumé gets you in the door for the interview, it's up to you to continue on, and the resumé becomes less important. So the only time you have to worry about deceptive omissions in your resumé is when the deception is of something that would *substantively* affect the interviewer's evaluation of you. Having too many degrees is not such a thing; having spent ten years in San Quentin for rape is. If it is this reader's opinion that she is the victim of age discrimination, for example, and that she can fight it by changing her resumé, then I think she should, and I wouldn't worry about such omissions. You want to be honest, but you don't want to roll up your sleeves to show your interviewer your newest wart!

Part of the reader's problem is a question of semantics. I don't like the stigma of the words "laid off," either. Her *job* was terminated. While this might be a fine distinction (since the result is the same), she should have explained her situation more fully than just saying she was "laid off." She should have explained that she had a good job and was doing good work and that her employer was happy with her but that there just wasn't enough work. That sounds better than just saying she was laid off, and it has the added virtue of being the truth.

Further, if I were she, I wouldn't say that I left to start my own business, because it's not true. Even more important, the reason she found herself on her own was not something that would be a negative. Had she slugged her boss in the nose and lost her job because of that, then she would have had something to worry about in trying to explain it in the best light, but what happened to her is not a negative; it just has to be fully explained when the question is raised.

DIFFERING INTERPRETATIONS

Most occurrences are subject to different interpretations. *What must be distinguished is the intentional misrepresentation of an established fact from the embellishment of the interpretation of the situation.*

Examples of misrepresentation are saying you made more money than you did, manipulating time periods in your resumé, or saying you finished higher in your graduating class than you did. If you misrepresent a verifiable fact that is not subject to interpretation and it is discovered, the interview process might end right there, or, if you have already been hired, you may find your job terminated.

But if the question calls for an interpretation, you can shade your answer so that you show up to your best advantage without actually lying. Once when I was interviewing at a western university, a student came up to me with a real problem. He was ranked third in his law school class, but he had not yet received a job offer, despite the fact that the recruiting season was almost over. He seemed to me to be eager, intelligent, and personable, so I asked him what he thought was behind his lack of success. He said it might be because he had been invited to try out for the *Law Review* and had declined and that the interviewers didn't like that. His explanation to interviewers was that the *Law Review* took a lot of time, and he didn't want to sacrifice his social life for all that work.

If I ever heard an answer calculated to turn off a prospective employer, that was it. I asked him if he spent all his time playing, and he responded, somewhat indignantly, that he did not. He spent most of his time studying, and what little leisure time he did have he needed to use just for leisure, not further legal work on the *Law Review*. I asked him if he had gone into this much detail when interviewers asked him his reasons for not applying to the *Law Review*, and he said that he had not.

I suggested to him that he tell the truth, but that it be the complete truth, not just a short, lazy truth. By shortchanging his answer he had left the impression that he didn't like hard work. By adding a few more details he could leave a completely different impression: that of someone who worked hard but was mature enough to realize that in order to work hard he needed leisure time to recharge his batteries.

The interviewer was asking for an explanation of why he did not try out for the *Law Review*. When asked for such an opinion, the interviewee should answer the question to his best advantage, which can result in the interviewer's evaluating him on the whole interview and not on one very bad answer that had a "halo effect." (For more on the halo effect, see chapter 15.)

Purpose of the Question

Remember what I said in chapter 5 about determining what the purpose of the question is? What might seem to be mendacity in answering a question can be justified if you are answering the question after considering what the purpose of the question is. In the example from chapter 5 a question was asked for the purpose of determining if the interviewee was smart enough to divine the correct answer (that the sports section was the first section of the paper the interviewee read). Any other answer automatically disqualified the interviewee from further consideration. Clearly, there is no dishonesty involved if you answer that the sports section is the first section you read, even if it isn't, because the question wasn't asked to determine what section the interviewee read, but to determine if the interviewee was smart enough to know how to answer the question. So if you get a question like this, think awhile before you answer.

EVASIVENESS

Reader Steven Shore of Columbia, Maryland, writes:

> I've been asked in interviews if I have ever done X. Of course, the interviewer has neither the interest nor the ability to take us both back in time, but is asking the question because he or she has made two implicit assumptions: that X is perceived as an essential skill in the job in question; and that the only way the candidate can actually perform X in the job is by having successfully performed X in the past.
>
> This type of question, in my opinion, allows only three basic answers: (1) "Yes, I have done X at _____; this resulted in $_____ of new product or service growth or $_____ of cost savings"; (2) "No, I haven't done X; however, I have successfully done Y, which resulted in [proceed as in answer 1]"; (3) "No, I haven't done X."
>
> I wish we lived in a world where answer 2 would be credibly received, but this is usually not the case. So under certain conditions—i.e., if I believe that I can accomplish X in the job in question—I will give answer 1.
>
> I would always prefer to give an honest answer. However, in more than one instance I have perceived that honesty really wasn't expected or appreciated by the interviewer, that in giving an honest answer to a question, I had removed myself from consideration for a position I

could function effectively in, and in an environment where I'd fit in quite well.

Mr. Shore's letter goes right to the heart of the matter, and the problem may be resolved in a way that is not dishonest. Very few questions ask strictly for facts. If someone asks you straight out if you've ever done X and you haven't and don't want to admit it, answer to your best advantage. You can answer as if you think the interviewer has asked you if you're *familiar* with X, or if you *think* you could do X, or how you would *approach* X if given the opportunity. What interviewees often fail to realize is that an interview is not a script. There aren't written questions and answers to which the interviewer can later refer. It's a dialogue, and generally, the interviewer is just trying to get the interviewee to talk.

Further, if you misinterpret the question (intentionally or unintentionally), the interviewer might immediately recognize that you're not answering the question he asked as specifically as he asked it. It's unlikely that he'll reask the question because (1) doing so can be insulting to the interviewee and (2) he might like your answer and not want to get another. Interviewers are not prosecuting attorneys and generally don't bore in until they get the specific answer to the specific question they asked. More probably, he'll just go on to other subjects and not repeat the question. Interviewers are as lazy as everyone else and might not want to exert the effort to try to force you to answer the question when you've already talked on the subject for a while. Another reason he might not pursue a specific answer, depending on how well you've vamped, is the time constraints of the interview. He might just want to go on to other things.

If you haven't done X and don't want to admit it, it's not dishonest to answer the question by talking about something else. The interviewer won't know if you are being evasive or misheard the question or if he asked the question properly. If he's really interested in the specific answer to the question, he'll ask it again, and then you don't have much choice but to answer it. If he's not, then answering a different question than what was asked has accomplished your purpose of not admitting that you haven't done X without lying about it. If you want to see how this works, watch politicians interviewed on television, especially on the Sunday morning interview shows. They are masters at giving an answer to a question that is actually an answer to another question and not the question that was asked. The late Senator Patrick Moynihan of New York was the only politician I've ever heard who would actually answer a question "yes" or "no." He had no fear of expressing how he felt on any issue.

A specific example of this technique that you can see on TV interview shows every day was an appearance by Senator Bob Graham on the *Today* show when he was campaigning for the Democratic nomination for the 2004 presidential election. He was asked by Katie Couric what he thought of a recent attack on President George W. Bush in a speech on the Senate floor by West Virginia senator Robert Byrd, who excoriated the president for a "mission accomplished" speech aboard an aircraft carrier. Couric asked specifically if Graham agreed with Byrd. After viewing a tape of Byrd's vitriolic attack, Graham responded, "That's a tradition of presidents. The first President Bush did it, too. What I think is more important is how the president pursues the war against terrorism . . ." And on and on, but never answering the question about whether or not he agreed with Byrd or what his position was on President Bush giving the speech on the aircraft carrier. It was the classic common method of not answering the question asked, talking instead in a vein that veered the conversation away from the question so that the interview continued without an aggressive follow-up to get an answer to the question.

Most politicians, unfortunately, fear expressing an honest opinion because they feel it's more important to their careers to avoid the possibility of offending a substantial portion of the electorate than it is to give an honest opinion. So when they're asked a question, their answer often has nothing to do with the specifics of what was asked. They "spin" and answer something else. Because most television interview shows have severe time constraints, politicians being interviewed can get away with this type of behavior. Your interview will most likely have similar time constraints. If it's good enough for our elected representatives, why isn't it good enough for you? There are two big advantages to being evasive in this way. First, you aren't giving an answer you don't want to give. Second, you aren't lying. Whether or not your evasiveness has been noticed is something you might never find out. Most likely, you'll be given the benefit of the doubt. The downside, of course, is that your evasiveness might be noticed, and the interviewer might form a negative impression from it. If it's a question you don't want to answer, however, you have to weigh this risk against how much giving a specific answer to the specific question might harm you.

Consistency

Inconsistency is a fault that can be almost as damaging as lying. You must take great care to be consistent in your interviews, especially in screening interviews when you are faced with trained personnel officers whose goal is to uncover the facts.

Remember, screening interviewers are looking for reasons to reject you. They are looking for inconsistencies on your resumé and in what you say. If they get a glimmer of something wrong, they may ask the same question over and over in different ways to test what you have claimed. If you have told the truth, you generally have nothing to fear. But if you have misrepresented something, or if you have hedged an answer to show yourself in the best light, you must be very careful that each time you discuss that topic you say the same thing. If you once vary from what you have said before, you may be rejected for that or you may have to justify the variance.

The selection interviewer is also looking for inconsistencies, although not with the same fervor that a screening interviewer is. Still, if he gets a red flag to one of his questions, beware. If you claim some accomplishment that he feels is beyond you, he may go into the subject in depth and probe the area to determine exactly what you did and how much you participated in the event.

For example, if I were interviewing the student who didn't try out for the *Law Review* and he told me he wanted to devote all the time he could to his studies, I would let some time pass and then question him on his outside interests. If I then discovered that he played intramural sports, never missed a first-run movie, went to all the football and basketball games, and dated a different woman every night, I'd conclude that his reason for not trying out for the *Law Review* was inconsistent with his actions.

Candor

The third element of honesty is candor. As a rule, interviewees look upon a selection interview as a one-way street. On the one side sits the interviewer who is picking a person to fill an available position. On the other side is the interviewee who is applying for the position.

But it works both ways: *You as applicant are also an interviewer seeking to find out if the position is right for you. If something bothers you about the position for which you are interviewing, you should be*

candid about your doubt and express it to the interviewer. I coun-
seled a man once who told me that he had turned down an
attractive job offer because the interviewer, the vice president
to whom he would report, was abrasive with a subordinate. He
felt that he would not react well if he were treated in a similar
manner. I asked if he had discussed the problem with the vice
president, and he replied that he had not. He had simply
declined the offer. He felt bad about it because what he knew
about the position stimulated him.

You should realize that when a job is offered, it is a compliment. The employer is saying, "I like you and I think you can
do a good job. I am so confident of this that I'm willing to pay
you to come and work for me." When a compliment is paid, it
should be treated with respect. If for some reason you decide
to reject the job offer, you owe it to both yourself and the
offerer to state the reasons for the rejection. First, it is courteous. Second, and more important, as far as you are concerned,
the offerer may wish to resolve the problems you have with the
job by making it more palatable.

The person I was counseling had a fear that the vice president would be difficult to work with. He made this judgment
on the basis of one incident and didn't give the man another
chance. It's possible that his interviewer had just been released
from the hospital, or a close relative had died, or he had lost a
lot of money in the stock market, or he could have had some
other disappointment about which the interviewee knew nothing, or the subordinate could have been completely incompe-
tent. If the interviewee doesn't raise the point, he isn't getting
the most out of his interview. He should try to get as much
information as he can.

Had he turned down the position by saying something like,
"I appreciate the offer, but frankly, I am very concerned about
how you and I would work together . . . I consider myself a

professional and, as a result, feel that I am due professional respect and courtesy . . . The way you spoke to Mr. Smith troubled me," he would have given the interviewer an opportunity to face the interviewee's main objection to the job and at least explain his actions.

Remember the advice previously given on assumptions. Don't base your decision on unqueried assumptions that may be erroneous. Be as certain as you can that your assumption is based on fact. You can do this by being candid and bringing your assumptions out into the open. If you think the job is an attractive one but you have grave doubts because of something about which you haven't spoken, bring it up and discuss it with the interviewer prior to making your decision.

One executive I knew made a terrible career mistake because he was not candid during the interview process. A reputable company had been trying to find a new vice president of finance. They had been interviewing for over a year to fill a vacancy that had had several occupants the preceding two years. Obviously, something was wrong.

The executive went to the interview, despite severe misgivings. He met the top management and was impressed. Still his doubts nagged.

He was made an offer that was beyond his wildest dreams: a large salary, a luxury car, bonus, and profit sharing, everything he had ever wanted. On the debit side was that he knew that the three people in the job before him had stayed only a few months before leaving. He also knew that the company had had the vacancy for more than a year. This troubled him, but he feared to bring it up.

Analyzing the situation later, he knew that his fear had two bases. First, he felt that a question about the turnover might offend the interviewer and cost him an offer. Second, he feared that the answer might cause him to have to reject an offer he wanted. So he didn't broach the subject, took the job, and immediately found himself in the eye of a storm.

Apparently, there were shenanigans with one of the recently acquired divisions that could subject the company to shareholders' derivative suits and the officers involved to extensive liability. Each of his predecessors had apparently discovered the problem quickly and resigned rather than become embroiled in such a dangerous situation.

My friend had large personal expenses and couldn't afford to quit. His resumé had so many job changes that he felt he couldn't put his name out on the street, so he had to try to survive without participating in the problem and thereby becoming an accomplice.

He was stuck in a miserable situation for two years before an offer appeared at a much smaller company for much less money. He grabbed it without looking back.

Had he been candid and expressed his doubts, he could have discovered the problem prior to taking the job. Of course, the company wouldn't have admitted such a thing to a job candidate, but he could have listened to their explanation and then told them he wanted to talk to the men who had held the position previously. That most probably would have terminated the company's consideration of him, or he would have discovered from his predecessors how sticky the situation was.

It's never wise to accept or reject an offer if you have unexpressed doubts about something. Bring them out into the open. They may be unfounded, and you will be able to start your new position with a clear mind. Or they may have foundation, in which case you're better off knowing about it and not proceeding further (or proceeding further with full knowledge of what you're getting into). In either case, you're much better off by being candid and expressing your doubts than keeping them to yourself.

Checklist

- Honesty consists of truth, consistency, and candor.
- When in doubt, tell the truth.
- An undiscovered lie will haunt you.
- A discovered lie can destroy your credibility forever.
- An employer does not want someone working for him whom he cannot trust.
- Failure to tell the truth reveals a character trait that cannot be remedied.
- Remember that you have no way of knowing how much the interviewer knows.
- A lie can change your personality as your guilty knowledge of it affects your performance.
- Distinguish between a question calling for a fact and one calling for an opinion.
- Always answer questions calling for your opinion to your best advantage.
- If you don't want to answer a question, you can intentionally misinterpret the question and give an answer to a different question, one that wasn't asked.
- Inconsistency can lead to an inference of a lack of honesty.
- Be candid about your doubts and bring them up to the interviewer.
- Determine what the purpose of the question is before giving an answer.
- A job offer is a compliment, and you owe the interviewer the courtesy of being candid.
- Don't base your decision on unqueried assumptions.

8

Mannerisms of Speech

There's a dichotomy that should be understood in determining how your speech affects your interview. There are basically two different sciences at work. The first is the point of view of pragmatics, which is what language means to the listener. The second is semantics, which is whether the speaker knows what he or she is saying when he or she speaks.

Obviously, in an interview situation both points of view must be considered. But for our purposes we are going to concentrate on pragmatics, which is what your words mean to the person with whom you are speaking, your interviewer. So I'm going to go over some common expressions we all use and tell you what they might mean to your interviewer. Sandor S. Feldman analyzed these in his classic work, *Mannerisms of Speech and Gestures in Every Day Life* (International Universities Press, 1959), a book I highly recommend that you read in full.

Mannerisms of Speech

1. "By the way"
Feldman tells of a person he was psychoanalyzing who told a story and then added a seemingly insignificant fact with the

introduction "by the way." The "insignificant" fact was actually the most important thing she said. So this way of saying something, by introducing it as if it's an afterthought, is, in fact, a clue that something very important is about to be said.

This is important to know in the context of an interview for several reasons. First, if your interviewer says "by the way," pay strict attention to whatever follows because it's probably very important. Your interviewer might not even be aware of what she's doing, but your knowing that "by the way" signals something important should jump-start your adrenaline. (In this chapter we'll assume the interviewer is a woman.)

Second, if there's something you want to say and you do not want to emphasize it, don't throw it in with a "by the way." Your interviewer might not be aware of what "by the way" really means, but, then again, she might be. In any event, a "by the way" statement is almost always remembered because it's usually somewhat different than what's gone before. If you want to make a statement insignificant, find some other way of doing it than by throwing it in as if it's something you've just thought of. As Feldman says, "usually the person who is using 'by the way' knows *in advance* the content of his or her comment, is even waiting awhile to mislead the listener as if the idea came into his or her mind suddenly. The aim is to pretend that what he or she says is not important. The truth is that it is very important to the speaker; it may be the most important thing in the whole conversation."

2. "Incidentally" and "As you are aware"
The use of these words indicates an inability to take credit for things you have done. Basically, they introduce things that you feel you want to minimize. But if they're important enough to mention, why minimize them by using such a mannerism of speech to deprecate what you are about to say about yourself?

You might be talking about your high school baseball career and say, "Yes, I played baseball in high school. Incidentally, I hit the first home run in the history of my high school." Well, why "incidentally"? You signal to your listener that this isn't much but you thought you'd mention it. In an interview context it indicates a lack of confidence in yourself, an inability to take credit when credit is due. It can come across as a weakness of character. How much better it would sound to say, "Yes, I played baseball in high school. One thing I'm really proud of is that I hit the first home run in my high school's history!"

3. "Needless to say"

According to Feldman, the use of this introductory phrase indicates an ambivalent, or mixed, feeling. Introducing a statement with this phrase shows that the speaker actually has two feelings, one positive and one negative, and he or she is hiding the negative to express the positive. If you're in love with someone, you're not going to say, "Needless to say, I love you!" However, what if you're having an affair? You see your spouse on some special occasion. You feel guilt about your affair. Now it might seem normal to say, "Needless to say, I love you." The "needless to say" expresses the unexpressed possibility that maybe I *don't* love you! You should avoid this expression in an interview. If you have a problem with dishonesty, you might say, "Needless to say, I'm honest." If, however, you have nothing dishonest in your background, it would never occur to you to introduce the statement of your honesty with "needless to say."

4. "To be perfectly frank," "To be honest," "To tell the truth," "Frankly, honestly"

Once again these introductory phrases indicate the opposite of what the speaker intends. If you're going to be honest or speak the truth, it would not occur to you to start out with one of these phrases. It's only if you do not intend to be honest or speak the truth that you might use one of them.

Further, these phrases also indicate that perhaps in other situations you might not be frank or honest or tell the truth. Otherwise, why would you use them with what you're about to say? Don't these phrases in themselves reveal that you sometimes don't tell the truth, that you're sometimes not honest?

These phrases don't gain you anything with an interviewer. Rather, they put the interviewer on guard that perhaps there's something amiss. When you're tempted to use one of these phrases, remember the tape of President Richard Nixon telling a press conference that "people have got to know whether or not their President is a crook. Well, I'm not a crook!"

What was the effect of that statement? It made everyone think he probably *was* a crook, whether he actually was or not.

5. *"Honest"*

This is another word to be avoided because it indicates exactly the opposite of what it expresses. If you say something and then add "honest," the listener suspects that what you said wasn't honest. Why else would you say "honest"? You tell a woman, "That dress looks great on you . . . honest!" or "I really like your hairdo . . . honest!" Why add "honest"? If the dress looks great, that's all you have to say. If you like the hairdo, you needn't say more. But when you say "honest," you're really saying, "I don't believe a word of what I just said."

6. *"Before I forget"*

Feldman says that there is rarely a legitimate reason for using "before I forget." One ostensible reason for using it is to try to convey to the listener that what you're going to say or do isn't very important to you. But what it really conveys is that it *is* very important to you. This is just another example of the speaker fooling him- or herself; belittling something by speech, which actually emphasizes it to the listener. The matter is important to you, which is why you brought it up. You're never going to forget it. It's probably the most important thing on your mind. So, since you're not fooling your interviewer, why fool yourself and telegraph something you apparently don't want to convey, which is how important whatever this is actually is to you.

7. *"As you (well) know" and "You know"*

These phrases have many uses. Their most common is to say something in such a way that you don't appear to be more knowledgeable than your interviewer. Because you don't want to appear to be condescending or in a superior position to her, you preface something with "as you know." In this way, you feel, you are inviting a comradely feeling with the interviewer, discussing something of which you are both aware, without appearing to be lecturing. This has the advantage of complimenting the interviewer by assuming her to be more knowledgeable than she is. Maybe she doesn't "know." If not, then it's up to her to let you know her state of ignorance by telling you—or not, as the case may be. In either event, you haven't put her on the spot so long as what you say is detailed enough for her to converse about it, even if she didn't "know."

Feldman says that "as you know" can have several meanings:

1. You better remember it.
2. I expect you to remember it.
3. I am sure you remember it.
4. Please remember what I say.
5. I would hate you if you were not interested in everything I say.

The problem with analyzing the use of speech mannerisms such as "as you know" is that the phrases have different meanings. The speaker might mean one thing; the listener might interpret it another way. If you are in the habit of using "as you know," in which of the five ways listed above do you mean it?

Regardless of your intent, you should realize that even though you might mean, let's say, number 3, "I am sure you remember it," your interviewer might interpret it as number 5, "I would hate you if you were not interested in everything I say." So you use these mannerisms at your risk. If the mannerism is ambiguous, as "as you know" clearly is, it's better not to use it.

Originally, "you know" was used to keep from mentioning something that the speaker didn't want to detail in specifics, but merely wanted to call to mind. Feldman uses the example of a patient of his who said that "my wife and I had problems, you know, and . . ." Feldman says that the "problems" stemmed from his relationship with another woman, which Feldman knew about but which the speaker didn't want to discuss specifically.

However, "you know" has become a phrase that is so much used it's misused. It's used as a pause in thinking while continuing to talk. I'll never forget the first television interview when ABC took over telecasting NBA games in the early 1970s. Milwaukee guard Flynn Robinson was the first to be awarded Player of the Game, and so he was interviewed after the game. I kid you not when I tell you that Robinson was so inarticulately nervous that the first thirty-eight words out of his mouth were nineteen consecutive "you knows"!

8. "I don't care"

Feldman says that there's rarely a time when this phrase should be used. Often it's a denial of a feeling one actually has, so it's hypocritical. If a lover dumps you, you might immediately say, "I don't care," when in actuality you care very much. In an interview situation it's also rarely a good idea to say, "I don't care." If true, it shows a lack of feeling. But generally, it's a denial mechanism that is all too obvious to the listener. Feldman says, "The use of the 'I don't care' affects all of our professional, social, and amorous relationships. Its effect is pernicious and spoils the mutual communication between people."

9. "Am I right?"

This is a terrible speech mannerism to use in an interview. What's the interviewer to say? "Yes, you are right"? "No, you are wrong"? If you're right, you're right. Why do you need support from your interviewer? Obviously, you don't. You're manipulating her to bolster your ego. Or to agree to something with which she might not agree. If the latter, then you're inviting an argument. If you're making an assertion, just make it and let it lie. If she wants to agree with you, she may do so at her discretion. If not, then you can go on. Don't force your interviewer to take a position.

10. "Of course"

Feldman says that "of course" is a limitation put on an affirmative answer. He uses the example of a wife asking her husband if he loves her. If he says, "Of course, I love you," it conveys, according to Feldman, the idea that, sure, he loves her, but not like he used to love her when he'd swim the widest ocean to be with her.

Feldman also says that "of course" can be a denial of what was just said. Here he gives the example of a doctor telling someone about a patient and what a beautiful body she had, then adding, "I looked at her professionally, of course." Feldman says when he adds "of course" to this statement, he's denying that he looked at her professionally! This is an example of how we aren't as smart as we think we are. By throwing in the "of course"—which we think will elicit agreement in the listener—we're actually creating just the opposite impression. The listener thinks, "Why did he say 'of course'? The only reason could be that he wants me to agree that that's the way he looked at her when in actuality he was looking at her sexually."

To me, "of course" generally signals something's wrong with what's being said. This is a phrase that is full of danger. Avoid it.

11. "It is not that . . ."

This is a personal put-down, a statement that you don't have the confidence in yourself to give yourself your due. Feldman gives the example of a doctor saying, "It is not that I'm such a great doctor, but in my opinion Dr. X is not a good doctor at all." What he's really saying is, "I am a good doctor, and my opinion, being a good doctor and able to judge who is and who isn't a good doctor, is that Dr. X is not a good doctor." This would be an honest statement. But introducing the statement with "it is not that" takes away from the impact of his opinion by putting himself down.

"It is not that" is an obvious ploy to a listener. But it is used time and again by people who don't want to appear to be arrogant, so they start off by putting themselves down and then making their point. How absurd! Exhibit confidence and pride in yourself when you're speaking. "It is not that" should be avoided.

12. "I am not boasting"

Of course, you're boasting! You start out denying it and then make some statement of something great you've done. "I am not boasting, but I can type 120 words a minute." "I am not boasting, but I wrote three short stories last week." And so on. Just say, "I can type 120 words a minute," or "I wrote three short stories last week." See how much better that sounds? You don't need to make a dishonest preface to your boast. If you want to boast, boast. There's nothing wrong with that. That's what you're supposed to do in an interview: tell why you're good, boast about your accomplishments. Don't preface the boast with a disclaimer.

13. "I cannot tell you how much" and "I cannot find the words to express"

Feldman says these phrases admit a lack of eloquence. Although you are trying to tell your listener that what you are going to say is so wonderful or exceptional that words don't exist to describe it, you are really just admitting that it is your own inadequacy that prevents a proper description. These are mannerisms of speech that should be discarded if they are part of your lexicon. They diminish you and what you're about to say.

14. "I only"

"Only" is a word that limits what you are about to say. "I only wanted to . . ." means that you wanted nothing further. It's rarely accurate. What it does, again, is diminish what you are about to say. "I only wanted to tell you that the water is cold." Why not, "I wanted to tell you the water is cold"? Or "The water is cold." Why preface it with "I only"? Probably because it's not honest. You really didn't "only" want to say that; you had some ulterior motive. As with the other mannerisms, this betrays something you think you have hidden by the use of the mannerism. It's the mannerism of speech itself that tips off your listener that you're being disingenuous.

15. "I just"

According to Feldman, "just" is acceptable only when it refers to time. "I just returned home" means that in the past few moments you returned home. However, many people use "just" as a limiting word, like "only." "I just wanted to ask you what you did when you were out" is a limiting statement. It demeans what you're saying. If your interviewer asks you what you did at your last job and you say, "I just negotiated a few contracts," what you're saying is that it's not important. Maybe you're asked why you had a disagreement with someone for whom you worked, and you respond, "I just gave a few suggestions," which in your mind minimizes what you did, telling your interviewer that you don't think the disagreement was so bad. This is a mistake in an interview. Don't diminish things you've done. If you had a disagreement with someone with whom you worked, it must have been important, so don't diminish it in your listener's mind by using minimizing words like "just." This holds true for any demeaning or limiting language you use to describe yourself or something you've done. As far as the use of the word "just" goes, don't use it unless you're referring to time.

16. "Bye-bye"

This is a particularly egregious phrase to me. It always irritated me, and I wasn't confident of my reaction until Feldman validated it. To bid someone adieu by saying "bye-bye" instead of "good-bye" or simply "bye" indicates to me a familiarity that is often lacking. I used to have a best friend with whom I played basketball and went to football games who always said "bye-bye" to me, and it always made me uncomfortable. A girlfriend could say "bye-bye" to me and it would be fine. But for a male friend to say it, it seemed to me, was wrong. This was something that lovers said to one another, not guy friends. And

Feldman confirms this: "Sometimes . . . the person to whom the 'bye-bye' is addressed finds the phrase irritating because he is uncertain whether he should allow himself to be trapped by the 'bye-bye' or whether he should maintain his authority and stick to the 'good-bye,' thus indicating . . . that she is in no position to say 'bye-bye,' which means more closeness."

Personally, I don't think a man should ever say "bye-bye" to another man. And a woman should be careful in saying it to a man in an interview because of the implications discussed here. Maybe I'm too sensitive about this. But that's the problem with an interview. You are dealing with personal feelings, and you don't know how the interviewer will react to something you say. I give you my feelings here, not because it's the way everyone feels, but to apprise you that your interviewer can react in ways you might not anticipate. So it might be better to avoid "bye-bye."

17. "In a way," "Maybe," "Sort of"
These words are qualifiers that allow you to back out of an answer if you change your mind. They can indicate to an interviewer that you don't want to take a position. Basically, these are words used to evade answering a question directly or taking a position. If the interviewer has asked you a factual question and is looking for a factual answer, use of these words to answer the question can be harmful to the impression she will form.

18. Begging the Question
This is a way to frame a question that requires the answerer to assume facts that are not necessarily facts. An example would be to refer to a fact with a judgment added, and then ask a question about it. How do you handle it, for example, if your interviewer were to say, "How do think a man as stupid as

Smith ever got to be president?" This begs the question because, although Smith might be president, there's no established fact that he's stupid. However, it might be a favorite ploy of anti-Smith people to continue to foist on the public, and it would never fail to irritate pro-Smith people. How to handle this? There are a couple of ways you could try, and remember, you're in an interview and you probably want the job. You can't make an assumption that your interviewer doesn't like Smith, because she might be deliberately imposing stress to see how you handle a difficult, controversial question. So there are two things you can't do: You can't rush to defend Smith's intellect, and you can't agree with the interviewer that Smith is stupid. So what do you do? Two choices are available.

First, you could immediately challenge the interviewer by asking, "Do you think Smith is stupid?" This now puts the interviewer on the defensive and doesn't reveal how you feel at all. It might end the inquisition right there because, in challenging the interviewer, you've switched the control of the issue from her to you. Now the interviewer is on the hook.

Second, you could attack the form of the question by saying something like, "Well, you've assumed facts that aren't in evidence," and leave it at that. Again you've snatched control of the issue from your interviewer and should have no further obligation to pursue it. If the interviewer pursues it, I'd avoid engaging on the issue, but concentrate on querying why she would ask such a biased, controversial question in a job interview. You could decline to answer by saying that you prefer not to discuss religion or politics with strangers.

Begging the question will only arise, generally, when the interviewer is trying to introduce stress into the interview. As we've said, the best way to handle stress is to recognize it immediately. If you're prepared for it, you're much better able to handle it.

19. ". . . and, uh . . ."
This is not on Feldman's list, but it is a killer. Someone asks you a question. You answer it. Then, instead of keeping quiet, you say ". . . and, uh . . ." This indicates to your interviewer that you have something further to say. However, generally, you don't have anything further to say, and it's really a pro-logue for rambling, which you don't want to do in an interview. But the interviewer, instead of proceeding with the interview, hears your "and, uh," so she sits and waits for you to say some-thing. The silence is compelling, so you add something. Gen-erally, it's something that's not terribly germane, and, not unlikely, you conclude this next rambling statement with "and, uh." You are on the slippery slope. And you have probably made a distinctly negative impression on your interviewer, who probably wants to get on with the interview.

The solution is simple. When you have finished your answer or whatever it is that you want to say, stop. Never, and I emphasize never, say ". . . and, uh . . ."

Gestures

Feldman also deals with nonverbal actions, or gestures, and what these can communicate.

1. Playing with the ring on the finger and with the handbag
Feldman says that this mannerism is pretty much confined to women and depends on intent and knowledge. If the person knows what she's doing. If she does it intentionally she is communicating something, often some sort of sexual thought. What is important in the interview environment is when she does it unintentionally. In that event, says Feldman, it "indi-cates a conflict, a tension in the person. It expresses a thought

which the woman does not like to have." Generally, playing with a ring especially, but also with a handbag, means that the woman is being bothered by something other than the topic at hand. In an interview it indicates a distraction, something you don't want to communicate to an interviewer.

2. Confusion around the hands

Feldman cites a colleague of Sigmund Freud, Sándor Ferenczi, who claimed that people with fidgety hands are communicating "unsuccessfully repressed inclinations to masturbate" and "other 'bad habits' like nail-biting, nose-picking, scratching oneself, etc." Feldman quoted this with approval. I think it's a bit far-fetched to think that someone who is uncomfortable about what to do with his or her hands is really communicating a desire to masturbate. Regardless of the truth of that, it does communicate a certain uncomfortability with oneself and should be avoided. In an interview you are generally sitting down. If you are worried about what to do with your hands, just keep them in your lap.

3. Pressing two hands to the temples

Feldman says that this gesture can "represent sadness, exhaustion, mourning, meditation in distress, and giving up hope for a solution," in addition to just having a headache. Clearly, this is a gesture that should be avoided in an interview.

4. Blinking and other eye anomalies

As the French say, *Les yeux sont le miroir de l'âme*, the eyes are the mirror of the soul. In a stress interview blinking and other eye anomalies can make a distinct impression. According to Feldman, when one lies, one blinks (apropos of nothing in particular, women blink nearly twice as often as men). But in an interview it's the full spectrum of eye anomalies that can be important. I remember negotiating with a builder in Charlotte Amalie, St. Thomas, U.S. Virgin Islands. The first time I met him his eyes were all over the place. He looked at me, he looked at my companion, his eyes were darting, and he was blinking like there was no tomorrow. I figured either he was high on some Caribbean drug or he was insincere, untrustworthy, and trying to put something over on us. It wasn't the failure to establish any kind of eye contact that bothered me (because he did occasionally establish eye contact; he just didn't hold it for more than a moment), it was the constant darting back and forth of his eyes and his continuous blinking that alarmed me.

As I got to know him, my initial impression was reinforced. He wasn't someone I could trust, and he had terrible power problems. He was around twenty-nine years old and was working for his uncles, who had assigned him to their holdings in the Virgin Islands. I negotiated a settlement of a big problem with one of the uncles, who was the boss in Florida. I had to take the contract to the nephew in Charlotte Amalie to sign, after his uncle had signed off on it.

After I landed and went directly to his office, he said he wanted to have his lawyer look at the contract before he signed it. That was too much for me. I told him that wasn't acceptable, that I had already negotiated the deal with his uncle, that it had been approved by his uncle's attorney, and both had already agreed to it, so what his lawyer thought about it was irrelevant. He threw a tantrum and physically threatened me. I left and went to the airport. I called his uncle and told him the deal was off. His uncle was incredulous and asked why and I explained it to him. He told me to go back and that the nephew would sign it without any further review by his lawyer. I did so and the deal was signed.

But the lesson was that my initial impression, caused mainly by the working of his eyes, was right on. This guy was trouble and the people for me to deal with were his uncles.

Unfortunately, some people have problems with blinking that are unrelated to truthfulness. If you have such a problem, it might be wise to tell your interviewer about it. For instance, I am allergic to perfume, which sometimes causes my eyes to water. If I were in an interview and my watering eyes caused me to have to blink a lot, I would explain why I was blinking, that it was a physical reaction to perfume, in order to keep the interviewer from drawing a negative inference from my blinking or watering eyes.

5. Coughing

Coughing is a nervous mannerism that is done by virtually everyone. We all feel that there's mucus in our throats and want to clear it. My experience is that the more one coughs to clear the throat, the more one has to continue to do it. If I feel the need to clear my throat and I know that I'm not sick or allergic to something, I try to repress it for a while and the urge generally leaves me. If I succumb to it, however, the urge returns almost immediately. This is something you want to avoid in an interview. You don't want to be constantly clearing your throat. If you don't have a cold or an allergy, be aware that the urge to clear your throat is probably a nervous reaction and try to conquer it.

This raises another issue, and I'm going to digress here and discuss whether or not you should go to a scheduled interview when you have a cold. My advice is not, and there are two reasons.

First, you are not at your best when you are ill. Shortly after *Sweaty Palms* was originally published, I was contacted by a national television talk show to come in for an interview. The day arrived and I was deathly sick with a cold. Despite the way I felt, I went to the interview and did not make a positive impression. The minute I walked in the door I knew I had made a mistake, but it was too late. It's better to postpone than to risk making a bad impression.

Second, you show little consideration for your interviewer if you come to the interview with an obvious cold or the flu. I'm not unusual in that I don't like to be around people who are coughing and wheezing with a bad cold. I immediately think that I'm going to get it, and when I get a cold, I'm suffering with it for two weeks. Your interviewer won't view you kindly if you expose her to your illness. And if she actually comes down with it, you are not going to be on her list of favorites. If you telephone and tell her that you have come down with a cold, you can give her the option of going forward with the interview or not. Maybe she isn't as sensitive as I am and will go forward with it. If she is like I am, she'll appreciate your consideration, and it should be a plus for you. Either way, whether she goes ahead with the interview or agrees to a postponement, your consideration will be noted.

Checklist

- Go over the list of mannerisms of speech and understand how their use can affect your interviewer.
- Go over the list of gestures and understand how their use can affect your interviewer.
- If you have afflictions that affect your eyes and they start to affect you during the interview, bring it up and explain to your interviewer.
- Don't go to an interview when you are ill unless you reveal your illness to your interviewer beforehand.

9

Confidence, Nervousness, and Relaxation

Believe in yourself. Even if you don't believe in yourself,
if you make the interviewer think that you do, you'll be
on the right track.

At a youthful twenty-five, Irving Thalberg was the head of production at MGM. It was the early twenties and Hollywood was in its ascendancy. Thalberg's pictures were enormously successful and profitable, and it was said that "Thalberg is always right." As one person described it, Thalberg exhibited "a glacial calm" when confronted with the decisions involving millions of dollars he had to make day after day. Did Irving Thalberg have confidence in himself? Did he ever doubt his judgment? This is what he confided to F. Scott Fitzgerald when he was at the height of his power:

> Supposing there's got to be a road through the mountain and . . . there seems to be a half-dozen possible roads . . . each one of which, so far as you can determine, is as good

as the other. Now suppose you happen to be the top man, there's a point where you don't exercise the faculty of judgment of the ordinary way, but simply the faculty of arbitrary decision. You say, "Well, I think we will put the road there," and you trace it with your finger and you know in your secret heart, and no one else knows, that you have no reason for putting the road there rather than in several other different courses, but you're the only person who knows that you don't know why you're doing it and you've got to stick to that and you've got to pretend that you know that you did it for specific reasons, even though you're utterly assailed by doubts at times as to the wisdom of your decision, because all these other possible decisions keep echoing in your ear. But when you're planning a new enterprise on a grand scale, the people under you mustn't ever know or guess that you're in doubt, because they've all got to have something to look up to and they mustn't ever dream that you're in doubt about any decision.

Confidence

Everyone has doubts. Irving Thalberg had them. Julius Caesar had them. We all have them. But keep them hidden, at least in an interview. This is one time when you must exude confidence in who you are and what you say. Elizabeth Araghi, a psychotherapist, says that in one of her interviews she had so much confidence that she "radiated." She says that when you radiate from within, your radiation expands to include the interviewer.

There are many ways to develop the appearance of confidence. Success breeds it. If you are offered some jobs, you'll begin to think that you're a pretty hot item, and you will enter interviews exuding it. But if you aren't made a lot of offers, *you can't let rejection erode your confidence in yourself.*

One of the best expressions of what I hope that you will get out of *Sweaty Palms* is contained in these words from Buddha.

> It is proper that you have doubt, that you have perplexity, for a doubt has arisen in a matter which is doubtful. . . . Do not be led by the authority of religious texts, nor by mere logic or inference, nor by considering appearances, nor by the delight in speculative opinions, nor by seeming possibilities, nor by the idea: "this is our teacher." But when you know for yourselves that certain things are unwholesome and wrong, and bad, then give them up. . . . And when you know for yourselves that certain things are wholesome and good, then accept them and follow them.

He then added that a disciple should examine even the Buddha himself, so that he, the disciple, might be fully convinced of the true value of the teacher whom he followed. I certainly can't say it any better than Buddha.

THE ART OF WAR

Although I had not read *The Art of War* when I originally wrote *Sweaty Palms* in the late 1970s, the similarity of thought in Sun Tzu's approach to war and my approach to the interview is striking.

Sun Tzu was not much interested in the numbers of warriors involved in combat. "Numbers alone confer no advantage," he said. Similarly, I do not feel that the questions and the answers are what is determinative of a successful interview. Sun Tzu felt that there were five fundamental factors in successfully waging war. The first of the factors is moral influence, which Sun Tzu defined as "that which causes the people to be in harmony with their leaders." Similarly, I feel that the most important part of the interview is your personal consciousness—that is, the ability for you to be comfortable with yourself and fashion a moral imperative, a calmness, within yourself so that you know yourself and are satisfied that you are who you are and you know who you are and, finally, that you don't want to change that.

Other books tell you how to answer specific questions. This, in my way of thinking, is counterproductive. How can an author know how you should answer a question? How can you accept having someone you don't know telling you how to answer a question? If you can accept this, you need a great deal of work getting to know yourself.

That's the most important part of an interview: getting to know yourself. The best way to prepare for an interview is not to memorize a bunch of answers to a bunch of questions you may be asked. This is a recipe for disaster (although it sounds good to an amateur). Your goal is to go into that interview with such sublime self-knowledge that you have the confidence that you can answer any question the interviewer might throw at you.

That was the objective of the original edition of *Sweaty Palms*. And that's the purpose of this latest revision: to tell you how to prepare yourself so that you can go into an interview confident that you can handle anything that's thrown at you.

The Subject of the Interview is You

In developing confidence you must recognize the things that tend to make you lack it. It is fear of the unknown that attacks and weakens your resolve. But there should be no such fear in being interviewed. First of all, an interview is centered on the subject you know best: yourself. The interview is much more of an unknown for the interviewer (and for this chapter let's assume the interviewer is a man). Most likely, all he knows about you is what is on your resumé.

If you have done your preparation as described in chapter 2, you'll know a good deal about the company and you might even know something about the interviewer if you've been diligent enough to do some detective work. You also know that the interviewer is probably tired and perhaps bored. He's interviewed many people and gone through this routine time and again, asking the same questions and getting the same responses. He doesn't know what you're going to say, but you know what you want to say. So there is no reason for you not to feel confident. You're better prepared than the interviewer is. You know far more about the subject under discussion than he does. The interview is yours.

If you've done your homework and are prepared for the interview, you have nothing to fear. Basically, the interviewer is going to ask you questions about yourself. What in the world could you know better than yourself? He can't ask a question that will stump you because he will limit himself to questions about your background and your ideas.

Appendix A contains three lists of questions that might be thrown at you in an interview. It's unlikely that an interviewer will come up with a question that is not at least touched upon in these lists. So go into the interview confident that he's not going to throw something at you from left field.

Advice of Others Can Hurt Your Confidence

Confidence is often shaken by the advice of others. They'll tell you that you can't do this and that and you shouldn't do that. They'll beat you down and get you to thinking negatively.

On December 12, 1890, a dinner party was given in New York City to introduce Charles Schwab, a thirty-eight-year-old Pittsburgh Steel man, to the East Coast banking establishment. The kings of the financial world were present, including J. Pierpont Morgan.

The hosts of the party, J. Edward Simmons and Charles Steward Smith, advised Schwab that the other guests would not be receptive to a long speech and told him to keep any remarks he might wish to make to fifteen or twenty minutes.

Schwab knew what he wanted to say and said it—for an hour and a half. And he kept his audience spellbound. After it was over, Morgan took him aside, and they conferred for another hour. The result was the formation of a steel trust that is known today as the U.S. Steel Corporation.

Had Schwab changed his mind in accordance with the advice given him by his hosts, he would not have achieved the enormous success that was his. He had the strength of character and confidence in himself to do what he had planned to do in spite of the warnings of his generous hosts.

Eddie Rickenbacker was exposed to this attitude after he got the job with Frayer. He progressed to mechanic and built a racing car that was entered in the Vanderbilt Cup, an elimination race among twelve American cars to determine the five American entrants. As mechanic, Rickenbacker rode in the car with Frayer, who was the driver.

Shortly after the elimination race began, the car developed engine trouble and had to drop out of the race. Frayer sat in the car for a long moment and then said simply, "We're through."

Rickenbacker was deeply impressed. He knew that an entire year of hard work had gone into preparation for entering the car in the Vanderbilt Cup and the car hadn't even survived the elimination race. Rickenbacker said, "I never forgot it. Gradually, over the years, the significance of that remark sank in, and I drew inspiration from it. To spell it out: *try like hell to win, but don't cry if you lose.*"

REJECTION MAY LEAD TO A JOB

Rickenbacker's inspiration should be the motto for every interviewee. Interviewing is a terrible shock to the ego because it results in so many rejections. Even outstanding candidates will be rejected by the vast majority of interviewers. The odds in interviewing are long. If you receive favorable attention in one interview out of ten, you are doing well. That means that you must come to grips with rejection nine times out of ten attempts. You've got to keep your head high and find ways to compensate for the beating your ego must take.

But you never know where a rejection will lead. When I was in law school, many classmates wanted to work in Europe for the summer, as did I, but nobody did anything about it but dream. Then one day I wrote letters to thirty law firms throughout Europe asking for a summer job. A month later some replies started dribbling in, mostly one-line letters of rejection. One man, Peter Crane, a London solicitor, was different. He wrote me a three-page letter telling me what it was like practicing law in London. He closed with a rejection, saying that they didn't hire summer clerks from America.

I wrote him a thank-you note. I felt that even though I had been unanimously rejected, I had learned something. But it didn't end there. Two years later I received another letter from Peter Crane saying that his firm had an opening for an American attorney and asking if I would be interested! From there I took a job that was the dream of probably every law student in America—working in a London solicitor's office.

Whenever you get down on yourself while going through the interviewing process, consider what Teddy Roosevelt had to say about trying and failing and trying again:

It is not the critic who counts, not the man who points out how the strong man stumbled and fell, or where the doer of deeds could have done them better. The credit belongs to the man who is actually in the arena; whose face is marred by dust, sweat and blood; who strives valiantly; who errs and comes short again and again . . . who knows the great enthusiasms, the great devotions and spends himself in a worthy cause; and at the best knows in the end the triumph of high achievement; and who, at the worst, if he fails, at least fails while daring greatly, so that his place shall never be with those cold and timid souls who know neither victory nor defeat.

Nervousness

There's no reason to be nervous going into an interview. If you do find yourself being nervous, let go. A friend of mine wanted to snorkel off the coast of Maui in Hawaii. She was terrified of water and found that the fear had taken hold of her:

I reasoned myself out of it. The Buddhist philosophy is to let go. I'm an existentialist, and so I treated this as the last day of my life. What did it matter what happened? I would never have another chance to snorkel if I didn't do it today because tomorrow may never come. So I let go. I just let my worries and nervousness go away. Almost immediately, my fear disappeared and I devoted my whole being to snorkeling.

Her boyfriend added, "I had to force her out of the water. She was having so much fun and enjoying herself so much that we'd still be there if I hadn't put my foot down."

The point is that you can control your nervousness. If you let your nerves and fears control you, your life will be miserable. French philosopher Jean-Paul Sartre said that you should treat each day as the last day you will live. In other words, you should live for, and enjoy, the moment. If you find yourself being terribly nervous over an interview, try to remember this and let your worries go.

SWEATY PALMS

Most interviewers expect a certain amount of nervousness on the part of those interviewing for lower-level positions. Certainly, a campus interviewer would think it normal that a student who has been through very few interviews and has never held a full-time job would be nervous. Sweaty palms and nervous speech would be understandable.

But if a person is being interviewed by the executive committee of a large corporation for the position as president of the corporation, nervousness would undoubtedly make a very poor impression. A candidate for a position at a high level is expected to be confident. The exhibition of nervousness through a sweaty palm or forehead or a nervous tic would be an indication of a lack of confidence and would be noted. An interviewer may not consciously exclude the candidate for exhibiting such a human weakness, but the impression would almost certainly lead to a negative judgment.

Leonard and Natalie Zunin, in *Contact: The First Four Minutes*, state that one personnel director told them that "regardless of the qualifications of a man he interviews, 'If his handshake is weak and clammy, he's out.'" The Zunins go on to comment: "Such reaction to body language is probably far more prevalent than we realize, as others assume many things about our glance, stance, or advance."

An honest interviewer will candidly admit that a sweaty palm makes his skin crawl. Even though he may recognize it as a normal sign of nervousness, it creates a less-than-favorable initial impression. Dr. Carlotta Mellon, who was appointments assistant to former California governor Edmund G. Brown, Jr., admits, "I react negatively to sweaty palms. People should try not to be so nervous. . . . They should probably have a handkerchief to wipe their hands. . . . I think that sweaty palms convey a lack of confidence."

The general counsel of a major New York Stock Exchange corporation once told me of an interviewee who was so concerned about his sweaty palms that just before entering the interview he went to wash his hands. Unfortunately, he didn't dry them sufficiently, and when they shook hands, the general counsel felt cold moisture that he said "made me cringe."

No one would refuse to make an offer to a superstar because of sweaty palms, but why start out an interview doing something that makes your interviewer cringe? It doesn't matter whether the moisture comes from nervous perspiration or insufficiently dried hands. Your first contact should be a positive one, and you should ensure that your hands are dry.

If you're nervous, no matter how many times you wash your hands or dry them off with a handkerchief, they'll still sweat. One method to reduce the moisture is to sit with your palms exposed while you wait to be called into the interview. If you have your palms covered, whether they are in your lap or in your pockets, the heat will increase the sweating. If you allow the air to get to them, the moisture will be kept at a minimum. I have found that if I sit with my hands dangling at my sides or with my palms in my lap but facing upward, sweaty palms cease to be a problem. These positions may feel awkward, but your interviewer isn't going to see you waiting, and what's important is that you not give him a wet hand when he offers his to you.

How Others Handle Nervousness

Different people deal with nervousness in ways that may seem uncommon, but work for them. Actor-director Gene Wilder says that he actually screams aloud to relieve tension and nervousness. To relieve tension before his performance, the late Sir Laurence Olivier used to utter the most vile words in the English language to the audience, although not so loud that they could hear. One prizefighter said, after the end of his career, that if he could have screamed at the spectators before his matches, he would have been a champion.

If you analyze nervousness, its causes and effects, you will recognize that it is a symptom of something else. Two successful men with similar jobs told how they handle nervous feelings.

As chairman of the board of Whittaker Corporation, Joseph F. Alibrandi had a grueling work schedule and a large load of responsibilities. He disdained nervousness and ways to combat it:

I don't look at the world that way. Sure, I get nervous, but that's part of doing it. See, the getting nervous is a symptom of the challenge of the problem. For me to sit back and work on curing the symptom just doesn't accomplish anything. What I've got to do is, there's something to be done and I've got to focus on getting that thing done. If there's nervousness as a symptom and perspiration and wet palms or whatever it is, that's fine, I'm not going to deal with those. They're just symptoms. I don't think there's a guy in the world who's not scared or what have you. I don't believe in Valium and all the other baloney. The problem is the problem and it's not going to change. If you've decided you've done everything you can do to optimize your probability to succeed, then you just jump in and do it.

The former president of another corporation looks at it this way:

My experience is that if you prepare yourself properly, you really don't have the time or inclination for the fright symptoms to appear.

Since we're dealing with human beings and there will be considerable gaps in their preparation, those things do occur. Among the things that I have found of some use is just before you come into the interview, give yourself some physical stress, even if it's only to the point of trying to run in place, or if you don't want to appear to be out of breath, do some isometrics of one sort or another. But do concentrate on the physical aspects rather than the mental aspects just before an interview. Just point out to yourself that any time you spend any of your own personal energy on the symptoms, you're just wasting preparation that you should have used for substance.

It's rather like trying to prepare for a classroom performance. There are all sorts of ways in which you can blow it. You can forget a half hour of material that you have stored up in your head, which can certainly be done that night. You're much better off to say, "Well, that's one circumstance about which there's very little control. My job here is to perform in as forceful a fashion to be of service to other people as possible." You don't make yourself of service to somebody else if you're not relaxed, if you're not sensitive to other people's needs.

How to Combat Sleeplessness

Nervousness attacks at different times, not just immediately prior to entering the interview room. Many people are so tense about an upcoming interview that they are unable to sleep the night before, tossing and turning and looking at the clock every ten or fifteen minutes.

Here are some suggestions for alleviating sleeplessness when the insomnia is caused by worry or tension:

- Muscular relaxation. When you are worried about something, your mind continues to function and tenses the muscles. But you will not be able to sleep until you can relax your muscles. Dr. Walter Alvarez, the noted medical writer, suggests taking a warm bath if you feel that your body is tense. The heat tends to relax your muscles and make you drowsy.
- Food or drink. Often people get sleepy after they eat. The physiological explanation may be that the blood rushes to your stomach to aid in the digestive process. Whatever the reason, sometimes a hot meal—or even a warm glass of milk—can cause drowsiness.
- Alcohol. Many people find that a glass of wine or beer before retiring allows them to relax and get to sleep quickly, but the quality of alcohol-induced sleep is

questionable, since alcohol can disrupt your sleep during the night.

- Drugs. Tranquilizers such as Valium and Librium are much in vogue as sleeping pills. Any drug such as these should not be taken unless a doctor has prescribed it. Even then, sometimes the side effects are worse than the cure. It is not at all unusual for a tranquilizer to cause drowsiness the next morning and a lethargy that is difficult to shake. Unless you are experienced in taking such drugs, the night before a big interview is not the time to experiment just for the sake of going to sleep. If you do ask your doctor for such a drug and plan on using it to ensure a good night's sleep before an interview, try it out a few nights before your interview so you know how it will affect you the next morning.

Even if you take a pill to get to sleep and do actually sleep, there's no assurance that it will do you a bit of good. Richard M. Coleman, who was codirector of the Sleep Disorder Clinic at Stanford University, states that "people who take the pill at night are actually *sleepier* in the daytime than if they'd just stayed up all night or had a bad night of sleep *without* the pill."

Coleman gives several rules for developing good sleep habits. You should follow them before interviews about which you are nervous.

1. Have a regular schedule.
2. The sleep environment should be quiet and completely dark.
3. Avoid alcohol after dinner.
4. Try to place some limit on the amount of coffee you drink. If you drink coffee in the daytime, you should

probably limit it to the morning hours. The more coffee you take, the more your brain needs that amount just to get to its basic level of arousal.

5. Exercise helps you sleep. It is best performed in the late afternoon between four and six if you plan to go to bed around eleven. If you exercise too close to bedtime, your sleep is likely to be disturbed.

6. Plan your time before you go to bed. You should try to wind down a little bit. If you are out and don't get home until your normal bedtime, stay up a little later that night. Take the time to unwind (not with alcohol) by relaxing and talking with someone, reading, or watching television before going to bed. Then get up at the normal time the next morning.

John Milton, in *Paradise Lost*, said, "The mind in its own place, and in itself can make a Heaven of Hell and a Hell of Heaven." Shakespeare's Caesar said, "Cowards die many times before their deaths; the valiant never taste of death but once."

Both were making the same point. Worry avails you nothing. As I've said before, preparation is the key to combating nervousness. If you've prepared well, you should not have to worry. An interviewer is only asking you about yourself, and no one on this earth knows that subject better than you. The best way to get to sleep is to forget the interview. By the night before the interview, you have done all that it is possible for you to do. If you haven't done all that you can, you may be justified in feeling guilty, but worry isn't going to allow you to do the preparation you feel you should have done. Just forget it and let it happen.

Energy

Interviewing can be fatiguing. Not only do you have the worry of trying to get the interview and then getting through the interview, you have the stress of the job search and the indecisions that invariably accompany it. Keeping your energy up is a very real problem, because if you're tired, you won't be presenting yourself at your best. Further, your tiredness or lack of energy can easily be perceived by the interviewer and negative perceptions formed. So it's essential that you take steps to keep your energy level at its optimum and that you don't allow your body and mind to be run-down.

Nutrition can be a very important aspect of maintaining your energy. Dr. Murray Susser is a Santa Monica, California, nutritional medicine physician, who is coauthor of *Solving the Puzzle of Chronic Fatigue Syndrome*. From his years of experience he makes the following suggestions on ways to maintain your energy.

First, he thinks you should avoid what he calls the "villains in the energy melodrama," sugars and caffeine. He lists the five Cs that provide the heaviest loads of our sugar intake—cola, coffee, candy, cake, and chocolate—along with loads of caffeine. Dr. Susser says that it's a myth that these provide energy. "They deceive us by borrowing from our reserve energy," he says.

But he also warns that it's not good to just go cold turkey on these things if you're used to relying on them. "You can get hypoglycemic, or low blood sugar, spells that cause light-headedness, foggy thinking, and severe fatigue," which are withdrawal symptoms caused by abruptly stopping these foods and drinks. You certainly don't want to be feeling these feelings while you're interviewing for a new job.

Fat is better than sugar, he says. Fatty foods, like cheese, red meat, milk, and eggs, give you a smoother energy boost than sugar. Sugar can cause an immediate, rapid boost in energy, but it quickly wears off and can leave you lower than you were when you started. And sugar isn't just the granulated kind. Your blood sugar is affected by eating refined foods like bread and rolls. Potatoes are one of the worst foods for having a rapid boosting effect on blood sugar. I know that when I eat potatoes, I'm left feeling like I'm lapsing into a coma. I used to think that I had some sort of blood sugar problem, but it turns out that I'm just very sensitive to changes in my blood sugar level. I hated to give up potatoes, because for years my entire diet revolved around potatoes. I had a delicious basic dish of sautéed potatoes and onions, to which I could add anything and cook it all together. I generally had it for dinner. After dinner it was impossible for me to stay awake. I'd go into a deep sleep. I never connected it with potatoes until I went to a doctor who told me of the deleterious effect that potatoes can have on one's blood sugar level.

I bring this up because I would often have french fries for lunch. If I'd been an interviewee invited out to lunch, I would have thought nothing of ordering french fries, which, however, would have knocked me out in the afternoon, and if the interview continued after lunch, I would have been out of it.

This is the type of thing of which you wouldn't be aware. I'd had some really bad afternoons because of my lunchtime potato intake, I now know, but never in a million years would I have connected the problem with potatoes.

I remember one time when I was an outside general counsel for a corporation. We were going to have a meeting, a fairly long meeting, after lunch. I never liked meetings and knew that I would need energy to get through it. So I made sure I had a good lunch, including french fries. I told my secretary, a new one, to get me a big cup of coffee because I knew I'd be fighting sleep and would need the caffeine to stay awake, so she brought me a huge Styrofoam cup of black stuff just before the meeting started.

The french fries took hold of me (I later realized; I hadn't yet learned how they affected me), and I felt myself falling into a comalike lethargy. So I drank from my coffee. I'd nod, sip, nod, sip, but the coffee seemed to have no effect. I asked my secretary for another cup. That meeting seemed to last forever. When I got out, I mentioned to my secretary how the coffee didn't have any effect on my sleepiness. She then told me that she had gotten me decaf!

The point of this is that the potatoes put me to sleep. I was relying on the caffeine to keep me awake (although at the time I just thought I was a bad afternoon person). Caffeine does have positive short-term effects on your energy. But, like sugar, when all is said and done, caffeine and sugar drop you off lower than you were before you started.

Serendipitously, as I was writing this segment, I had an experience that validates sugar's effect on me. I went to a movie that I really liked, a comedy. Because I'm tall, I get to theaters early so I can get an aisle seat. This time I was a half hour early. I usually get a small package of M&M's to eat while I'm waiting, which I did. It took me a little over half an hour to get through the little package. The movie had started. Initially, I felt great. Suddenly, I was asleep. I wasn't bored. I was laughing. But a horrible sleepiness grabbed me. I only slept for a few minutes, and when I awoke, I was refreshed and had no further sleepiness during the rest of the movie. But, probably because I was writing this segment, I thought about how horrible it would have been to have had this occur shortly after the start of an interview. This was a sudden surge in my blood sugar, as explained in *Suzanne Somers' Get Skinny on Fabulous Food:*

Simple carbohydrates [like sugar] cause a sharp increase in blood sugar. This surge of blood sugar gives us a "sugar rush" or a "sugar high." As we now know, when the blood sugar is elevated to such a high level, insulin tries to store the sugar in the cells, but if they become filled with sugar, they will not accept any more. Then the pancreas secretes even more insulin to attempt to balance the blood sugar. This results in an excess amount of insulin in the bloodstream, which causes a condition called "hyperinsulinemia." . . . After extra insulin has sent the sugar to the fat cells, eventually our blood sugar is lowered to even below its starting point. That's when we feel the letdown or the "sugar low." This sugar low leaves us feeling tired, listless, and artificially hungry. During this time we often feel like taking a nap, or we reach for something sweet or caffeinated to give us more energy—then the vicious cycle repeats. Sugar goes in, blood sugar goes up, pancreas secretes insulin, then blood sugar drops and we feel tired and hungry again.

Dr. Robert Atkins agrees in *Dr. Atkins' New Diet Revolution:*

Excessive carbohydrate intake results in high amounts of blood sugar and may, in turn, overstimulate insulin production. When this happens, it causes a drop in blood sugar, robbing the body of energy for the cells. The result of the process is destabilized blood-sugar levels, quite possibly causing fatigue, brain fog, shakiness and headaches.

So, in order to control your energy, you have to control your blood sugar.

Another deleterious effect of sugar is how you react to it at nighttime. I can tell you my personal experience. I love sugar at night. It might pick me up for a few minutes, but it's not long before I'm asleep. So you might think it would be good to eat sugary foods if you want to go to sleep and have a good night's sleep. For me, it will put me to sleep, but then I'll awaken at around 2 a.m. and be wide-awake with no hope of returning to sleep. Alcohol affects me that same way. It makes me sleepy, but it ruins my night's sleep because it awakens me in the middle of the night and keeps me awake.

You increase your blood sugar level when you ingest large quantities of refined white flour and simple sugars. Foods containing refined white flours are often disguised as foods generally thought of as healthful, like pasta, bread, bagels, and cereals. An increase in blood sugar level will initially give you a boost of energy. But after this ingestion of foods that spike your blood sugar, the burst of energy quickly crashes, and you're left in a state of deficient energy level, both mental and physical.

Bread is a real villain here. You have to become a label reader. I see loaf after loaf of bread proclaiming it to be "wheat bread" or even "whole wheat bread." But when I read the label, I see that the first ingredient is white flour. Sure, it contains some wheat flour, but if it contains white flour, it's not what you want. I now buy my own flour and make my own bread, so I know that it contains only 100 percent whole wheat flour. And that's what a label must say if you want to buy commercial bread: "100% whole wheat." If it says anything else about the flour, like "refined flour" or "enriched flour," stay away from it, because eating it is just like mainlining sugar into your blood.

So what foods spike your blood sugar, and what foods don't? What should you eat to control your blood sugar? First off, protein—meat, fish, eggs, and cheese—don't have a deleterious effect on your blood sugar. But carbohydrates can. So the carbs to eat are what are called slow-burning carbs—that is, carbohydrates that don't spike your blood sugar instantly upon ingestion. Some of these are whole grain cereals, like oats, grits, and cream of wheat. Other slow-burning carbs are legumes like beans and peas, and vegetables like artichokes, asparagus, beets, broccoli, and tomatoes.

WHAT TO AVOID! I put this in capital letters because, well, it's important (duh!). Don't eat anything with white flour in it, and this includes cereals, bread, rolls, pasta, and pancakes. Don't drink soft drinks with sugar in them. Don't eat desserts (unless they are fruit). And if they're fruit, make sure it's fresh fruit and not something canned, because canned fruit is often packed in such heavy syrup that you might as well just eat a spoonful of sugar.

Don't eat candy bars! I wish I had had this advice when I was driving down to my properties. I owned a lot of real estate in Riverside County, about a hundred miles from Los Angeles, and I had to drive down there on a weekly basis. I'd start in the morning, tour my properties, take care of any problems, have lunch, and start back in the early afternoon.

Lunch would usually consist of a sandwich made out of white bread. I'd then get sleepy driving back, so I'd eat a candy bar, thinking that the sugar would awaken me. Not the right idea! The candy bar just helped me for a few minutes. I would have to pull over to the side of the road and take a ten-minute nap before I could continue. The white flour I had for lunch, buttressed by the sugar in the candy, made me so sleepy I felt as if I were going into a coma. Sometimes I'd drink a cola (with sugar, naturally), thinking that the caffeine would help. But the caffeine would help for only a short period before two things happened. First, when the caffeine high wore off, I'd be lower than before I started drinking the cola, and, second, the sugar spike from the cola caused my blood sugar to plummet. I'm just lucky that I didn't fall asleep at the wheel. There is nothing so bleak as the feeling that you simply cannot stay awake.

One thing to remember, however, is something that helped me immensely. When I was hit by one of these blood sugar lows, I discovered that if I could just go to sleep for ten minutes, I would be almost completely revived. I'm one of those people who can lie down for a nap and say to themselves, "I want to awaken in seven minutes," and seven minutes later, to the second, I'll awaken. I'll be in a deep sleep, then awaken instantly at exactly the time I told myself I wanted to awaken! I have no idea how this works, but I've done it so often that I take it for granted.

A corollary to this type of relief is that if I allowed myself to sleep longer than a short period of time, like ten or fifteen minutes, I awakened horribly groggy, and it sometimes took me more than an hour to get back to normal. So the rule was, take a short nap, and be certain that it's a short one. If you can't program yourself to awaken when you want, have some sort of alarm with you that will go off to wake you up. You can buy a watch with a timer on it or a small kitchen timer and set it for ten minutes.

Just be sure that you don't oversleep. If you have an interview and you're taking a nap as a respite, but you oversleep, you might go into the interview groggy, and that could be curtains for the interview.

So, while a short nap can rejuvenate you from a blood sugar low, a long nap, involving deep sleep, can be disastrous, because it can make you groggy for an extended period. You don't want to go into an interview groggy. If you decide to take a short nap for its regenerative purpose, be sure that you set an alarm to awaken you after not longer than fifteen minutes. That won't be long enough for you to go into a deep sleep, but it should be long enough to get rid of the blood sugar low and put you back to normal.

The Glycemic Index measures how fast a food may raise your blood sugar. Apparently, if you want to keep your blood sugar from dropping, you would limit your carbohydrates to those with a low Glycemic Index and a longer action time. Basically, "slow carbs," those with lower Glycemic Index numbers, are the foods that will prevent rapid drops in your blood sugar. There are many Glycemic Indices, and the numbers may vary, but they will be close. Again, if you want to protect against a rapid drop in your blood sugar over a period of hours, you should limit yourself to foods with lower numbers and avoid those with higher numbers. To access a Glycemic Index online, go to http://www.glycemicindex.com.

Another thing to consider is when to schedule your interview. If you are aware of your circadian rhythms, you should try to schedule the time of your interview in accordance with them. I'm a morning person. I'm at my best before lunch. Maybe what I've been eating for lunch messes up my blood sugar. I don't know. But I know that I've always been at my best, my most alert, in the morning. So if I were to have an interview, I would try to schedule it for before lunch.

Others, however, are not like me, hard as that is to believe. Some people are terrible in the morning but shine in the late afternoon. If you're like that, try to schedule your interview for the late afternoon. Remember that even though someone calls you and suggests a time for the interview, that time is not set in stone. It's not a command performance that you have to drop everything to meet.

Even if you don't have something scheduled, if the interviewer's initial request is for a time when you know you aren't at your best, just respond that the time suggested is not convenient and then, instead of waiting for the interviewer to make another suggestion, make the suggestion yourself. Then, if the interviewer says that's no good, either, and suggests another morning time, tell her that morning is generally not convenient for you and ask if it's possible to schedule it in the afternoon.

Generally, something like that will work without your being offensive. But if the interviewer insists on scheduling an interview at a time when you're not at your best, you should go along with it. Remember, you're always being interviewed whenever you have contact with your interviewer. So when you're communicating about when to set up the interview, that's part of your interview! If you come across as inflexible and uncooperative, either you won't get an interview or you will create a negative feeling that might be difficult to overcome. So do your best to schedule the interview for a time when you are at your best, but if you see that the interviewer clearly wants to schedule it for a different time, go along with it. It's better to have an interview when you're not at your best than to have no interview at all or to leave a negative impression on the interviewer.

You've Got Nothing to Lose

Nervousness and lack of confidence are often caused by fear of losing. But what have you got to lose? People are nervous going into a job interview because they fear that they will not get an offer or be invited to return. But they didn't have an offer before the interview. If they still don't have an offer after the interview, they are no worse off. So why worry?

Throw caution to the wind. Look at the downside. What is the absolute worst that can happen to you? You won't get an offer. Well, right now you don't have an offer, so the downside is simply a maintenance of the status quo. That's nothing to worry about. Go into the interview forgetting about yourself.

For fifteen minutes exude confidence. Take a chance. If you recognize that not getting what you hope for is no disaster, you will be much looser and will try things that may work. If they don't work, you're no worse off.

When I was a young lawyer, I once left a job with a law firm because I was intensely bored. After a summer of contemplation in the South Bay area of Los Angeles, Manhattan Beach, I decided that I wanted to work in a corporate law department. I made calls and wrote letters and finally got an interview with a vice president and general counsel of a major airline company.

He was courteous, but at the end of the interview he said that he just didn't have enough work to justify another attorney. I returned home and wrote him a long letter volunteering to work for nothing. I told him that at that stage of my career the experience was worth more than the money. It was, truly, an outstanding letter, and I waited confidently for his reply. How could he possibly turn down such a magnanimous offer?

Well, I found out it was pretty easy for him to turn it down. He replied that he just didn't feel like he wanted to accept that responsibility. It can be crushing when someone tells you he doesn't want you to work for him for free! But I didn't let it dissuade me. I kept plugging and finally got a much better job. The point is that you've got to try. If you can see something you want, go after it in any way you can. You can't worry about rejection, and you can't let rejection get you down on yourself.

I didn't hang my head and hide because of his refusal to hire me. I knew that I had done all that I could to get a job I wanted. I hadn't lost anything. Before I wrote the letter I didn't have a job. Afterward I still didn't have a job, but I was no worse off. I had been honest and aggressive. If you do your best, if you take your best shot and still miss, you have nothing to feel bad about. I felt exhilarated. I knew I had fought the battle.

Relaxation

Relaxation is as important as any of the other techniques suggested in this book. But it almost needs to be treated with an admonition, because the more one tries to achieve it, the further one tends to move in the opposite direction.

This virtue is important not only in interviewing but in virtually every endeavor you undertake. Above all, relax! That's easy to say. Here you're reading this book that emphasizes how important the selection interview is, and now you're told to relax. How in God's name can you relax when so much is riding on your interview?

The answer isn't easy, but it's one that each person must determine for himself or herself. No matter what you try, you do it better if you're relaxed. Tennis players do much better when they're playing someone they know than when they're taking on the club champion. Suddenly, their forehands are sailing into the fence, their backhands dribble off the frame, and they end up with the ball in their teeth while attempting to volley. Why? Because against their friend, they are loose and aren't concerned with making mistakes. Against the club champion, mistakes are all they think about. As a result, that's what they do: make mistakes.

Timothy Gallwey, in his book *The Inner Game of Tennis*, advises his readers that the way to stop thinking mistakes on the tennis court is to concentrate on minutiae, such as focusing on the seams of the ball or saying "bounce" each time the ball hits the ground and "hit" each time the ball hits the racket.

Judgments Cause Tension

Gallwey probes the reason why we become tense and make mistakes. *He says that it is the judgments that we make on ourselves that keep us from relaxing:*

> What I mean by judgment is the act of assigning a negative or positive value to an event. . . . What is important to see here is that neither the "goodness" nor "badness" ascribed to the event . . . is an attribute of the [event] itself. Rather, they are evaluations *added* to the event in the minds of the players according to their individual reactions.

If you apply this to your everyday life, you will discover its truth. If you simply observe something, you attach no value to it and you're totally relaxed.

But why do we make judgments? It's because when we do something, we expect certain results. If we don't achieve the desired result, then we make the judgment that it was bad. If we achieve the result we wanted, then we make the judgment that it was good.

In an interview how can we keep ourselves from making judgments and then tying ourselves up in knots when we do not achieve our artificially imposed result?

View each interview as pragmatically as possible. Sure, you have a goal. But most people mistake their goal. Most of us going into an interview are completely inwardly directed. We say, "I'm going to an interview. I hope I get an offer." Already we've imposed a result upon the event that is not only not probable; it is not justified.

You Are Interviewing Them

Remember what was said earlier: An interview is a two-way street. Certainly, they are interviewing you to see if they want to offer you a job. But you are also interviewing them to see if you want to work for them. You are going to make some decisions on them, just as they will make some decisions on you. You must approach each interview in this frame of mind. If you do, you will eliminate the prime cause for tension: your artificially imposed objective of getting an offer. You don't know if you want an offer! *Go into the interview with the objective of finding out something about them.* Tell yourself, "I want to find out what it would be like to work for this outfit. Then I'll make a decision after I've gotten the data I need and thought about it for a while."

If you take this approach to an interview, you'll find that your frame of mind before an interview changes dramatically. No longer will you be worrying about your sweaty palms or what you say when you meet the interviewer. You won't be worrying about yourself. You'll be concerned about finding out about your interviewer and his company. You'll be outwardly oriented. You won't be setting objectives for your performance and the interviewer's evaluation. You won't be making judgments on your own performance, so you'll be relaxed.

When you are tense and you strain, your mind blocks and you don't respond in a normal manner. Don't worry about what you're going to say and how you're going to say it. If you have a general idea of what you want to cover, let it go at that and just be ready.

Years ago Maxwell Maltz dealt with the mysterious effects of relaxation in his book *Psycho-Cybernetics:*

> You must learn to trust your creative mechanism to do its work and not "jam it" by becoming too concerned or too

anxious as to whether it will work or not, or by attempting to force it by too much conscious effort. You must *let it* work, rather than *make it* work. This trust is necessary because your creative mechanism operates below the level beneath the surface. Moreover, its nature is to operate *spontaneously* according to its present need. Therefore, you have no guarantee in advance. It comes into operation as you act and as you place a demand upon it by your actions. You must not wait to act until you have proof—you must act as if it is there, and it will come through. "Do the thing and you will have the power," said Emerson.

Gallwey talks about this process on the tennis court. He says that you must trust your inner self and "let it happen." If you're trying to be funny, you're not. If you're trying to be profound, you sound silly. Just relax and trust your normal reactions. An interview is, in essence, the interrelationship between two people. Each must react to the other.

Mean Joe Greene played defensive tackle for the Pittsburgh Steelers in their "Steel Curtain" days. The first half of the 1976 football season was a bad one for him. He played subpar football, and the Steelers suffered, losing several games in a row. Suddenly, things turned around. Greene became the player he had been, and the Steelers, who had lost four of their first five games, won eleven in a row, allowing only twenty-eight points in their next nine games. What had caused the turnaround? "I was trying too hard not to make mistakes," Greene said. "In the past, I never gave a damn about mistakes. I used to play about 70 percent by design and 30 percent freelance. I'd take a chance now and then."

Once Greene forgot about himself and how he was performing, he resumed playing at the caliber he had achieved in the past. Thinking about what he wanted to do and worrying about mistakes caused him to make the very mistakes he was worrying about.

How to Relax

Everyone must find his or her own method of relaxing in potentially stressful situations. Even though the interview is important, it is not Armageddon. Look upon it as an experience. Afterward analyze how you reacted to the interviewer's questions and try to determine how he reacted to you. If you can adopt a clinical approach to what's going to happen, if you can view it as a test from which you are going to improve yourself with new knowledge and awareness, you may tend to relax.

The process of being interviewed inevitably involves a period of waiting. This is the time when the most intense nervousness attacks. Your mind is racing a mile a minute trying to remember all the things you want to say and do. You're trying to keep your hands from sweating. You want to make sure your hair is not mussed, that your clothes are neat. Your heart is beating at a faster pace than normal. Your blood pressure is probably elevated. Above all, your mind is working overtime, telling you to check all the things you've previously thought of in preparing for the interview—and adding a few more.

Since it's too late to do any more preparation, you must relax your mind. The first step in achieving this is to relax physically. Close your eyes and concentrate on relaxing each muscle in your body, beginning with your toes. Once your toes are relaxed, think about your ankles, then your calves, then your knees, then your thigh muscles, then your hips. Progress to your stomach muscles, your chest. Take some deep breaths. Then relax your neck. Lay your head back.

When your body is finally in a state of relaxation, cleanse your mind. Try to think of something calming and pleasant like a waterfall or the waves at the beach or a snowcapped peak with the deep blue sky beyond.

If you concentrate on relaxing your muscles and ridding your mind of all but pleasant thoughts, you should be able to feel the tension drain from your body. Your heartbeat will slow, the sweating will diminish, your mind will cease to race.

Fran S. Wickner, Ph.D., M.F.T., a licensed marriage and family therapist in San Francisco, lists nine ways to best manage stress in your life:

1. Stay healthy. While this may seem obvious, if you maintain proper weight and blood pressure, you will be positioning yourself to better handle stress when it appears. If you're overweight or your blood pressure is elevated, stress makes things worse, and these abnormalities exacerbate stress.

2. Reduce caffeine, sugar, and alcohol intake. Caffeine is notorious for making people high-strung. We have discussed the deleterious effects that sugar can have upon your system and your psyche. Alcohol is a depressant that makes stress worse. Unfortunately, our society has educated us to take a drink when things go badly. That's exactly the wrong thing to do because alcohol depresses your entire system and makes you less able to fight off bad things, including bad thoughts.

3. Relax (e.g., read a book, listen to music, meditate, go outdoors). The idea here is to get your mind working on something other than what's causing the stress. If you're worried about an upcoming interview and you've already done your preparation, there's no reason to continue thinking about it. So if you find that it continues to invade your thoughts, that's a good time to do some serious relaxing. Do whatever it is that you enjoy. Maybe

it is reading a book or listening to music. Maybe it's playing golf or tennis or bridge. Maybe it's needlepoint or embroidery or crochet or cooking. Whatever it is that gives you enjoyment, go do it and get your mind off the interview.

4. Practice visualization. Close your eyes and imagine the most relaxed place you have ever been. When you begin feeling stressed-out, try to bring this special place to mind. For me it's the bridge over the Merced River under Vernal Falls in Yosemite. So many times I've hiked up to this bridge in the first warming days of spring and just lain on the bridge looking at the falls. What a relaxing feeling! When I close my eyes, I can return to that spot. If you have a spot like that, go there. If you don't, find one!

5. Take slow, deep breaths. This is a yoga technique that rarely fails. If you've ever taken yoga, you know that breathing is an important part of relaxation. Whenever you're feeling stress, this is a wonderful antidote. Try it; you'll like it!

6. Learn to manage time. This may seem strange, but if you can manage your time efficiently, you will gain a respect for yourself and what you're doing that will be remarkable. I know how I feel when I let my desk get the better of me. Then I look at that pile of paper and just don't want to wade through it. But after I've gritted my teeth and disposed of everything, I feel like I've just hit a home run!

7. Exercise. This is one of the best managers of stress. When you're worried and stressed, if you go outside and run or you lift weights, or even if you just take a long walk, it gets your heart to beating and your blood to pumping. The more vigorous the exercise, the better,

because if you're exercising strenuously, you don't have time to worry about anything.

8. Laugh. The best medicine. Do you have a favorite movie that always makes you laugh? If so, get a DVD or videotape and watch it to get yourself laughing. The first half hours of *The Producers* (with Gene Wilder and Zero Mostel) and *A Touch of Class* ("Is this any way to treat a hotel?") do it for me. It's marvelous therapy.

9. Surround your space with positive images.

Know When to Stop Preparing

In order to relax, you must at some point cease preparing for the interview. As a student in law school I recognized this when I studied for exams. I would completely drop out of everything preceding exams. I stayed in my room and spent the entire time memorizing my class notes, comprising hundreds of pages. I had a strict schedule that I followed religiously.

But the day before my first exam, I put away all my notes. That day I played basketball or tennis. That night I went to a movie. I did not return to my notes. I knew that I had studied enough either to know it or not. If I did not know it by then, it was too late to learn it. If I did know it, I couldn't know it any better. The most important thing for me at that time was to relax. I knew that my mind was trying to get me to check out this point or that point or to clarify something. The only way I could conquer this battle with myself was to throw myself into an activity totally unrelated to my courses. I worked on my jump shot or forehand instead of the law. At night I further relaxed with James Bond or Marilyn Monroe. As a result, when I went to my exams, my mind was completely relaxed, and the secret mechanism worked perfectly. I was confident that when I read the exam, my mind would perform, and I let it.

It's the same with an interview. If you have done adequate preparation, stop, relax, and just let it work. You will react in accordance with your ability and preparation. As a result, you will be yourself rather than something your mind is telling you you should be.

Maxwell Maltz has some things to say about relaxation that are to the point:

Conscious effort inhibits and "jams" the automatic creative mechanism. The reason some people are self-conscious and awkward in social situations is simply that they are too consciously concerned, too anxious, to do the right thing. They are painfully conscious of every move they make. Every action is "thought-out." Every word spoken is calculated for its effect. We speak of such persons as "inhibited," and rightly so. But it would be more true were we to say that the "person" is not inhibited; but that the person has "inhibited" his own creative mechanism. If these people could "let go," stop trying, not care, and give no thought to the matter of their behavior, they could act creatively, spontaneously, and "be themselves."

Checklist

- Continue to tell yourself that you are doing well.
- Even if you don't believe in yourself, try to make the interviewer think that you do.
- Keep your doubts to yourself.
- An interview is centered on the subject you know best—yourself.
- Don't let rejection erode your confidence.
- The interviewer knows less about you than you do.

- If you've done your preparation, you know more about the interviewer and his company than he knows about you.
- Don't let the advice of others shake your confidence in yourself.
- Interviewers expect a certain amount of nervousness.
- Try to avoid sweaty palms by sitting with your palms exposed to air.
- Combat nervousness by relaxing your muscles and getting enough sleep.
- Remember: Before the interview you don't have an offer. The worst that can happen is that after the interview you still won't have an offer.
- If you see something you want, go after it.
- Don't worry about failure.
- Don't look back.
- Don't make tension-causing judgments.
- Go into the interview with one of your objectives being that you are also interviewing the company to find out about it.
- Trust yourself to react properly.
- In order to relax mentally, you must first relax your body.
- Stop preparing the night before the interview at the latest.

10

Dress

The initial impression you make on the interviewer (and in this chapter let's assume the interviewer's a woman) creates a presumption in her mind that will have a strong effect on the rest of the interview. She will look at you and form an opinion about you based on your appearance. How you are dressed will make up 80 percent of that opinion, and it will be formed before you open your mouth. If there is something bizarre or slovenly about your dress, it may be a deciding factor in the result of the interview.

Phil Jackson was an NBA basketball coach who won more championships than any coach other than the Boston Celtics' Red Auerbach. He coached Michael Jordan with the Chicago Bulls and Shaquille O'Neal and Kobe Bryant with the Los Angeles Lakers. One wouldn't think he would have ever had a problem getting a job. One would be wrong.

Sam Smith tells the story in his book *The Jordan Rules*. Bulls general manager Jerry Krause asked the then Chicago Bulls coach, Stan Albeck, to interview Jackson for the position of assistant coach during the 1985–86 season. At the time, Jackson had coached in the minor-league CBA but couldn't interest anyone in the NBA to hire him. Smith reports:

Jackson came to his interview with a beard that made it look as if he was eating a muskrat and wearing a big Ecuadoran straw hat of which he was very proud; it had a big bird feather looping out of the brim, and Jackson tried to tell Albeck a story about the tropical bird from which it was taken. Jackson's long, bony face was nearly black from the sun of Puerto Rico, where he was then coaching, and his hair was still longish.

Albeck told Krause he wasn't interested in hiring Jackson. Clearly, this decision had nothing to do with Jackson's qualifications. It was based almost entirely on Albeck's reaction to Jackson's appearance. And it doesn't necessarily mean that he rejected him just because he looked bizarre. No, he could have reached his conclusion for one of two reasons, both of which were based on how Jackson dressed. First, he could have concluded that anyone who dressed in such an outlandish manner showed poor judgment, and he didn't want to hire someone with poor judgment. Second, he could have concluded that anyone who dressed in such a way for an interview would have a difficult time communicating and getting along with NBA players. So the way you dress can lead to the interviewer making assumptions about you that may or may not be true.

This story epitomizes two truths about the interview process. First, the interview is more about the feeling the interviewer develops for the interviewee than about the interviewee's ability to do the job. Second, how you dress is extremely important, and a mistake can destroy your chances.

You should dress with consideration for three factors: (1) Dress to your advantage; (2) dress to suit your interviewer; and (3) dress appropriately for the position for which you are interviewing.

Dress to Your Advantage

Dressing to your advantage means that you should dress in a manner that puts you in the most favorable light and does not offend. Your attire can speak for you as strongly as what you say. Your choice of colors should blend well. If they do not, this will be a point that could stand out in your interviewer's mind to your detriment. Do you want to be remembered as "that person wearing purple and pink"? A garish combination of colors will probably make more of an impression than any profound argument you make. How would you react if you were an interviewer and someone walked in wearing a red-checked sports jacket, a purple-striped shirt, and a pink polka-dot tie? Your lasting impression would probably be of the horrendous outfit he chose to wear, and your confidence in his judgment would be permanently impaired.

If you lack confidence in your judgment, seek the advice of someone qualified, like a friend whose style of dress you admire, a wardrobe consultant, or a department store salesclerk who exhibits good taste.

Dress for the Interviewer

Remember the story I referred to earlier of the law school student who came to an interview with me dressed in an old sweatshirt with holes in it, dirty blue jeans, and scuffed sneakers? *Don't try to make some childish point of being antiestablishment or independent by dressing in a manner that will offend your interviewer.* If you care enough to go to the interview, why blow it by dressing in a manner that tells the interviewer, "I don't give a damn about you"?

Don't dress in a manner that will cause your interviewer to draw an unfavorable impression from your dress prior to starting the interview. If you stick to conservative dress, you're going to be safe.

Jocelyn Young, who was national accounts manager for Datapro, a division of McGraw-Hill, offers a few tips:

For mid- to high-level positions, you can expect to go through at least four interviews in one day. My main advice may sound trivial, but it's actually very practical: Don't wear anything that wrinkles easily! You need to look "together" for a full day. Don't try to dress to please any one audience, either. Coworkers as well as those who would be in positions above and below you will probably interview you. Your best bet is to find out what the standard of dress is where you are interviewing and not deviate too much from it.

Jolly Mansfield-Young, who was area systems manager for Tandem Computers, says that all prospective employees at their Dallas headquarters, from the lowest to the highest positions, underwent two preliminary screening interviews. Those who passed the screening process were invited back for a second round of interviews. They could expect to be interviewed by at least five employees of the company all on one day, and their interviewers came from all levels of the organization. Mansfield-Young did a fair amount of interviewing herself, and in terms of dress, this is what she said:

Don't wear clothes that will detract from you as a person. You don't want the interviewer to focus on your clothes rather than your abilities. On the other hand, avoid an overly packaged "dress for success" look. This always sets off an alarm for me and causes me to probe a little more deeply than I ordinarily would because I feel I need to find the person under the wrappings. Whatever you decide to wear, make sure that it feels comfortable to *you*. The interview day is going to be long and stressful, and you don't want to be fidgeting with buttons or tight cuffs or shoes you've never worn before. You always want to give the interviewer the impression that you are completely at ease and in control, but if you're fussing with your clothes or have a pinched look, you'll destroy that illusion right away.

Color

There is a great deal of disagreement as to whether color has any effect upon a person with whom you come into contact. If you dress for an interview as if you are going to a funeral, you'll be at a disadvantage with one who dresses like springtime, unless Dracula is your interviewer.

Color matching is important when dressing for an interview. Here's a short synopsis for men, thanks to www.askmen.com:

When matching shoes and pants, the following chart is helpful:

Pant/suit color	Shoe color
Black	black, tan, camel, oxblood
Gray	black, oxblood, camel
Brown	any shade of brown, black, camel
Navy	black, camel, tan, oxblood
Earth tones	any shade of brown, camel, black

How about socks? The general rule is that socks should match the shoe, not the pants. In addition, your shoes and socks should not be lighter than your top. One result of this rule is that you should never wear white socks! (Sorry.)

As to belts, askmen.com says that the belt color should match the shoes, or, alternatively, the pants. Standard usage is to wear a black or dark brown belt with a navy suit. However, the trend now is for funky looks, like a beige belt with navy and gray. Do not wear a belt and suspenders together.

Askmen.com has some terrific articles on what colors to wear and other fashion tips. I recommend you check it out.

Consider that some people do make judgments based upon appearance. Movies have educated us to expect certain professions when we see specific types of dress. A trench coat conjures images of a private detective. White tie on a dark shirt equates to a gambler. Black leather jacket over a white T-shirt means a motorcycle tough.

I remember attending a meeting with a client who was looking for millions of dollars in financing. He had been told that the person with whom we were meeting had access to Middle Eastern money. We set up a meeting with him at a restaurant in Los Angeles, but when he showed up, I immediately sensed that we were wasting our time. He was dressed in a loud sports coat and a cravat. He hadn't yet uttered a word, but my reaction to him was that he was a flaky promoter.

Unfortunately, my initial impression proved to be accurate. We were forced to sit and listen to his pitch for more than two hours, two hours of name-dropping and grandiose schemes to finance my client's enterprise. I didn't say anything after he departed but asked my client what he thought. His reaction was instantaneous: "Two hours of nothing" he said.

SCENTS

Other questions arise regarding grooming. If you're a woman, how much perfume, if any, should you wear? If you're a man, should you wear an aftershave or cologne or neither? Scents are important.

If you wear perfume or aftershave or some other substance that emits an odor, there are two cardinal rules. First, make sure that none of it is on your hands so that it is not transferred to the interviewer when you shake hands. Second, remember that the interviewer is going through many interviews, and she may work in the room in which she interviews you, so be sure that what you wear is not so strong that it will waft through her room the rest of the day. You don't want her to remember you because of a lingering smell, no matter how much what you are wearing cost.

You should also be aware that the interviewer might be allergic. I can speak from experience, because I'm extremely sensitive to perfume. If a woman has any kind of perfume on, or a man a strong aftershave, it will cause my eyes to water, or my nose to run, or a fit of sneezing. You obviously can't ask in advance if your interviewer is allergic, so this is a good reason to go lightly with the aromas. It's safer not to smell wonderful than to risk an allergic reaction in your interviewer. (Just be sure you don't smell bad.)

Dress for the Job

Another thing to consider when it comes to your mode of dress is the kind of job you are interviewing for. Although generally an interviewee should avoid extremes, this is not always true. For example, if a woman is interviewing for a job as a cocktail waitress, part of the qualification for the position might be sex appeal, so dressing for the interview in a way that highlights your sensuality could be a plus for several reasons. First, it would relieve the interviewer of having to ask whether or not you would be willing to dress in a sexually provocative way. This is a question that could cause the interviewer to worry about your filing a claim for sexual discrimination, especially if the interviewer is a man. Relieving him of the burden of asking it by the way you dress could be a big help. Second, it would show the interviewer how you look without him having to guess or ask you to put on the costume he might want you to wear. Third, it indicates in a nonverbal way that you know what's involved in the job and that you are experienced.

On the other hand, dressing for an interview for a position in industry in a sexually provocative way could leave a distinctly negative impression, since sex appeal would have no earthly relationship to such a job. It could communicate the wrong impression or, worse, be seen as an invitation, or the interviewer could draw the conclusion that you feel you aren't qualified for the position but are trying to get the job on the basis of sex appeal.

No matter what kind of job for which you're interviewing, you should dress neatly. Even if you're interviewing to be a laborer or ditchdigger, dressing in a clean and neat manner will indicate that you have enough interest in the job to take the time to dress well. It's never a plus to show up in dirty, unkempt clothes, no matter what the job.

For most positions the safest bet is to dress conservatively. It is risky to wear trendy styles. It takes a long period of time for a fad to become a style. Wait until it's accepted before you adopt it for an interview.

Lisa Converse, a development director for a clothing company in Florida told the *Los Angeles Times Careerbuilder* in fall 2004 that women should pair a clean, classic outfit with modern accessories, such as antique-inspired brooches, simple pumps in subtle colors, and silk scarves.

Tips for Men

Here are some comments about men's dress by some real people from an article by Peter McQuaid in the *Los Angeles Times Magazine*.

Roberto Benabib, TV screenwriter, *Ally McBeal*, who has to pitch story ideas:

If you walk into a room dressed like Cary Grant, they're going to think you're nuts. It's sneakers, jeans, a T-shirt under a button-down, under a sport jacket. However, you want the best sport jacket you can afford . . . staples: the perfect three-button black jacket; the simple gray V-neck sweater; the crisp, white shirt; all stuff that is basic, but executed in a way that it always looks really sharp. You finish this off with well-tailored jeans . . . and some good sneakers—like Pumas or Adidas—but never, ever running shoes. Basically, what you're doing here is combining some very un-sloppy clothes in a sloppy way. To sell myself—to other writers as well as the "suits"—I have to look like a young, educated, creative type. The truth is I would rather wear something more interesting, but there really is a uniform. You can update it, you can improve it, you can make sure it fits really well, but it is still a uniform.

John C. Siciliano, director of global institutional services, Dimensional Fund Advisers Inc., whose job is to get people who control vast sums of money to invest with his firm:

My suits are very conservative: dark charcoal pinstripe or solid navy, or low-key plaids. The only thing men can do is wear a shirt and tie that's different. Red is my all-time favorite color, but for shirts I love pink and I love yellow—for ties too. I have to dress a certain way, and I think color makes the difference between looking nice and respectable and looking nice and respectable with a little flair. I don't want to look boring, but you also don't want to look too frou-frou for the old-line LA crowd.

Since I travel to New York a lot, I go to Saks and Bergdorf Goodman, but I've also recently gone back to Brooks Bros. They've really come back in a big way, and I just bought a sport coat in blackwatch plaid from them, very classic. I wear loafers from Cole Haan and Ferragamo—I get them at their outlet store—and I'm notorious for my socks: polka dots, light yellow, plaid. It's another way to express some individuality and have some fun. But you have to keep in mind that the rules about what is appropriate business attire and what isn't are very clear.

Brian Leitch, independent advertising creative director for companies such as Banana Republic and the Gap, who creates visual images that will give a product the image that it's hip, prestigious, and fun:

In my business . . . you have to have the confidence not to wear the Gucci or Prada shoes to the meeting or the job interview . . . you really have to look like you think for yourself. Showing up in a total head-to-toe designer look doesn't demonstrate creativity: it only shows that you can afford the clothes, or that you've been eating tuna fish for the past 10 weeks. I tend to wear really inexpensive clothes with really expensive clothes that look like they've just been pulled out of a Dumpster. I have these shoes from Paul Harndon, a cobbler in England, that are handmade, cost a thousand bucks a pair—it was a real intake of breath when I plunked that down for a pair of shoes—and a friend of mine calls them my "clown shoes." They're scuffed up, and they were scuffed up when I bought them. But they're great, and they're unique, and you won't see them on everyone else. That's what I like, and that's my style.

I would never package myself for a situation that didn't feel natural for me to walk into. If someone admires my weird shoes, I know I'm in the right place. I also love this line called Carpe Diem; they make shirts and jackets that are somehow 18th century-looking without being costume-y; it's just different and really beautiful. . . . You don't want to think about this too much. Assuming you're good at what you do, think about being who you are.

David Pollick, publicity and marketing consultant, who directs publicity for movie stars and producers:

This is the image business, and I need to look hip or, at the very least, like I know what is hip. In my business, you need to look like you're conversant with what's hip. Part of that is convincing your clients who are hip and cool, or want to be, that you are—and if need be, you can show them how. I wear jeans almost daily, Helmut Lang or Levi's with Pumas. Whether I'm marketing a film or an actor, many of the people I meet with are in their 20s, and me in a Brooks Bros. suit is not going to cut it. I'm 42, and I'm not going to even try to wear [rock-star designer] Roberto Cavalli, yet at the same time, I'm not going to show up in Armani, which really defined Hollywood fashion for a period. I offer a certain hipness factor, and that is communicated by the clothes I'm wearing as well as what comes out of my mouth.

Ted Mitchell, president of Occidental College, part of whose job is to persuade people to contribute money, another part is to work with faculty members, and a third is to deal with students:

> For me, each day has a central focus, and that's where I aim my wardrobe. If there's a donor meeting, I'm in a blue, gray or olive suit from Brooks Bros. And Florsheim lace-ups in black or brown, a tie, and a white or light-blue button-down shirt from Lands' End. [If there are no outside meetings] it's a pretty structured range, though I do like to have fun with ties—I will buy them anywhere, be it Brooks Bros. or an airport tie store. I also have a huge collection of reading glasses—and the more outlandish, the better: purple, multicolored flecks, you name it, though I keep a few dignified pairs in metal for meetings. They all come from [a drugstore], so I figure I can indulge myself.
>
> You interact with a lot of different people, and you can't pretend to be part of their club, but you can make them comfortable. This point was impressed upon me several years ago when I was still working at UCLA and had to come across town to meet with some Occidental alums. I was wearing a black turtleneck, which is fine on the Westside of Los Angeles but not really what you want to wear to a meeting in Pasadena. As was pointed out to me.

Women in Management

As women move up the ladder in management, problems relating to gender are evolving, but it's still the fact that there are far more men than women in upper management. Women who are interviewing for positions in management have unique problems. One Los Angeles attorney, a woman, who has worked for a major Wall Street law firm and a major New York Stock Exchange corporation says:

I'm a fanatic on how women should dress for an interview. I never wear pants and I always wear very conservative dresses, on the long side, never anything short, never anything low-cut, never anything too flamboyant. Most of my things are solid colors. I dress in pastels or navy and black and brown. It's hard to tell me from a secretary anyway. If I go in dressed too much like a secretary, I get taken for a secretary. It also makes me look more professional. I want to look good in what I buy. I certainly don't tie my hair back and wear horn-rimmed glasses and no makeup. But I think it looks more professional and businesslike and gains me better acceptance to dress conservatively.

She varies this theme, however, when interviewing with someone near her own age:

When I know I'm going to be interviewing a man who is close to my own age, I try to wear something softer, like a baby blue or light green, maybe even a pink because it makes me seem less threatening to him. It looks more feminine. It looks softer. It looks less professional and therefore he feels less challenged by me.

She has had several interviewing experiences where the combination of her gender and aggressiveness cost her offers. One firm made her an offer and then withdrew it; the younger members in the firm argued that she threatened to wreck the close, noncompetitive atmosphere that they had created in the firm. She combats this feeling by looking more feminine and therefore less aggressive when she interviews younger men. She puts a large emphasis on colors. Her experience has proved to her that the way she dresses has a very important effect on the interview.

Cleanliness

There is one constant that applies to both men and women. No matter what your gender and no matter what type of job you are interviewing for, be neat and clean.

- Be sure that your fingernails are properly cut and clean. Dirty fingernails can result in a feeling of revulsion in an interview that you will be unable to counter.
- Ensure that your hair is neat. If you have to park outside the building where you are having the interview, the wind may mess up your hair. Try to visit a restroom and inspect your coiffure before going into your interview.
- Your clothes should be neat and pressed, and your shoes should not be scuffed. Jeri Long, a Bank of America executive, says, "Scuffed, dirty, and poorly maintained shoes account for the highest rejection percentage of all clothing atrocities."
- Be careful about the amount of jewelry you wear. An armful of bracelets and a handful of rings can leave a negative impression.
- If you have bad breath, take a breath mint before entering the interview. If your interview is in the afternoon, don't have a cocktail at lunch. The smell of liquor on the breath will not be received favorably. Also be careful of what you

eat before your interview. You don't want to come across as one huge garlic clove.

- Be sure you bathe before the interview. There is probably no bigger turnoff for an interviewer than to interview someone who has body odor. If you've got this problem more severely than others, try to bathe just before leaving for the interview and use a deodorant-antiperspirant.
- Your clothes should be fresh. If you have a suit, shirt, or dress that you've worn once and feel that you can get another wearing out of it before sending it to the cleaners, save the additional wearing for some other occasion. If you wear freshly cleaned and pressed clothes, you won't have to worry about your clothes being spotty, wrinkled, or smelly.
- Try to look yourself over in a mirror immediately before entering the interview. Things can happen to you after you leave your home of which you might be unaware. And there's nobody looking out for you once you arrive. Ask the receptionist if there's a restroom you can visit. Then take a good, sharp look at yourself in the mirror. Make sure that your nose is not running or dirty and that your clothes look neat and fresh.

Robert H. Lentz, former vice president and general chief counsel for Litton Industries, sums it up well:

Personal appearance and personal habits are very important. If an interviewee has bad breath or body odor, I'd say that it implies a certain sloppiness that's personal. I think that there's an inference of some value that if a person is sloppy in appearance or has a greasy tie, for example, or a very cavalier outfit going out for a job interview, it implies that the person is possibly sloppy in many ways. I would consider that a very definite negative. I think that personal appearance is highly important. Even though it's a first impression, people have to realize that when they're being interviewed, they're trying to convey as much as possible to the interviewer in a very limited amount of time. Proper dress and good personal appearance are both important.

Checklist

- Dress to your advantage.
- Dress to suit your interviewer.
- Dress for the position for which you are interviewing.
- Consider the effect your choice of colors will have.
- Your colors and patterns should coordinate.
- Do not dress sensually unless sex appeal is part of the job.
- Dress conservatively.
- Your fingernails should be clean and properly cut.
- Your hair should be neat and combed.
- Your clothes should be fresh, neat, and pressed.
- Your shoes should not be scuffed.
- Your jewelry should be sparse.
- If you have bad breath, take a breath mint.
- Before the interview don't drink liquor or eat foods that will leave an odor on your breath.
- Bathe and use a deodorant-antiperspirant before the interview.
- Check out your appearance in a mirror before the interview.

11

Silence and Power

In the late nineteenth century Adrian "Cap" Anson was the premier baseball player in the National League. He batted more than .400 and fielded flawlessly. But one thing bugged Anson, and in 1888 he did something about it.

Anson organized a group of fellow baseball players and demanded that African Americans be prohibited from playing in the National League. Because of his prestige and the tenor of the times, an unwritten law was maintained, and thereafter no African American's name graced the box scores of the major leagues, despite such standout players as Josh Gibson, Satchel Paige, and James "Cool Papa" Bell.

In 1945 a grizzled baseball executive had a plan. Branch Rickey was general manager of the Brooklyn Dodgers, and he told his scout, Clyde Sukeforth, to go to Chicago, check out a player's arm, and, if satisfied that his arm was sound, bring him to Brooklyn for an interview.

Sukeforth returned a few days later, and he and Jackie Robinson entered Rickey's office. Sukeforth told Rickey that he hadn't seen Robinson's arm but had brought him in for Ricky to interview anyway.

After introductions, Rickey subjected Robinson to intense study. No one said a word as Rickey stared at Robinson for several minutes. Finally, Rickey told Robinson that for years he had been looking for a great black baseball player, that he had a feeling that Robinson was his man. But he said that he needed someone who was more than a great athlete; he needed someone who could take insults and abuse and have the courage not to fight back. He described the terrible abuse that Robinson would have to take from everyone—fellow players, fans, sportswriters, even his own teammates. But Rickey said if the first black man to play baseball in the National League in fifty years fought back, he'd set the cause back twenty years.

When Rickey was through, he waited for Robinson's response. But Robinson didn't say anything. For five minutes the room was enmeshed in silence as Robinson thought and Rickey waited. Sukeforth said that Rickey was immensely impressed that Robinson did not give a quick answer.

Finally, Robinson told Rickey that he had no doubts about his ability to play baseball in the National League but that that judgment would be up to Rickey. He promised that if Rickey was willing to take the risk, there would not be any incident. Thus ended a classic interview, one that changed not only the complexion of the sporting world but the opportunities of African Americans in all professions.

Jackie Robinson was a man of power, as was Branch Rickey. Their initial meeting emphasizes the manifestation of power through silence. Each used silence, but in a different way and with different purposes.

Silence by the Interviewer

When they first met, Rickey said nothing, staring at Robinson for several minutes. Rickey was applying stress before he uttered a word. Robinson responded by withstanding the scrutiny with silence and confidence. It was Rickey's move. Had Robinson fidgeted or shown discomfort, Rickey's impression would probably have been less favorable. Rickey had been looking for forty years to break the color line. A few more years wouldn't matter. He had to have the man who could stand the tension under which he would be put. He had to have a man of power and restraint.

THE THINKING SILENCE

After Rickey had put the facts before Robinson, Robinson was silent. He had the confidence in himself to think the problem through, and he wasn't intimidated by the powerful man across the desk from him. The room was filled with silence for five minutes. Someone who is uncomfortable with himself, or is intimidated, or lacks confidence, will find five minutes of silence in the same room with a man of power and decision an eternity. But Robinson thought the problem through. He didn't rush out with a rapid acceptance, which could have been his undoing. He thus showed Rickey that he had the confidence in himself to consider the proposition as something that could expose him to great risk and that he wasn't going to jump at an opportunity without considering the consequences.

Each of these men conveyed his power to the other through silence. Although Rickey used silence as a tool, Robinson was not trained in interviewing and was reacting from within. His silence was a genuine indication of the man inside.

Most people think it is their obligation to fill gaps in conversation. They feel an urge to talk when there is silence. Sometimes silence on the part of an interviewer invites initiative by the interviewee. Other times it does not. It's important to distinguish one from the other.

Silence You Should Not Break

In the Robinson-Rickey interview it was clear that Rickey's initial silence did not invite conversation from Robinson. It's very rare that in an employment interview a candidate will be met with such a stressful imposition of silence upon introduction.

If you are alert, you may be able to distinguish an invitation from an evaluation. In *Contact: The First Four Minutes* authors Leonard and Natalie Zunin say, "Once people are talking, they look at their partners less often than when they listen. To look away while speaking is natural. . . . A pause while glancing away usually means an incomplete phrase, signaling, 'I have not yet said all I want to say; don't interrupt.'"

Silence as a Plea for Help

Often silence does invite initiative. I remember an interview I had with a potential client. The president of the company was fairly shy. I accompanied the vice president to the president's office, and the interview consisted mostly of my talking with the vice president while the president observed.

Nobody asked me questions. We were introduced, and the three of us just sat there looking at one another. It was clearly an invitation for me to take over the interview, so I started discussing a real estate project I was working on, which I had discussed previously with the vice president. We chatted about this, and then I slowly introduced other areas in which I had worked that I felt were germane to the operations of the company.

The president hardly uttered a word. After I felt that I had established my credentials, I asked the president to tell me something about his company and its problems and why he felt that he needed a lawyer.

The dichotomy between the initial silence of this situation and the Robinson-Rickey silence was determined by the ambience of the confrontations. There was nothing friendly about the Rickey silence. It was plainly evaluative. On the other hand, the silence that greeted me in the president's office was expectant. Had Robinson started to talk while Rickey was staring at him, or had I remained silent while the president waited, we each would have misjudged the situation and most probably blown the interview.

Successfully handling silence in an interview is a most convincing demonstration of power and self-confidence. If you get into a silence situation and use it properly, you can't help but win. If the interviewer knows what he's doing, and you know what you're doing, your feeling of having handled the situation properly will be instantaneous.

Some interviewers are actually more nervous than the people they are interviewing, in which case a long silence may mean they can't think of anything to say and that they'd be grateful if you would help them through these awkward pauses. You must learn to recognize whether you are talking to a sophisticated interviewer or to an inexperienced one so that you can distinguish a deliberately imposed silence from a plea for help to keep the conversation flowing.

One of the keys to look for in making this determination is whether the interviewer looks at you. If he does, and says nothing, he is obviously introducing stress, and you should act accordingly. If, on the other hand, he looks away, fidgets, or exhibits other nervous mannerisms, he probably can't think of anything to say and is wondering how he's ever going to get through this interview.

Don't delude yourself by thinking that this situation never happens. Many selection interviewers are inexperienced, and more than you might imagine are terrified of interviews. They are on uncertain ground, and a lot of them are just as worried that they are going to make fools of themselves in front of you as you are that you're going to make a fool of yourself in front of them.

In such a situation you should come to the interviewer's rescue by telling him you have some questions. He will undoubtedly ask to hear them, and you can then inquire about the job, the company, or the interviewer himself. He should feel relief and indebtedness to you for saving him from embarrassment and for not exposing his inexperience.

How to Endure Stressful Silence

Silence is a powerful phenomenon that can produce intriguing effects. Using it as an interview technique is simple. Sometimes around the middle of the interview, the interviewer (and, for this chapter, let's assume the interviewer is a man) will ask a question requiring a short answer. He gets the short answer. Then he does not respond. Nothing. He just sits there, looking at you but saying nothing.

The predictable result is that the silence will cause you to think about your frailties. You will begin to worry that you have said the wrong thing, or that your nose is running, your clothing is unbuttoned, or your hair is out of place. So without thinking you rush to correct whatever it is that is worrying you. You restate something you said earlier, wipe your nose, brush the hair back. All of these actions are telltale signs of insecurity in the face of silence.

Since the cause of insecurity is derived from an active mind, the cure is to keep your mind busy with other matters. You know that the best way to handle silence is simply to return the interviewer's stare with a calm, anticipatory look. Don't let your mind race around trying to determine which weakness he's focusing on. Keep your mind too busy to think about your weaknesses.

The best way I have discovered to do this is to become aware of the silence and see how long it lasts. The moment that you recognize that the interviewer is imposing silence, start counting to yourself. I'll guarantee that the silence won't last longer than fifteen seconds. Start counting to yourself "one thousand one, one thousand two" and so on until the interviewer breaks the silence. You'll be so busy counting that your mind won't focus on your runny nose or falling hair. Your demeanor will reflect a calm anticipation, and suddenly, your test will be over and the interviewer will continue the interview by breaking the silence with another question.

Don't Retract

The most common reaction to the deliberately introduced stressful silence is to conclude that you've somehow stuck your foot in your mouth. You hastily review the answer you just gave, and your instinct is to retract or qualify it. *Don't!* Don't retract! Don't change what you've said, even if you think the interviewer doesn't agree with you or is looking for a different answer.

A small digression here may emphasize this point. It is said that in the first year of law school the professors try to scare you to death. Law school is generally taught by the Socratic, or question-and-answer, method where the professor quizzes a student about a case the class has read. The professor will get the student to take a stand and then caustically tear the position to shreds.

When I was in my first year, contracts professor Richard Speidel was feared at Virginia Law School for his brutality to the students' psyches. It was the rule rather than the exception that he would keep a student standing for the entire hour, grilling him on points of contract law. Sometimes he would start the next class with the person who had been destroyed the previous session, so you could never relax.

But there was a rule to Speidel's game, and it is a cardinal rule that is also applicable to interviewing. If you stuck to your guns and didn't change your position when he attacked you, he'd let you sit down after about fifteen minutes.

One day he called on me and had me brief a case about the crew of a merchant ship who agreed to ship out for a certain rate; when the ship hit the high seas, the crew struck for three times the rate previously agreed upon.

"Well, Mr. Medley," said Mr. Speidel, "what would you do if the ship's owner called you for advice?"

"I'd tell him to go ahead and agree to pay the rate and then renege when the cargo was unloaded at destination," I replied.

"What!" exploded Speidel. "You'd have the ship's owner make a commitment he never had any intention of honoring?"

"Well," I countered, "I'd say that he was acting under undue duress and that he wasn't bound because the crew's actions were a breach of contract."

"Do you mean, Mr. Medley, that he honor only the commitments he wants to honor, those that work to his advantage, and ignore those that work to his disadvantage? What is this, Mr. Medley," he attacked with devastating vitriol, "the two-edged sword of Damocles?"

He leaned against the blackboard and waited. "Well," I thought, "he's certainly got a good point. Maybe I should reconsider. Maybe he'll like me better if I agree with him and he will treat me more easily." But then I remembered how he had changed and destroyed people before. If I change, I decided, he'll keep switching and I'll never sit down. Taking a deep breath, I gambled on a little show of strength and confidence in my position. "Not for my client," I replied. "He would be sticking by the original agreement."

He glared for a minute and then, with a smirk, said, "You may sit down, Mr. Medley." My ordeal for the year was over; it had lasted less then ten minutes.

When silence is used as a method of challenging your belief in your statements, you can be devastated. If you are faced with this situation and if you've taken a position, don't backtrack. Just sit and wait. Often, in an interview it's not what you say when you voice your opinions; it's whether you have confidence in them.

Don't Mutter

A second mistake that is made in the face of silence is to start to mutter. You may have given an opinion and the interviewer just sits there looking at you. So you add something onto it. He still says nothing, so you add something else.

If you've said what you have to say on a subject, stop. If the interviewer doesn't immediately pick up the conversation, you have no obligation to continue talking. Muttering and frivolous talking in the face of silence indicate a lack of confidence and the fact that the tension he has created is getting to you. So don't add taglines to your opinions. If you're through talking on a subject, let it be.

Just Wait Calmly

Silence is easy to handle if you recognize it quickly for what it is: a ploy. The interviewer is testing you. The best way to survive it is to sit calmly and wait for him to continue the interview. Don't fidget. Don't look down or around. Just sit and look at him expectantly. The silence cannot last long because the interview is for a short period of time, and there are many things he wants to cover. If you're not ready for the silence, it may seem to last an eternity. If you are prepared and recognize it, it will be over in a few seconds and you may have conveyed more than you could have with thousands of words.

A sophisticated interviewer will introduce stressful silence at a time when you least expect it. People apply stress in many different ways. Byron Atkinson, who was dean of students at UCLA for nineteen years, said, "If you really want to unnerve someone, stare at one corner of his hairline. Or look him in the eyes in a fixed gaze. Your partner will be so ill at ease he'll start fumbling for words." If you are prepared for it and handle it properly, you will get one of the warmest positive feelings you'll ever receive out of an interview. If you remember what has been said here and if you're relaxed and confident, you should be able to handle stressful silence whenever it's introduced.

BREAKING THE STRESSFUL SILENCE

There are two good ways for an interviewee to handle silence introduced into an interview as an imposition of stress. The first is to sit expectantly, as I've explained. The second involves a risk and must be handled adroitly. You have finished your answer to one of the questions and the interviewer just sits and stares, and you recognize that stress has been introduced. *Who should break the silence?* As we have seen, changing your statement or backtracking or muttering can be interpreted as a lack of confidence in yourself and what you have said. If a few seconds pass and you know the interviewer is using silence as stress and not just thinking over your answer or preparing a new question, you may ask, "Do you mind if I ask a few questions about your company [or the job or you]?" This breaks the silence in an acceptable manner without revealing an insecurity on your part or an inability to handle the silence. It also takes the silence as a weapon away from the interviewer.

By asking a question pertinent to the interview, you are telling the interviewer that you recognize that the interview is for a finite period of time and you want to cover as many areas as possible. There is quite a bit of information you wish to obtain from him, and this seems like a good spot in the interview to get it. You tacitly don't recognize his imposition of stress for what it is. Instead, you are telling him, "Well, if you're through, there are some things I'd like to ask."

Just remember: If you break the silence, don't do it by volunteering more information, either on the subject just finished or on a different subject. If you do, you will indicate a lack of ability to deal with the silence, and this can be a big negative. If you have communicated by your method of speaking that you have finished talking on the subject under discussion (which is generally done by pausing and looking at the interviewer), you must keep it closed. By bringing the subject up again in response to the silence, you will probably have failed the silence test. Similarly, by bringing up an entirely new subject after you have signaled that you have finished speaking, you express your insecurity. After you have indicated that you've finished speaking, don't begin again unless it's to ask some questions.

Silence by the Interviewee

It is possible for you, the interviewee, to introduce silence into the interview for your own benefit. In chapter 5 I suggested that pausing not only gives you time to think over your answer but also indicates to the interviewer that you are a deliberative person, not given to making snap decisions. Eisenhower, you remember, requested several hours to contemplate. Robinson took five minutes to think over and formulate his answer. Each man used silence as a tool to indicate self-confidence and restraint. Most important of all, each conveyed his power through the use of silence.

The way you answer a difficult question may convey more than the answer itself. If you give a quick answer, for example, you may leave a bad impression. An answer given too quickly, without sufficient thought, may lead the interviewer to think you are a person of little depth.

Perhaps the most important aspect of Rickey's evaluation was the fact that Robinson sat silent for five minutes before answering. Remember, Rickey had not offered him a job. He had merely said, "I have reason to believe that you're [my] man." Unquestionably, the manner of Robinson's response was what decided the day. Had Robinson said without a pause that he wanted the job, Rickey would undoubtedly have concluded that Robinson either did not recognize the turmoil into which he would be entering or was insincere in his promise to avoid incidents.

But Robinson thought through what he had just heard. By his silence he conveyed to Rickey the fact that he recognized the risks and the tremendous self-control that would be required of him.

Look at it from Rickey's viewpoint. African American ballplayers had been yearning for more than fifty years to get into organized baseball. He was making an offer that thousands of African American men had dreamed of for a half century. Rickey knew that Robinson was no different from any other African American ballplayer. He wanted to play in organized baseball, where the money and fame were. But Rickey had to be convinced that Robinson recognized the risks involved and what would be required of him.

The fact that Robinson did not jump for the plum but thought about it for a long period before replying convinced Rickey probably even before he heard the answer that Robinson was his man. It was the silence, not the words, that did it.

Other Impositions of Stress

There are other ways that stress may be introduced into an interview. For example, you could be asked to perform without any notice or preparation. If you're interviewing for a bookkeeping job, for example, you might be asked to show what you can do by being given some work to perform.

I have used this occasionally. I actually used it to interview a bookkeeper. I had some work that needed to be done, and I was interviewing a woman who seemed nice, but I wasn't sure of her expertise. So I asked her if she wanted to do some bookkeeping for me while she was there, and I offered to pay her for it. She agreed and made some entries onto my books, taking about an hour. I paid her. I looked at her work and found it satisfactory. It was one of the better interviews I've had because I found out what she could do and I got something done that needed doing.

Or maybe you're interviewing for a sales position. I used this tactic for a salesman. I was looking for someone to help me sell my videotape interview service (which was the inspiration for this book) because I didn't like doing it myself. So a salesman was recommended to me, and I had him come in for an interview. Like most salesmen, he was a likable guy. But I couldn't judge how he'd sell my service, so I asked him to sell it to me. He immediately went into his sales mode, but I wasn't convinced and didn't hire him.

Sportscaster Andrea Kremer was subjected to extreme stress when she applied for a job with NFL Films, as reported in *ESPN: The Uncensored History*, by Michael Freeman:

> Kremer . . . returned for an interview, which consisted of a written and verbal test. One question was to define a trap play. Kremer's answer was lengthy and exact, need-

ing extra space, filling a full page. She noted that the Pittsburgh Steelers probably ran a trap play better than anyone. NFL Films was so impressed that they stored Kremer's test answers for future reference and offered her the job seven days later.

I mention these examples because a performance test is something for which you should always be prepared. Whatever job it is that you're trying for, one of your interviewers might ask you to prove what you can do.

Checklist

- Silence by the interviewer is generally an imposition of stress.
- Silence by the interviewee is a manifestation of confidence.
- If you recognize that the interviewer is inexperienced and his silence is a plea for help, break it by asking questions.
- Don't break a stressful silence imposed by the interviewer except to ask a question.
- The interviewer will cue you as to when he wants you to break the silence.
- If the silence is not imposed as stress, it's your obligation to break it.
- Don't retract in the face of silence.
- Don't mutter in the face of silence.
- Wait through a stressful silence by counting the seconds it lasts.
- Don't fidget through a stressful silence.
- Be prepared to perform whatever task you're interviewing for.

12

Sex

Even though there could probably be improvements, women's position in the marketplace has changed for the better over the years. Following is an except from the July 1943 issue of *Mass Transportation*. It was a serious article written for male supervisors of women in the workforce during World War II.

ELEVEN TIPS ON GETTING MORE EFFICIENCY
OUT OF WOMEN EMPLOYEES

There's no longer any question whether transit companies should hire women for jobs formerly held by men. The draft and manpower shortage has settled that point. The important things now are to select the most efficient women available and how to use them to the best advantage. Here are eleven helpful tips on the subject from Western Properties:

1. Pick young married women. They usually have more of a sense of responsibility than their unmarried sisters, they're less likely to be flirtatious, they need the work or they wouldn't be doing it, they still have the pep and interest to work hard and to deal with the public efficiently.

2. When you have to use older women, try to get ones who have worked outside the home at some time in their lives. Older women who have never contacted the public have a hard time adapting themselves and are inclined to be cantankerous and fussy. It's always well to impress upon older women the importance of friendliness and courtesy.

3. General experience indicates that "husky" girls—those who are just a little on the heavy side—are more even-tempered and efficient than their underweight sisters.

4. Retain a physician to give each woman you hire a special physical examination—one covering female conditions. This step not only protects the property against the possibilities of lawsuit, but reveals whether the employee-to-be has any female weaknesses, which would make her mentally or physically unfit for the job.

5. Stress at the outset the importance of time—the fact that a minute or two lost here and there makes serious inroads on schedules. Until this point is gotten across, service is likely to be slowed up.

6. Give the female employee a definite daylong schedule of duties so that they'll keep busy without bothering the management for instructions every few minutes. Numerous properties say that women make excellent workers when they have their jobs cut out for them, but that they lack initiative in finding work themselves.

7. Whenever possible, let the inside employee change from one job to another at some time during the day. Women are inclined to be less nervous and happier with change.

8. Give every girl an adequate number of rest periods during the day. You have to make some allowances for feminine psychology. A girl has more confidence and is

more efficient if she can keep her hair tidied, apply fresh lipstick and wash her hands several times a day.

9. Be tactful when issuing instructions or in making criticisms. Women are often sensitive; they can't shrug off harsh words the way men do. Never ridicule a woman— it breaks her spirit and cuts off her efficiency.

10. Be reasonably considerate about using strong language around women. Even though a girl's husband or father may swear vociferously, she'll grow to dislike a place of business where she hears too much of this.

11. Get enough size variety in operator's uniforms so that each girl can have a proper fit. This point can't be stressed too much in keeping women happy.

One of the most controversial aspects of interviewing for a job involves sex. Since the original publication of *Sweaty Palms* in 1978, there has been a revolution in the treatment of sex. In 1978 sex in the job market was still treated with a wink and a nod. *Sweaty Palms* was one of the first to raise the issue and deal with it head-on.

There are three basic ways that sex may become an issue in a job interview. The first is alleged sexual harassment by the interviewer. The second is the use of sexual attractiveness by the interviewee to get a job. The third is the pursuit of a sexual relationship by the interviewer, which is part of sexual harassment but will be dealt with separately in this chapter.

Sexual Harassment

Sexual harassment in the workplace has been clearly defined and outlawed by both state and federal law. As an example, California law now defines sexual harassment as unwanted sexual advances, or visual, verbal, or physical conduct of a sexual nature. The California Department of Fair Employment and Housing has compiled a list of offensive behavior that includes unwanted sexual advances, leering, making sexual gestures, making or using derogatory comments and jokes, verbal sexual advances or propositions, and touching.

Both federal and state law recognize two types of sexual harassment: *quid pro quo*, or the grant or denial of employment based on sexual favors, and *hostile work environment*, or the deprivation of the right to work in an environment free from discriminatory intimidation, ridicule, and insult. Even someone not personally subjected to the harassment may make a claim if forced to work in an atmosphere where harassment exists.

Today any relatively sophisticated interviewer should be aware of the risks involved in including any kind of sexual elements in an interview. But the fact is that many interviewers are unaware of what may and what may not be done in an interview. It's not improbable that an interviewee will be faced with a sexual harassment issue in an interview without the interviewer even knowing that the issue has been introduced. It's also possible that an interviewer will *intentionally* violate the rules against sexual harassment. The question is, if you're presented with the problem, whether innocently or intentionally (and that distinction may not be something that you will find easy to determine), how should you handle it?

Before I go on, I want to emphasize that this applies equally to men and women interviewees. However, because of the preponderance of men in upper management, most sexual harassment occurs with women as the victims. As more and more women become involved in management, this is changing, but the fact is that, at present, women are still far and away more often victim that victimizer.

In a job interview sexual harassment most commonly occurs

in the form of an offensive question. When you are asked a question that offends you, the first thing you must determine is whether there is a business reason for the question. If you think there is none (like asking you if you are sleeping with anybody), then you should handle it in the manner discussed in chapter 5.

The problem with the offensive question is that more often than not it is not intended to be offensive. The perfect example of this is a question that is asked primarily of women: "Have you completed your family?" Or its corollary: "Do you plan on having any [more] children?" (The legality of this question is covered in chapter 14 on discrimination. The problem is that, legal or not, it is often asked, and you must be prepared to handle it properly.) Many women immediately react by thinking, "They don't ask men this question, so why are they asking me? It's discriminatory and demeaning." Undoubtedly true, but you must realize that there may be a business reason (maybe it's not legitimate, but it *is* a business reason) for asking. Put yourself in the place of an employer. You are interviewing to fill a vacancy that happens to be a key position. You have budgeted that this position will be filled by a person who will assume a large responsibility load; that person is needed every day. You have also budgeted that the person filling this position will be absent from the job for two weeks every year for vacation and probably an additional five days because of illness. So you are counting on the person to be on the job forty-nine weeks each year.

If you're interviewing a young married woman who has a two-year-old child, you may think, "Well, she's young and married and already has a child. If she gets pregnant, she'll probably have to miss several weeks while having her child. That's on top of her vacation and normal illnesses. Who's going to fill in for her while she's off? Do I have to train someone just to be her stand-in while she has children?"

If you as interviewee recognize this worry, you might not be able to answer the interviewer adequately, but you won't make the mistake of reacting with hostility—and that's the worst thing that you can do. Try to recognize that the question is not necessarily being asked to put you down or to discriminate against you, but to voice concern.

A reader from Shawnigan Lake, British Columbia, writes about how she was subjected to what she considered sexual harassment and how she felt and reacted:

> I was already employed as a secretary, but when the manager's job for a local tourist association came open, I decided I would try for it. (I have a bachelor's degree in mass communication and have experience as a newspaper editor and reporter.) I sent in my resumé and got a copy of the association's yearly publication to learn the names of the board and whatever I could about the association's goals and past successes. I went so far as to plan some ideas that could be used to help publicize the region (one of their main goals). After doing all that, I felt confident that I could at least present myself as an intelligent person who could do the job.
>
> I was interviewed by a panel of three; each person in turn asked me a series of questions they had written down on a piece of paper. I felt I answered the questions well and was able to present my ideas, which they all seemed interested in and even enthusiastic about. Then it happened!
>
> One of the interviewers started asking questions that I didn't want to answer like, "Your resumé doesn't say, but are you married?" I answered this question but thought it had no relevance to the job. The next question was, "Does your husband have a good job?" I asked him to clarify

what he meant. "Is he going to be transferred out of the area soon?" I answered that he worked for a hospital and they didn't have a transfer policy that I knew of. Then he asked, "What are your family plans?" Right then I knew I should have said something like, "I think what you're asking is if I will be committed to this job and the answer is yes," but I was so stunned by the question all I could answer was something about my husband and I not having decided what we were going to do since we hadn't been married that long. I finished the interview pleasantly, but I was furious! How dare they ask those questions!

Well, they offered the job to another candidate, and I just continued on in my secretary's job. I did go back to one of the interviewers and asked why I didn't get the job. According to him, it was because I couldn't work Friday nights and Saturdays due to my religion. He also said I was an excellent candidate for the job and that if it ever came open again, I should try for it. (Which to me didn't make sense because I wasn't going to change my religion for the job.) At that point I told him that I regarded their questions about my personal life as not relevant to the job and in addition they were in direct violation of the Labor Rights Act. I gave him a brochure with a list of questions you can't ask during an interview or on a job application. . . .

Choosing the person with the best ability to do the job should be the only factor businesses take into consideration, not the sex of the individual. Young women can offer the best abilities to many companies, but if they are not hired simply because they might get pregnant, then not only does the woman suffer but the company does and so does society. Instead, it seems for men it's a competition to figure out who can do the best job; for women it's a competition to see who's least likely to get pregnant.

I guess what I'm trying so desperately to tell you is that I felt degraded that my abilities to do a job weren't as important as my private life. . . .

This woman's letter is typical of a lot of the mail I receive from people who didn't know how to answer a question that they considered offensive and have written to tell me of their problems and their real feelings. The solution? The expression of her real feelings to me in her letter should have been how she answered the questions!

You must realize that some of the questions interviewers ask are to resolve genuine concerns that they have. My advice is not to legitimize offensive or illegal questions; it is to explain the reasoning behind the questions so that an interviewee might be better prepared when hit with them. Maybe the interviewer's concerns are unfair; maybe their questions are illegal; but the concerns are there, and you are ahead of the game if they state them. The law can prohibit them from asking the question. The law can prohibit them from discriminating against you. But what the law cannot do is keep them from having the concerns, and the practical result of an unrectified concern can be your not being offered a job.

It's very easy for a prospective employer to refuse to hire a young woman on a pretext when the real concern is that she might get pregnant and want maternity leave or that her husband might get a job and they'd move somewhere else. If that occurs, it's up to you to prove that the reason was bogus and then go through litigation to try to win and recover damages. But is that the way you want to spend the next five years of your life?

Isn't it better to deal with the illegal question or the unexpressed fear openly and honestly? Had my reader expressed herself in her interview the way she expressed herself to me, she would have been much better off. Her eloquent expression of her feelings could only impress an interviewer. After all, the concern about her fecundity already existed. The way for her to combat it was to deal with it head-on, as she did in her letter to me.

Use of Sex by the Interviewee

Sex is a two-headed coin. Not only may an interviewer use sex as a form of harassment, a job seeker may use it to try to get a job. This is a possibility that's rarely mentioned. I do not encourage people to go after a job using sex as a ploy, nor do I condone the practice. I'm only recognizing the existence of this tactic and pointing out the pitfalls from both sides of such a tawdry encounter.

Many counselors will advise that sex in the office is a bad thing and that if you get a job because of it, everything will turn out poorly. Barbara Walters, in her book *How to Talk with Practically Anybody About Practically Anything*, says:

> When to be sexy, and when not. When not is when applying for a job, or when trying to keep one. . . . The beddable look does not lead to the door marked President, but to the one marked Exit. Be sexy on your own time; working hours and job interviews require the crisp and cool version of you.

The Walters theory is based on the hypothesis that all interviewers are professional and are looking only for someone who can do the job. This may be true in a great many cases, but there are many interviewers who have a more hedonistic outlook on life. Something that happened to me epitomizes the problem and its effects on all involved.

When I was a young attorney, I had just joined a division and had to hire a secretary. I was sent one of the most beautiful, sensuous women I had ever seen. She was an absolute knock-out. I interviewed her, and while she played games with her eyes, I had enough self-control to determine that she couldn't type very well, wasn't very good at shorthand, didn't seem to be very well organized, and had very little experience in what I needed for a person to run my office. Reluctantly, I told her that I didn't think she was qualified for the job.

She was a friend of the person in charge of secretarial employment, so she got a job as a typist. Whenever an executive was looking for a secretary, she was the first one to be interviewed. Finally, after work one day, she met an executive who had one of the most efficient secretaries in the office. But the executive was the man for whom she was looking. He looked into her eyes and fired his secretary the next day.

She worked for him for several months. He became very morose because his work fell off. Then she received an offer to become secretary to the president of another company and left. She found a home as a window-dressing secretary to a company president who had others do the real work. The last I heard, everyone was happy except the guy who originally hired her. He never found someone who managed his office the way his first secretary did.

There is a much-diminished chance that a job obtained on the basis of sexual attraction will last as long as the one based upon ability. You should recognize the pitfalls if you are going to base your strategy on this. Walters thinks that office affairs inevitably lead to problems: "Most bosses are married men and so, unless it turns out to be for keeps and he goes the whole route of divorcing his wife and marrying you, the only way to end the affair will be to fire you."

If you get your job because of sex, your performance will be subjected to the spotlight of attention once the sexual attraction ceases. If you're not performing in your job and there is no more sexual attraction, you're probably going to be back in the job line pretty soon. If you enter on this path, you'll be changing jobs pretty regularly.

The woman referred to above was wise: She made her move to a better job while she still had good credentials. Moreover, her boss was beginning to cool on her, and, given his mental outlook, it was easier for him to give a good recommendation to get rid of her than to be truthful to the prospective employer.

If all you have to offer is sex, and you decide this is the route you're going to take, be sure you know the rules of the game, but be prepared to ride the roller coaster.

Interviewer's Sexual Propositions

If you are attractive, articulate, and ambitious and are being interviewed by a person who might find you sexually alluring, there may come a time when you feel you are being pursued for your sexual attractiveness rather than your capabilities. It may not be because of something overt; it will just be a feeling that you have. What should you do? Should you bring it out in the open? Should you react with indignation? Should you accept an offer for a job if it is tendered?

Don't follow the first two alternatives. If your intuition is wrong, bringing the question of sex out in the open or reacting with indignation would result in an insult and almost certain withdrawal or lessening of interest. In this situation you must both analyze yourself and evaluate the interviewer. If you have conducted a good interview yourself, you should have gained enough insight into the interviewer to make a judgment. Is the interviewer a professional or one with hedonistic leanings?

If you're not sure whether the interest in you is because you're capable or because of a sexual attraction, but you conclude that even though there are hedonistic leanings and ulterior motives, the interviewer is still a professional and will recognize and reward accomplishment, and if you're confident you can do the job, you should leave your doubts unspoken and pursue an offer. If your intuitions prove correct and there were ulterior motives, you can disabuse them in a tactful way after you have the job. In the meantime, if your performance has been good, you should have won a respected place in the organization. You may never be sure that the offer was made because of sex, but what difference does it make? So long as you respect the interviewer's professionalism and can handle the sexual advances when they come, you have achieved your objective—a job—and the fact that you may have gotten it because you're attractive is irrelevant. You should trade on what you have and use all your assets.

If, on the other hand, you do not gain a measure of respect and confidence in the interviewer's professionalism, you should trust your intuition and turn down the interest. A job that is taken on the basis of sex, when you want it on the basis of capability, can only lead to disaster if you don't want to participate in sexual games and your potential boss is not professional enough to recognize your talent in spite of your unwillingness to play. In this situation trust your intuition and move on to interviews with others.

Interviewer's Insensitivities

Reader Debbie Laskey lists the following questions and comments to which she has been exposed during her career. Some of these might seem unbelievable, but they certainly prove that you may encounter interviewers who (1) don't have a clue about what they're doing, (2) don't know the law, (3) are rude, (4) are inconsiderate, and (5) are stupid. But, as I've emphasized throughout *Sweaty Palms*, many interviewers are unsophisticated in the interviewing process, so you have to be ready for anything. Here's Ms. Laskey's list:

1. You will never get a job because you do not show enough skin.
2. We have a problem here. You are a superstar and we are just average.
3. Education is not important.
4. We do not have an appropriate job for you here. I just wanted to meet you.
5. Most women enter the hospitality industry because of the glamour.
6. When women who work here are tested for lead levels in their blood, their levels are not normal and are hazardous to women of childbearing age. But we did not want to tell you that over the telephone.
7. Where do you live? (A man asked this as he put his foot on his desk and looked at me leeringly. Obviously, he could not read. The address was on the resumé.)
8. Can you get here in time for work?
9. Do you drive?
10. Are you married?
11. When I asked a president of a company, "Where do you see the company in five years?" and he answered, "I don't know," I knew that the company had no vision.
12. What was your GPA in elementary school? (Appropriate question for college or graduate school, but not elementary school!)

13. A woman from a woman recruiter service advised me to do the following: She said that I should ask an interviewer to rate me on a scale of 1 to 10, with 10 being "a sure hire." If the interviewer responds that I am a 7 or 8, I should lean toward the interviewer, shake my chest, and ask, "What must I do to be a 10?"

14. When I asked an interviewer to stop smoking during the interview, he was extremely insulted that I should ask such a thing and ended the interview.

15. I was told that "women find the president attractive."

16. I was asked by an HR woman, "How do you do in presentations?" I replied, "This interview is a form of a presentation," but that statement was over her head. She did not understand.

17. Since you are married, are you free to travel?

18. Why did you go to school to get an M.B.A. degree?

Ms. Laskey sums up, "Although I have had some unpleasant experiences, I have also learned from all of my interviews. The most important lesson is that I would not have wanted to work for these companies, and that lesson may have saved me from sexual harassment lawsuits, unproductive companies, and countless headaches!"

Caveat

We live in a litigious society. Many who feel that an interviewer is acting unprofessionally and pursuing an agenda more related to romance than to the job are quick to react with hostility, and immediately think about sexual harassment.

Dr. Benjamin Spock, in a passage that everyone in the job

market should remember, said that people should have "sufficient sexual and romantic maturity to allow a person—man or woman—to show, whenever they are dealing with a member of the opposite sex, that they can be appropriately attentive and charming, without implying an intention of further seductiveness."

There is little that is more offensive than to have a well-intended compliment flung back in the face. If you think about it, your looks are just as important an asset as your brains or your grades or your experience. If you are a sensuous person, why downplay it?

The job market is a difficult field at best. In days of rising unemployment and expanding availability of workers, any asset you have should be used to your advantage. Sex must be used subtly, but it should not be ignored. If you've got it, don't flaunt it, but let it work naturally to your advantage.

Checklist

- Be aware of the rules relating to sexual harassment.
- Try to determine whether your interviewer is applying sexual harassment *intentionally* or *innocently*.
- If asked an offensive question, determine whether there is a business reason to ask it.
- If asked an offensive question, answer with your honest feelings without being disagreeable.
- Evaluate the interviewer's motivation.
- Don't be overly sensitive.

13

Salary

Probably nothing worries an interviewee more than how to handle the subject of salary and benefits. For some reason, most job hunters seem to feel that it is insulting to the employer to discuss salary. In fact, they often feel apologetic about it. On the other hand, a few job seekers are very aggressive when it comes to salary negotiations and look upon it as a challenge to push the stakes to the limit. There is no reason to feel apologetic, but the subject of salary is something that you should handle very carefully.

Don't Bring It Up Yourself

Salary is one subject that you should not bring up yourself, at least not in the early stage of an interview when the interviewer (and in this chapter let's assume the interviewer is a man) is still sizing you up—trying to find out if you have the qualifications for the job and whether or not you are compatible. At this point no interviewer, however inexperienced, wants to waste time discussing salary. So if you broach the subject yourself before he determines that he is interested in you, you run the very real risk of turning him off.

If there are several applicants interviewing for the same position, the interviewer has another reason for postponing discussion of salary. If he quotes a high salary to you, it makes it more difficult for him to negotiate salaries with the other applicants, who might have been happy with a lesser amount, or who might have been less qualified than you and therefore not worth the same high salary.

So leave the subject of salary for the interviewer to bring up. If, as the interview winds down, he asks you to come in for further interviews, or otherwise indicates that you are still being considered for the position, then you can risk bringing the subject up yourself. Simply ask what range of salary the position pays. Don't beat around the bush.

When You're Asked How Much You're Making

One of the roughest problems faced by an interviewee comes when the interviewer asks how much the interviewee is making. Generally, you are not making as much as you want to make or as much as you want your interviewer to offer you. As a general rule of thumb, someone who changes jobs wants an increase of salary of at least 20 percent. But what if you feel you are grossly underpaid and you want a much larger increase? What do you do when you are asked how much you are making?

It's a sad fact that employers will base their compensation more on what a candidate is making at his or her present job than on what the candidate is worth. If, for example, he has budgeted the job at $50,000 or $60,000 a year, and he finds out that you are making $28,000, it's unlikely that he'll offer you more than $34,000, even though he was willing to pay a lot more. Why? He knows he's in a buyer's market and your alternative is to stay where you are and continue making $28,000.

He's not about to offer you a 50 percent increase when he can probably get you for a 20 percent increase.

So what do you do when he asks what you're making?

What you do *not* do is lie. You always run the risk of his verifying what you tell him. If you decide to answer the question, but tell him you're making more than you actually are and he asks you for a W-2 or tax return or payroll stub, what can you say? If you refuse, he'll assume that you were lying and will probably reject you on that basis alone. Once you've answered the question, you're in a difficult position to deny his efforts to verify what you have told him.

An exception is that you can always refuse to supply a copy of your tax return when an interviewer requests it. Simply tell him that you never reveal such private and confidential information to anyone. He has no legal authority to ask for such a legal document, and you have no obligation to supply it. The problem is that if he wants to verify what you've told him, he'll ask for some other type of verification, and you can't logically refuse a request he might make to have your present employer supply verification.

You do have one ploy you can try if he asks you for salary information before discussing what he is willing to pay for the position. Before you reply, you can ask what the position pays. This turns the tables on him. The problem with asking this is that you risk being offensive. But if you are earning a very low salary in relation to what you want and what you think he's willing to pay, you've got to try something that will deflect him from his course of finding out your salary. It's possible that this query will permanently keep him off the subject, although it's not likely.

The advantage is that if he's broaching salary by asking how much you make, he's indicating he's interested. You must try to get him to reveal a salary range before you reveal how much you're making. If he tells you the range before you tell him that you make much less than that, it would be difficult and awkward for him to offer you less than the range he reveals. If you tell him your salary before he reveals the range, when he does indicate the range, it'll be a lot lower than it was before you revealed your salary.

So the one rule to remember if you have a very low salary is to try to get him to tell you the salary range of the position for which you're interviewing *before* you tell him how much you're making.

That said, however, the best advice I can give is, don't reveal your salary and don't be coy. Don't enter into a game with all its attendant evasive language. In the end I can't see any objection to just raising the issue directly. If you're asked, there's nothing wrong in saying something like, "I'm really uncomfortable discussing what my salary was in the past or what it might be where I am now. Frankly, I don't think it should be relevant to what you might be offering. Let's say that you are offering a huge salary, far above anything I've ever made in the past. Would what I made in the past have any effect on whether or not you hire me or pay me the huge salary?"

Then I'd wait for a response. Then I'd go on, if the interviewer persisted in asking for salary information, and say, "I just don't want to discuss my salary history. I'm not ashamed of it, but it has nothing to do with what I can do for you. I might be willing to take less if I think this job has a lot of potential. On the other hand, if I feel like I'm grossly underpaid, I would obviously want more. But neither of those possibilities has anything to do with how well I can perform."

If I got an interviewee who was articulate and diplomatic like this and who stood up for what he or she thought was right, I'd admire it. It would be a plus.

There comes a time when you must have the courage of

your convictions. And your conviction here must be that how much you make is nobody's business and has no relevance to your qualifications for the job. This might be difficult for you to assert and maintain because an interviewer might aggressively pursue the information. In fact, the interviewer might take the position that the information is required and that if you don't give it, the interview will come to an end. I feel you should stick to your guns.

Here's a situation that was faced by sports agent Bob Woolf, relayed in his book *Friendly Persuasion: My Life as a Negotiator* (G. P. Putnam's Sons, 1990). Woolf was in the running to be picked as the agent for Larry Bird, who was just coming out of Indiana State University. He had been drafted after his junior year by the Boston Celtics and needed someone to negotiate for him. A committee had been formed in Indiana to help Bird pick his agent. Originally, there were sixty-five people on the list of potential agents. Over time it had been whittled down to two, Woolf and Cincinnati attorney Reuven Katz, who represented baseball immortals Johnny Bench and Pete Rose.

Woolf went through several board interviews. At the last one, a meeting at which Bird was present, Woolf answered all the questions. When the meeting ended, Bird drove him back to his hotel. Woolf picks up the story:

I was surprised and pleased when Bird drove me back to my room at the Holiday Inn. In the car, I told him that I admired his loyalty to [former Los Angeles Dodgers and New York Yankees Pitcher] Tommy John and his sense of decency. He responded with a shrug, but he talked easily the rest of the ride and I felt we had made genuine contact. I was almost certain I would get Larry as a client.

Back in my room, I called home to tell my wife, Anne, about the meeting, and how confident I felt about the prospect of representing him. My entire family was happy for me. We were all Boston fans and sensed that Larry Bird was going to be very special for Boston.

I had no sooner hung up and propped myself on the bed, when the phone rang. "Bob, this is Lucien Meis," the voice said. He was the department store owner on the committee. "Larry and some of us would like to come over to the motel and chat with you again." I couldn't tell whether this was good news or trouble and during the time it took them to reach my room I began to feel extremely anxious.

When the group arrived, Meis was the spokesman. "Look, Bob, this is the situation," he said. "The selection has been narrowed down to you and Reuven Katz. . . . We have got to know from you exactly what you are going to charge as your fee for representing Larry. Will it be $10,000? $40,000? Give us a dollar figure. We have got to know exactly what it is. Mr. Katz has given us a figure and we need one from you."

I felt my stomach tighten. The question had come up before. When they pressed, I had resisted answering. There was no way I could even approximate a figure that far in advance. I had no idea how long the negotiation would take or what the actual work would involve. I had explained to the committee that I did not work on a flat-fee basis. I have always worked on a percentage, with a maximum fee of 5 percent of the client's annual salary. The fairness of this practice has been upheld time and again over the years. This was the working relationship I had established with all my clients.

"Look," I said, addressing Meis, "I understand why you're asking me and I respect Larry's desire to know how much it will cost him. But I want to work with Larry the same way I have worked with everyone else. At the end of the negotiations when Larry has a contract, then we will agree upon a fee. I cannot give you a figure now. It wouldn't be fair to my other clients if I was to make a special adjustment in order to work with Larry. I want to represent him very much. I consider this a special opportunity. But I just can't give you the answer you want."

Meis stared at me. "Well, look, we just want to be sure that you understand the consequences," he said. The consequences, of course, were that I would not get Larry Bird as my client. Meis continued, "We're asking you again, give us a set figure and we can wrap this up. Chances are, I've got to tell you, that without it you will not be representing Larry Bird. Please give us a figure." Bird was sitting there watching.

Quickly I tried to calculate the possibilities. In Boston, where I lived, Larry Bird was already being canonized and his potential was unlimited. But if I compromised my basic way of working with him, then I shortchanged every one of my clients.

I took a deep breath. "I can't give you a figure," I said. "I can only repeat that my fee will be reasonable and I will work hard on Larry's behalf. But I will not treat Larry Bird any differently than anyone else I represent and I am prepared to accept the consequences." We all shook hands and they walked out of the room.

You can only stand and look at a door for so long. I felt righteous but miserable. I called home again and told Anne, "You won't believe what just happened." But she did, even the part about my apparently losing Bird as a client. My son Gary, then a teenager, picked up the extension phone and said, "It's all right, Dad. I'm proud of you. You still have your principles and I'm glad that's what you did."

The principles might strike some as slightly fuzzy, but you cannot tailor your standard to fit that day's opportunity. It appeared that I had kept my principles, but at the cost of some substantial figure earnings and prestige. It sounds mighty noble to talk about putting honor above profit, but as clear a choice as that is supposed to be, in the real workplace it isn't.

Five minutes later, the phone rang.

"Bob, this is Lu Meis. I just wanted to tell you we've made our decision. We thought we shouldn't wait until morning to let you know."

"Yes?" I felt weary and drained and not very talkative. I braced for the bad news.

"We've decided on you."

I was shocked . . . and thrilled. "You're kidding!"

"No, Bob," Meis said. "We know how much you want to represent Larry, how much it means to you and how much time and effort you put into coming here. We decided that if you would stand up to us the way you did, stick to a position and just walk away, you are the kind of man we want negotiating for Larry against Red Auerbach" (the legendary General Manager of the Boston Celtics, with a reputation as a tough bargainer).

If you make the decision to keep your salary confidential and not reveal it to anyone, stick to it. If you once take the position and then relent, you could be showing weakness that might not be respected. My feeling is that this is the best way to handle the revelation of your salary if you are making less than the job pays and you think that knowledge might hurt you. Two benefits are likely to result from this. First, you won't be revealing information you think could hurt you. Second, you could be showing yourself as someone with principles.

I don't give this advice lightly, and I follow it myself. A woman I was dating knew that I had been in a relationship with another woman, a woman she knew, and that I had almost married the other woman. One evening she started querying me about my prior relationship and what had happened to cause us not to marry. I told her I didn't feel comfortable discussing it with her. She persisted. I repeated that I just didn't feel right talking about something that was personal to someone else. She said, "Well, if you don't tell me these things, how am I going to get to know you?" I replied by asking her a rhetorical question. "How," I asked, "would you feel if we went together for a while and then broke up and then I discussed the reasons with some other woman?" I wasn't going to compromise my principles to continue the relationship with her. If it was going to cause an end to a budding relationship, so be it. I wasn't interested in pursuing it if she wasn't intelligent enough to respect the fact that if I could be discreet about a prior relationship, I would also be discreet about ours.

On the other hand, I would be remiss in not mentioning that this strategy could result in your not being considered further. It's a decision you must make.

When You're Asked How Much You Want

If you are sure you know how much you want and you express this in an interview, you must stick with it. Backing down will leave the impression that you are indecisive and lack integrity.

Many years ago, when a lawyer's pay was much lower than today, a young lawyer told me about his experience. He had interviewed with the general counsel for a fairly large corporation, and when the subject of salary came up, he said that he would accept nothing less than $30,000. The interviewer said that this was beyond his budget, and tried to persuade him to accept $25,000. The candidate was firm. He wanted $30,000. Impressed, the interviewer recommended the candidate to the general counsel of another corporation who was also looking for an experienced attorney.

The interview with the second company went well, too, and when it came time to discuss salary, the young lawyer again said that he wanted $30,000. The interviewer, a dynamic individual, said that $26,000 was tops. The candidate hesitated. He was very interested in working for this second company, and the salary offer was closer to his goal. Besides, he had already priced himself out of one job and was probably afraid it might happen again. So he asked for time to think about it.

The next day, the second interviewer called and told him that the offer was no longer open. Then the candidate called the first interviewer to see if the $25,000 offer was still good and was told that he was "too heavy" for the job. From having two corporations pursuing him, he was down to zero. What had happened? Simple. He had come across very strongly as a man who knew his worth and was willing to walk away from any offer less than $30,000. This was impressive and earned him the respect of both interviewers. But when he showed interest at a lower figure, it was a sign of equivocation that caused the interviewers to lose respect for him, resulting in rejection.

Had the young lawyer been more sophisticated or analyzed his position more carefully, he would have recognized the $26,000 offer as a blatant ploy. Since the first general counsel had recommended him to the second company, he could safely assume that the second counsel already knew that he wanted $30,000 and had turned down an offer of $25,000. He should have drawn the conclusion that the second company was willing to pay him what he wanted or they would not have wasted time interviewing him. The $26,000 offer was simply a part of their interview technique to test his character.

Once you present something as a requirement, you cannot back down, so don't paint yourself into a corner by trying a bluff you really don't believe in and are not willing to back all the way. Oscar-winning director Frank Capra tells of his first interview with Mack Sennett, the "king of comedy" in the 1920s, and it is a good example of setting a requirement and sticking with it.

Capra had been writing "Our Gang" comedies for Hal Roach. But he wanted to be a director, so a friend arranged an interview with Felix Adler, the head writer at Sennett's production company. After a short conversation with Adler he was introduced to John Waldron, Sennett's accountant, who offered $35 per week. Capra turned it down, saying that he already got $40 at Roach.

Waldron wasn't impressed, saying that the rule was that beginners start at $35. Capra responded that he felt to take less than what he had been making would be going in the wrong direction. Waldron icily replied that one works for Sennett, he's at the top, and that $35 was his only offer. Capra could take it or leave it.

Capra said, "I swallowed hard [and said], 'Then I'll leave it, Mr. Waldron.' . . . My knees shook. I blew it. My big chance to work at Sennett's—and I blew it."

On the way out they stopped by Sennett's office. Waldron mentioned to Sennett that Capra wouldn't accept the beginner's $35 and that he wanted $45. Sennett asked Capra why he thought he was worth $45. Capra said, "Mr. Sennett, what's the difference what you pay me? If you don't think I'm worth it you'll fire me in two minutes anyway."

Sennett said that it was $35 or nothing, that he wouldn't break any of his own rules.

Capra replied, "Mr. Sennett, I'm not asking you to break *any* rules. John Waldron starts me on the books at $35. Okay? Tomorrow you raise me to $45. Everybody's happy and no rules broken."

Capra got the job. He knew what he wanted and was willing to walk away from the job rather than compromise. He stuck to his guns and got what he wanted.

But there's something else to be learned by this story. Capra wasn't just adamant about what he got. He recognized that Sennett had a problem, too, a rule that everyone started at $35. Instead of just demanding $45, he came up with a solution that took care of Sennett's problem, but got him what he wanted, starting at $35 and being raised the next day to $45. This is an essential part of negotiating, trying to work together to resolve each party's concerns. Capra was smart enough to figure out a way to get what he wanted by finding a way to work with Sennett's requirement.

How Much Money You Need

In order to come out of the salary negotiation phase of your interview with self-respect, you need to plan and prepare by looking deeply into yourself and deciding the parameters of what you *must* have and what you would *like* to have. In discussing what you *must* have, you aren't losing anything by taking a firm stand. In discussing points that you desire but can survive without, always leave yourself an escape so that you can give in without losing face.

Determining the difference between your needs and your desires is an essential part of your preparation, and it requires an honest analysis of yourself. How much money you need and how much you desire are two completely different things.

You can determine how much you need by preparing a simple budget. How much does it cost you to live? Write down your rent or mortgage payment, how much you spend on food each month, what your car payments are, how much you spend on clothes, utilities, gasoline, cleaning, and so forth. Then check this with your monthly bank reconciliations for the past year. You may find that your memory is faulty and you're spending more than you realize. In any event, know exactly how much you have to earn in order to live. This is your basic salary requirement. You may *desire* more money (don't we all?), but you can live on this amount. So if worse comes to worst and an offer is made for a job you would enjoy and it meets this amount, you can take it without feeling that you are making a financial mistake.

Ensure That Your Wants Are Logical

Many years ago I was advising a friend of a friend who was a job applicant. We took a break for lunch, and he drove me to a restaurant on the beach. He drove a truck, which at that time was unusual for an attorney, and en route I asked him why. "Money doesn't mean anything to me," he replied. "I don't have to work, so I just do what I want. As a result, I can't afford a big car, so I drive this truck."

During lunch our counseling session continued, and he revealed that he had just been offered a job with great opportunity but had turned it down. When I asked why, he said that they were offering him only $27,500 and he felt he was "worth more than that."

I asked him how much he made at his last job, and he said $23,000. He was currently making less than $20,000. The reason he felt that he was worth more was that his friends all

earned more than that. This is the way many people judge
their worth, but it's completely irrelevant unless the friends all
have the same background, education, training, experience,
and personality. Here was a man who had never made more
than $23,000 in his life turning down an attractive job offer for
20 percent more than he had ever made, because it wasn't
enough money.

Had I been interviewing him for a job, I would probably
have dropped him right there. First, he told me he didn't care
about money, and then he said he turned down an attractive
position solely because of money—an apparent inconsistency.
Second, he had a grossly inflated value of himself based upon a
false syllogism: My friends make more than $27,500; they are
my friends; therefore, I am worth more than $27,500.

The error of this reasoning is clear. But it was not his faulty
reasoning that would have spelled the coup de grâce for him
with me. It was the inconsistency in his telling me how he disdained money, yet the sole reason he had for rejecting a fine
offer was money.

You cannot base your salary upon what other people are
making. For one reason, pay for the same job varies widely
from company to company and from location to location. Just
as an example, at one point the lowest pay for an administrative
assistant/executive secretary in Bakersfield, California, was
only 70 percent of the highest pay for the same job in Los
Angeles. Lowest pay for a secretary was 62 percent of the highest pay for the same job in Los Angeles. A receptionist with
typing skills in Bakersfield made only 73 percent of what was
paid for the same job in San Francisco.

You have a right to expect to be paid a reasonable salary and
benefits in return for your work, and you shouldn't be shy
about discussing them frankly and openly. But you must be
pragmatic about what you want and what you feel you are

worth. Don't worry about what your friends are making. That's irrelevant to what you should earn. Determine what *you* need, what *you* want, and what *you'll* settle for and know these three figures going into the interview.

Women's Pay

In October 2003 the most comprehensive government study to date on women's earnings, by the congressional General Accounting Office, shows that the gap between men's and women's earnings has stubbornly persisted over the past two decades, even when employment and demographic factors are taken into account.

Workingwomen today are paid an average of eighty cents for every dollar that men are paid, even when such factors as occupation, industry, race, marital status, and job tenure are accounted for. This gap remained consistent from 1983 to 2000, despite a sense of continued progress toward gender equality in the workplace.

Women in the workforce are also less likely to work a full-time schedule and are more likely to leave the labor force for longer periods of time than men, further suppressing women's wages. These differing work patterns lead to an even larger earnings gap between men and women—suggesting that workingwomen are penalized for their dual role as wage earner and homemaker.

Men with children appear to get an earnings boost, whereas women with children actually lose earnings. Men with children are paid about 2 percent more on average than men without children, according to the GAO findings, whereas women with children are paid about 2.5 percent *less* than women without children.

The following was prepared by the office of Carolyn Maloney, congresswoman from New York:

THE MORE THINGS CHANGE . . .

	1983	2000
World population	4,690,492,539	6,079,006,982
Total number of Internet hosts	562	93,000,000
Dow Jones daily average	1,190	10,729.4
Mobile phone subscribers in U.S.	First introduced	109,500,000
Most-watched television show	*Dallas*	*Survivor*
Woman's earnings for every male dollar	80.4 cents	79.7 cents

There is continuing controversy about the level of women's pay compared with men's. The theory of comparable worth has been developed to eliminate what many consider to be an insidious form of sex discrimination.

Comparable worth, however, is a concept that is, at present, mostly talk, and not something upon which you can rely. Some laws have been passed to make things closer to being equal. The Equal Pay Act of 1963 ensures that women who perform the same work as men will receive the same pay. This covers employees engaged in commerce or the production of goods for commerce and includes all state and local government employees and most federal employees. But it does not cover equivalent work that is not identical.

Title VII of the Civil Rights Act of 1964 makes it unlawful to discriminate against any individual with respect to compensation, terms, conditions, or privileges of employment, because of such individual's sex. Anyone complaining must prove that the employer's wage policy has a disproportionately adverse impact on a group protected under Title VII for disparate treatment or for disparate impact.

Lynn Weir, a Seattle attorney, summarizes how an aggrieved party can prove liability under Title VII:

> In a disparate treatment claim, a plaintiff seeks to prove that an employer intentionally treats some people less favorably than others because of their race, color, religion, sex, or national origin; in a disparate impact claim, a plaintiff challenges employment practices that are facially neutral in their treatment of different groups but that in fact fall more harshly on one group than another and cannot be justified by business necessity. To prevail on a disparate impact theory, a plaintiff need not prove a discriminatory motive.

I include this short and superficial mention of Title VII so that you will realize that when your interview turns to a discussion of salary, you may still be at a disadvantage and that, even though there are laws that attempt to grant equal treatment, they are not perfect, nor do they adequately solve the problem of unequal pay.

What's important in the context of the job interview is that you are aware of the problem. How you handle it—whether you want to fight for equal rights and equal treatment as opposed to getting a job regardless of whether or not a man doing similar work makes more—is up to you. The important thing is for you to be prepared for the difference. Even if you feel you're being treated unfairly, handle it as professionally as you can. Consistent with what I've said earlier, if you feel strongly about an issue such as this, it's much better to deal with it head-on and express your emotions than to sublimate them. Just express them in an agreeable manner. No matter how firmly you speak, you should do it cordially.

Negotiation Rules

Fred Allen once said that an agent's heart would fit in a flea's navel with room left over. Maybe, but that description wouldn't fit sports agent Bob Woolf, discussed earlier. Woolf was an agent with ethics (quoting Arnold Glasgrow, "Don't part company with your ideals. They are anchors in a storm"). If money got in the way of principle, Woolf let his client go somewhere else. It was Woolf's emphasis on ethical behavior that made him the best. He had a list of 101 rules on how to negotiate. They're listed in his excellent book *Friendly Persuasion*, which you should read if you're negotiating salary. I'll mention the more important rules here.

1. Try to get the other side to make the first offer. As we've noted, this is extremely important, because once you've mentioned what you want, you've almost certainly set a maximum on what you can get. And that maximum could be well below your interviewer's minimum! I can speak from experience. When I was a young lawyer in the early 1970s, I had just resigned from Litton Industries to start my own practice and I was short of work. One day an executive with whom I had worked at Litton called. He had taken a new position as president of another major corporation, needed some legal help on the East Coast, and wondered if I was available for a few weeks. I said sure. He asked how much he'd have to pay. I thought for a while. He broke the silence by saying, "Don't hold me up, now." I quoted him $500 a week plus all my expenses, which was a lot more than I had been taking home at Litton. He didn't say much but told me to meet him at the plane in a couple of days for the trip East. I was happy. When he got to the plane, he said he had discussed my fee with his controller, and neither thought I should be paid so little, so they were going to pay me $700 a week. I later found out that they were expecting to pay between $1,000 and $1,500 per week.

I learned an important lesson from that experience. It wouldn't have hurt me at all to have turned the tables on him by responding, "Make me an offer." That puts the ball in his court. If he persisted in trying to get me to state what I wanted first, I could have responded, "It's difficult for me to set a figure because I don't know what's involved. You are in a far better position to tell me what it's worth for me to do some work for you, so I'd really appreciate it if you would tell me." At that point, I think he would have offered $1,000, and I would have been in much better shape. At least it would have told me what the starting point was and maybe I could have asked for $1,100 or $1,200, always knowing that I would gleefully accept the $1,000 (which I eventually got, but it took several months), if that was his bottom line. Of course, the ability to ask your interviewer to make you an offer depends on the status of the negotiations and your relationship with your interviewer. In this situation, he had approached me and we had a prior relationship.

2. Don't get angry because the offer isn't what you wanted.

3. Determine how much room the other side has to move. Hearken back to my earlier advice about needs and desires. If there's a big difference between the two, you've got plenty of room in which to negotiate. Further, the first offer is just that, an offer. You can diplomatically test the waters to see how firm it is.

4. Try to assess the other side's weaknesses. Has the job been open very long? How many people have been interviewed? If they've been looking for a while and have talked to a lot of people, this gives you a strong position, because either they are very particular or the people they've been interested in haven't been interested in them. This means that they might need you more than you need them.

5. Assess your leverage. Are the job qualifications unique? Are your qualifications unique? If the job is one requiring specialized skills or qualifications and you have them, then your leverage is pretty high. If the job is one that could be done by a large number of people, and all they're looking for is a personality fit, your leverage is probably not too good. But if the person for whom you would be working is difficult to get along with and you have the unique ability to get along in a difficult personality mix, your leverage improves.

6. Make your presentation logically. When it gets down to actually talking numbers and you're far enough apart, you should be able to present your case as to why you're worth what you want in a cogent and reasonable manner. Lay out why you're worth it in terms of qualifications, personality, experience, and whatever other attributes you feel are relevant. But discuss each facet in turn. Don't shotgun the presentation, or the interviewer may think you're just talking off the top of your head, mentioning anything that floats in. It's much better to present each reason as a separate entity and discuss it rationally and fully before moving on to the next.

7. Start high but don't be ridiculous. As we've said, the theorem "I want $X because my friends all make that much" won't get you very far. If you've done your preparation as I've suggested, you should have a good feel for the range that the job should pay. There's nothing wrong in asking for the top of the range, but if you ask for something that's way over the top, you'll probably not be seriously considered any further, no matter how interested they were in you at first.

8. Don't give information, try to get information. Ah, this is where the skill of the interviewee comes to the fore. If the interviewer broaches the question first by asking how much you want, you can easily turn the tables on him by asking him some questions about the job. You can rationally say that before you arrive at that conclusion, you need to know more about what the job entails and how profitable the company or division or activity is. You can definitely ask what the company pays employees in similar positions, along with the salary range that is being considered. Resist, if you can, mentioning your needs or desires before you get this information.

9. Make sure the other side knows you want but don't *need* a job. Maybe that's not the case, but if you're in desperate straits and your interviewer knows that, you almost totally destroy your negotiating position. You've got to appear to be looking, not begging. Remember that the interview is a two-way street. Not only are they interviewing you for a position, but you're interviewing them to see if you *want* to work for them. If you can keep it on this level, your negotiating position will be on more even footing than you may feel it is.

10. Be flexible. If you present yourself in the light of, "This is what I want and I'm not going to consider anything else," you are doing extreme damage to your interview. Not only will you risk getting the response of, "Well, thanks for coming in, but we can't afford that," but you also give the impression of being intractable and stubborn, and this could result in an unfavorable inference that could ruin the good you've done up until then. So learn how to present your desires in a friendly, nonconfrontational manner, leaving yourself room to backtrack without losing face.

11. Keep a record of each conversation. I mentioned this earlier and it's vitally important. You might have many interviews with many different people or many interviews with the same person, and you don't want to be inconsistent. It's easy to forget what you've said and the numbers you've mentioned, especially if there's a substantial difference between your needs and your desires. So make a record of each interview as soon as possible after the interview ends and be as detailed as possible.

12. Never raise or lower your demand before you've been asked to do so. This might seem pretty elementary, but a sophisticated interviewer can make you feel like you want him to like you, so you might want to show your good faith by lowering your demand. This can be a big temptation, especially if negotiations have gone on for an extended period. It's like when you own a stock. When it goes up, and you should be considering selling, the urge is to hold; when it goes down, and you should be considering holding, the urge is to sell. So, too, in an interview the urge is to reach agreement and you feel the best way to reach that agreement is to give a little. Don't do it unless you're prompted to by a request from the other side.

13. Don't give tit for tat. This is a corollary to the prior rule. If the person with whom you're negotiating raises the offer voluntarily, your impulse might be to come down an equal amount. Don't. There's no logical connection between how much your interviewer comes up and how much you come down. In fact, you don't have to come down *at all*. People sometimes think that in order to show good faith when the other side moves, you have to move. Not true, and don't succumb to it. Perhaps a countermove by you is called for. But perhaps it's not. Whatever, a countermove by you is not automatically called for in response to a move by the other side.

14. Don't split the difference. Another corollary. You might be $X apart, and he offers to come up halfway if you'll come down half, so you think, "What the heck, let's get this over with." Or "That's fair; he's giving and I'm giving and it's equal." But if you think about it, your interviewer has made a major mistake. He's already given you a number and raised it, and you haven't come down a penny! Woolf calls this a major point. "Don't snap at the bait, no matter how tempting it may be as a way to get nearly all you want and end the negotiation. Be a smart negotiator and you will earn a little more without offending anybody."

15. Don't let them intimidate you. You shouldn't have to think too much about this point. They wouldn't be negotiating salary with you if they were not very interested. So there's no way they can intimidate you if you always keep this truth uppermost in your mind during the negotiations.

16. Be patient. Unless they give you an ultimatum, you have plenty of time. No negotiation is much fun, and you will almost always feel self-imposed pressure to end it. Try to resist this feeling as much as you can. The negotiations will continue until you reach an impasse. That impasse will be reached when you've got them as high as they're going to go. When you know that, then you can make a decision. But they are the ones who need the employee, so, unless you're starving, you should view time as your ally, not theirs.

17. If you have what you want, don't let it go further. Or, put another way, don't be greedy. While you don't want to accept less than their minimum, as I did years ago, if you've had fairly detailed negotiations and finally have what you want and need, take it and start work. If you prolong the negotiations, you run the risk of alienating them to the point where they might withdraw the offer, or, worse, they might find someone they want more than they want you.

18. Don't be afraid to leave something on the table. So what if you don't get the absolute maximum they might have been willing to pay? That's something you may never find out. And rather than risk losing an offer that would satisfy you in the hope of getting a few more dollars, it's better to grab what you want when you can get it and leave something on the table. If it's true that they got you for a little less than they were willing to pay, they'll feel they got a bargain, and that can result in better treatment and a good atmosphere.

19. Don't ever burn your bridges. You never know when you might want to come back and ask for a job again. So if things don't work out, depart on a cordial note. Thank them for their time and interest. If they reject you, take it with good cheer. Put yourself in their place. It's not easy to turn someone down, so this will leave a good taste in their mouth and you can never have too much goodwill. If you do the rejecting, do it as gently as possible with a good, cogent explanation and depart with thanks and in a friendly manner. As I said, sometime down the line, you could be looking for work there again.

I have another personal example to tell about this point. I was representing a major NYSE corporation that was wrapping up a housing development operation in Clearwater, Florida. They had built a low-income housing project, but the transfer to the Local Housing Authority had been stalled because of a sinkage problem and the insistence that my client construct an outflow line to the tune of almost $100,000.

Although I had been retained only as an attorney, I had volunteered to act as project manager on several troubled projects to get them completed and conveyed. This one was proving to be horrible. People on the other side seemed to react irrationally to everything I proposed to settle the matter.

Finally, we arranged a meeting in Jacksonville, Florida, with HUD representatives. My client's corporate controller was there representing the company, since I wasn't an employee, even though I was in charge. After we went through everything that we had discussed before, I said that the city engineer for Clearwater had a document to which we had agreed and which I understood would solve the problem. The HUD representative was dubious and wanted to see the document.

This was in 1974 and we were in the midst of a horrible oil shortage. It was also before fax machines. I had to go to Clearwater to get it. It was 4 p.m. and the next meeting was at 8 a.m. the following day. I couldn't fly because it was springtime and the Tampa Airport was often fogged in. I asked the controller if he wanted to drive over with me, a round-trip of approximately four hundred miles. He said yes.

So we drove to Clearwater, arriving around midnight, and called the city engineer, awakening him. He said he'd be glad to meet us at City Hall and give me the document, which he did. Now we had to get back, but we didn't have enough gas, and all the gas stations were closed. So the city engineer volunteered to take some gas out of his boat and give it to us. We drove to the Clearwater Marina and siphoned gasoline from his boat into our car and drove back to Jacksonville, arriving at around 7 a.m., just enough time for me to shower and shave and get to the eight o'clock meeting.

I showed the document to the HUD representative, and he threw it back at me, saying, "This isn't worth the paper it's printed on." I thanked them all and said there was no further reason to continue the meeting and left.

When we got out of the room, the controller was almost apoplectic. "What's all that 'thank you' nonsense? Why were you so calm? I couldn't believe it!" he told me. I said that getting angry wouldn't accomplish anything, that we had done the best we could and now we should think about what else we could do, although there wasn't much left to consider.

Almost immediately, the administrator of the Local Housing Authority in Clearwater contacted me, we met, and within two weeks I was at a party celebrating the conveyance of the property to the Local Housing Authority. The administrator came up to me and asked if I had noticed a change in attitude. I said that I certainly had. He asked if I knew why, and I said I didn't have a clue.

He explained to me that everyone who had held my position before me had said whatever they could to get the LHA to agree to do things, but their promises were always unfulfilled. So when I came into the picture, they all thought I was just another corporate guy who would continue to make false representations. But when I drove all night to get that paper, it made him and everyone in Clearwater realize that I was really trying to solve the problem and that I was honest and reliable. They realized that they could trust me and work with me, which they did.

I could have easily lost my temper and burned a bridge when

the HUD representative treated me so rudely. But you never know how people are judging you or how they are thinking. I certainly didn't do what I did to impress anyone. That's just the way I work. But, unknown to me, they were always judging me, and this was a result that was totally unforeseen, a result that wouldn't have occurred had I burned my bridge by reacting as the controller suggested.

Never burn a bridge.

20. Use common sense.

Vacation

Don't refrain from asking about vacation. Employers do not expect their employees to work fifty-two weeks a year (they may want them to, but they don't expect it). Vacation is one of the most important elements of a job, and you should not shrink from asking about it. Most of the interviewers with whom I've spoken expect—and welcome—questions about vacation. You will not be jeopardizing receiving further consideration by letting the interviewer know that you are interested in the vacation and other job benefits. It's much better for you to ask about it before you receive an offer. Where are you if you take a job and then find out that you get one day off a year? If you knew that before, it would probably have kept you from accepting an offer.

R. E. Taylor, who was vice president of personnel administration for the Bank of America, stated a typical view:

> It's not a negative to ask about vacation. It's our experience that it's very important to people today. When I applied for a job, I just wanted a job. We find that people's

expectations are greater and more varied than they were. Leisure time is important to them. They're concerned about the environment and where they want to live and work. It's very important to them. We have people asking, "Can I work downtown in the Towers?" "Can I work by the beach?" I don't think we can afford to have that type of question be a turnoff.

The general rule relating to vacations and benefits is that, like salary, they are items you should not bring up until the interviewer has raised the subject or has let you know that he is definitely interested in you. Once you have determined that, you should find out as much as you can about the job—what it pays and what the responsibilities and benefits are.

Checklist

- Don't bring up the subject of salary yourself until they have shown keen interest.
- The interviewer won't want to discuss salary until he has made an initial determination that he is interested in you.
- If it appears that the interview is ending with his expressing interest in seeing you again, then you can ask about salary.
- If you raise the subject yourself, don't beat around the bush.
- You must do research into yourself before you go into the interview.
- Make a budget to determine how much money you must have.
- Don't base what you want on what your friends are making.

- Make a list of the things you have to offer an employer.
- Try to find out what the job pays before you reveal what you want.
- Feel free to be adamant about not revealing your salary and wage history.
- If you decide to take a position that you will not reveal your salary and wage history, don't back down.
- Don't give the interviewer a copy of your tax return.
- After he has revealed his interest in you, ask about vacation and benefits.
- Don't burn your bridges.

14

Discrimination and Legal Remedies

The law relating to what may and may not be asked is simple. Questions may not be asked for the purpose of discriminating on the basis of race, color, religion, sex, national origin, birthplace, age, disability, or any other protected class.

Federal laws don't expressly prohibit an interviewer from asking questions about your race, color, religion, or national origin, but the Equal Employment Opportunity Commission (EEOC) has issued a statement saying that it regards such inquiries with "extreme disfavor." It also says:

> Except in those infrequent instances where religion or national origin is a bona fide occupational qualification reasonably necessary for the performance of a particular job, an applicant's race, religion and the like are totally irrelevant to his or her ability or qualifications as a prospective employee, and no useful purpose is served by eliciting such information.
>
> Accordingly, in the investigation of charges alleging the commission of unlawful employment practices the

Commission will pay particular attention to the use by the party against whom charges have been made of pre-employment inquiries concerning race, religion, color, or national origin, or other inquiries which tend directly or indirectly to disclose such information. The fact that such questions are asked may, unless otherwise explained, constitute evidence of discrimination, and will weigh significantly in the Commission's decision as to whether or not [the law] has been violated.

Basically, what you need to remember is that all questions should be job-related. The United States Supreme Court has said that "the touchstone is business necessity."

State laws on the subject are more specific. Each state has laws relating to employment practices. They are generally known as fair employment practices laws and forbid employment bias based on race, color, sex, age, religion, national origin, birthplace, or physical disability.

Most states prohibit employers from asking questions that might prove prejudicial. California law, for instance, prohibits "any non-job-related inquiry, whether verbal or through the use of an application form, which directly or indirectly limits a person's employment opportunities because of race, color ancestry, national origin, citizenship, age (40+), physical and mental disability, cancer, pregnancy, religion, gender, marital status, sexual orientation, military status, political affiliation, and genetic characteristics." Employers are to confine themselves to questions related to the applicant's qualifications for the job or potential for the job. It is all right to ask, "Can you perform the essential functions of the position for which you are applying with or without reasonable accommodation?" But it is illegal to ask, "Do you have any physical disabilities or handicaps?" It is all right to ask if the job seeker speaks a second language (if such skill is directly related to the position), but it is illegal to ask what the applicant's mother tongue is.

Most states publish lists of legal and illegal questions as a guideline for employees. Following are the lists for California and New York. For your state's list, contact the Fair Employment Practices Commission in your state. It may not be called that in each state (in New York, for instance, it's called the State Division of Human Rights), but a phone call to your nearest state employment office will guide you to the right office. If you have a question, don't hesitate to call your state office or the EEOC.

California
Pre-employment Inquiries

A list of acceptable and unacceptable inquiries employers may make prior to hiring an individual is reproduced below. The list has been issued by California's Department of Fair Employment and Housing.

The California Fair Employment Practice Act prohibits any non-job related inquiry, either verbal or through the use of an application form, which directly or indirectly limits a person's employment opportunities because of race, color, religion, national origin, ancestry, medical condition (cancer related), disability, marital status, sex, or age (40+). The regulations of the Fair Employment and Housing Commission define this to include any question which:

- Identifies a person on a basis covered by the Act; or
- Results in the disproportionate screening out of members of a protected group; or
- Is not a valid predictor of successful job performance.

It is the employer's right to establish job-related requirements and to seek the most qualified individual for the job.

It is presumed that the information obtained through application forms and interviews is used by the employer in making selection and assignment decisions. For this reason, the employer should make only those inquiries necessary to determine the applicant's eligibility to be considered for employment. Documents required for legitimate purposes which reveal protected information (such as birth certificates, naturalization papers, or medical histories) may be requested at the point of hire, not before. (The point of hire is reached once the employer has decided to hire and so informs the applicant.)

This guide is not intended to be an exhaustive compilation of all acceptable and unacceptable inquiries. The examples listed are representative of questions frequently asked. Those considered unacceptable are likely to limit the employment opportunities of persons protected by the FEP Act. For further detail, consult the Commission's Employment Regulations. These regulations and answers to questions on pre-employment inquiries can be obtained by writing to the Department of Fair Employment & Housing, 1201 1 Street, Sacramento, CA 95814.

COLLECTING APPLICANT FLOW DATA

It is now unlawful for an employer to collect applicant-flow and other record keeping data for statistical purposes. Employers are encouraged to solicit this information on a voluntary basis in order to comply with federal and state requirements and for affirmative action efforts.

It is recommended that the material be collected on a separate form or tear-off portion of the application and be filed separately. Misuse of this data constitutes a violation of the FEP Act.

ACCEPTABLE	SUBJECT	UNACCEPTABLE
Name. "Have you ever used another name?" or "Is any additional information relative to change of name, use of an assumed name, or nickname necessary to enable a check on your work and education record? If yes, please explain."	*Name*	Maiden name.
Place of residence.	*Residence*	"Do you own or rent your home?"
Statement that hire is subject to verification that applicant meets legal age requirements. "If hired can you show proof of age?" "Are you over eighteen years of age?" "If under eighteen, can you, after employment, submit a work permit?"	*Age*	Age. Date of birth. Dates of attendance of completion of elementary or high school. Questions which tend to identify applicants over age forty.
"Can you, after employment, submit verification of your legal right to work in the United States?" or statement that such proof may be required after employment.	*Birthplace* *Citizenship*	Birthplace of applicant, applicant's parents, spouse, or other relatives. "Are you a U.S. citizen?" or citizenship of applicant, applicant's parent, spouse, or other relatives.

ACCEPTABLE	SUBJECT	UNACCEPTABLE
		Requirements that applicant produce naturalization, first papers, or alien card *prior to employment*.
Languages applicant reads, speaks, or writes (if directly related to the position for which the person is applying).	*National origin*	Questions as to nationality, lineage, ancestry, national origin, descent, or parentage of applicant, applicant's parents or spouse.
		"What is your mother tongue?" or language commonly used by applicant.
		How applicant acquired ability to read, write, or speak a foreign language.
Name and address of parent or guardian if applicant is a minor. Statement of company policy regarding work assignment of employees who are related.	*Sex* *Marital status* *Family*	Questions which indicate applicant's sex.
		Questions which indicate applicant's marital status.
		Number and/or ages of children or dependents.
		Questions regarding pregnancy, childbearing, or birth control.
		Name or address of relative, spouse, or children of adult applicant.

ACCEPTABLE	SUBJECT	UNACCEPTABLE
		"With whom do you reside?" or "Do you live with your parents?"
	Race *Color*	Questions as to applicant's race or color.
		Questions regarding applicant's complexion or color of skin, eyes, hair.
Statement that photograph may be required after employment.	*Physical description* *Photograph*	Questions as to applicant's height and weight.
		Require applicant to affix a photograph to application.
		Request application, at his or her option, to submit a photograph.
		Require a photograph after interview but before employment.
State by employer that offer may be made contingent on applicant passing a job-related physical examination. "Can you perform the essential functions of the position for which you are applying with or without reasonable accommodations?"	*Physical condition* *Disability*	Questions regarding applicant's general medical condition, state of health, or illnesses. "Do you have any physical disabilities or handicaps?" Questions regarding receipt of Workers' Compensation.

ACCEPTABLE	SUBJECT	UNACCEPTABLE
Statement by employer of regular days, hours, or shifts to be worked.	*Religion*	Questions regarding applicant's religion. Religious days observed, or "Does your religion prevent you from working weekends or holidays?"
"Have you ever been convicted of a felony, or, within (specified time period) a misdemeanor which resulted in imprisonment?" (Such a question must be accompanied by a statement that a conviction will not necessarily disqualify applicant from the job applied for.) Note: California law prevents employers from seeking information concerning certain convictions, including convictions for marijuana use that are more than two years old.	*Arrest* *Criminal record*	Arrest record, or "Have you ever been arrested?"
Statement that bonding is a condition of hire.	*Bonding*	Questions regarding refusal or cancellation of bonding.

ACCEPTABLE	SUBJECT	UNACCEPTABLE
Questions regarding relevant skills acquired during applicant's U.S. military service.	*Military service*	General questions regarding military service such as dates, and type of discharge. Questions regarding service in a foreign military.
	Economic status	Questions regarding applicant's current or past assets, liabilities, or credit rating, including bankruptcy or garnishment.
"Please list job-related organizations, clubs, professional societies, or other associations to which you belong. You may omit those which indicate your race, religious creed, color, national origin, ancestry, sex, or age or any other protected class status."	*Organizations* *Activities*	"List all organizations, clubs, societies, and lodges to which you belong."
"By whom were you referred for a position here?" Names of persons willing to provide professional and/or character references for applicant.	*References*	Questions of applicant's former employers or acquaintances which elicit information specifying the applicant's race, color, religious creed, national origin, ancestry, physical disability, medical condition, marital status, age, or sex.

ACCEPTABLE	SUBJECT	UNACCEPTABLE
Name and address of person to be notified in case of accident or emergency.	*Notice in case of emergency*	Name and address of relative to be notified in case of accident or emergency.

New York
Sample Questions
Application for Employment

Personal Information
Date
Social Security Number
Name
Present Address
Permanent Address
Phone No.
If related to anyone in our employment, state name and
    department
Referred by

Employment Desired
Position
Date you can start
Are you employed now?
If so, may we inquire of your present employer?
Have you ever applied to this company before?
Where? When?

Education
(For grammar school, high school, college, trade, business, or
    correspondence school)
Name and location of school
Did you graduate?
Subjects studied
Subjects of special study or research work
What foreign languages do you speak fluently? Read? Write?

Activities (You may exclude those which indicate the race, creed, sex, marital status, age, color, national origin, or physical disability of its members.)

Former Employers
(List employers, starting with the most recent.)
Date (from/to)
Name and address of employer
Position
Reason for leaving

References
Name
Address
Business
Years Acquainted

Other
In case of emergency notify (name, address, phone no.).
I authorize investigation of all statements contained in this application.
I understand that misrepresentation or omission of facts called for is cause for dismissal.
Signature and date

Pre-employment Inquiries
The following Rulings on Inquiries were reflected in a pamphlet issued by the state Division of Human Rights on August 1, 1988.

Directly Revelatory Inquiries
The Law expressly prohibits employers,[1] employment agencies, landlords, and real estate sellers, brokers and salespersons, and creditors from asking certain questions either in an application form or in a personal interview before selecting an employee, apprentice or tenant or making a real estate or lease, or extending credit. The following are examples of different types of inquiries that have been ruled lawful or unlawful.

SUBJECT	LAWFUL	UNLAWFUL
Age	Are you eighteen years of age or older? If not, state your age.[2]	How old are you? What is your date of birth? What are the ages of your children, if any?
Arrest record	Have you ever been convicted of a crime? (Give details)[3]	Have you ever been arrested?
Birth control	None	Inquiry as to capacity to reproduce, advocacy of any form of birth control or family planning.
Disability[4]	None	Do you have a disability? Have you ever been treated for any of the following diseases . . . ? Do you have now, or have had, a drug or alcohol problem?

(It is *unlawful* to inquire, either directly or indirectly, about an applicant's/employee's disabilities. An employer may inquire only whether a prospective employee can perform specific tasks in a reasonable manner. An employer may not disqualify an applicant/employee because of suspected *future* risk to his/her health of performing a specific job.)

The above limitations apply equally to questions which may be asked of an employee who applies for or is under consideration for promotion, transfer, upgrading, etc.

They also apply equally to questions asked by a prospective employer, either orally, by telephone, in writing or otherwise, of a former employer, with reference to an applicant or a person under consideration for employment.

SUBJECT	LAWFUL	UNLAWFUL
Marital status	None	Do you wish to be addressed as Miss? Mrs.? Ms.? Are you married? Single? Divorced? Separated?
Marital status	None	Name or other information about spouse.
National origin	None	Inquiry into applicant's lineage, ancestry, national origin, descent, parentage, or nationality. Nationality of applicant's parents or spouse.
Race or color	None	Complexion or color of skin. Coloring.
Religion or creed	None	Inquiry into applicant's religious denomination, religious affiliations, parish or church, religious holidays observed. Applicant may not be told "This is a (Catholic, Protestant, or Jewish) organization."[5]
Sex	None	Inquiry as to gender.

INDIRECTLY REVELATORY INQUIRIES

It is unlawful to ask questions the answers to which will indirectly reveal information as to race, creed, color, national origin, sex, marital status, disability, age, or arrest record in cases where such information may not be asked directly. In making such rulings, the Division has applied a rule of reason, taking into account the need for the information asked as well as the danger that it will reveal other information that should not be considered in selection.

The following are Division rulings on inquiries indirectly revelatory of race, creed, color, national origin, sex, marital status, disability, or age:

SUBJECT	LAWFUL	UNLAWFUL
Address or duration of residence	Applicant's place of residence. How long a resident of this state or city?	
Birthdate	None	Requirements that applicant submit birth certificate, naturalization, or baptismal record.
Birthplace	None	Birthplace of applicant.
		Birthplace of applicant's parents, spouse, or other close relatives.
Citizenship	Are you a citizen of the United States? If not a citizen of the United States, do you intend to become a citizen of the United States? If you are not a United States citizen, have you the legal right to remain permanently in the United States? Do you intend to remain permanently in the United States?	Of what country are you a citizen? Whether an applicant is naturalized or a native-born citizen; the date when the applicant acquired citizenship. Requirement that applicant produce naturalization papers or first papers. Whether applicant's parents or spouse are naturalized or native-born citizens of the United States; the date when such parents or spouse acquired citizenship.

SUBJECT	LAWFUL	UNLAWFUL
Driver's license	Do you possess a valid NYS driver's license?	Requirement that applicant produce a driver's license.
Education	Inquiry into applicant's academic, vocational, or professional education and the public and private schools attended.	
Experience	Inquiry into work experience.	
Language	Inquiry into languages applicant speaks or writes fluently.	What is your native language? Inquiry into how applicant acquired ability to read, write, or speak a foreign language.
Military experience	Inquiry into applicant's military experience in the armed forces of the United States or in a state militia.	Inquiry into applicant's military experience other than in the armed forces of the United States or a state militia.
	Inquiry into applicant's service in particular branch of United States Army, Navy, etc. Did you receive a dishonorable discharge?[6]	Did you receive a discharge from the military in other than honorable circumstances?

SUBJECT	LAWFUL	UNLAWFUL
Name	Have you ever worked for this company under a different name?	Original names of an applicant whose name has been changed by court order or otherwise.
	Is additional information relative to change of name, use of an assumed name or nickname necessary to enable a check on your work record? If yes, please explain.	Maiden name of a married woman. If you have ever worked under another name, state name and address.
Notice in case of emergency	None	Name and address of person to be notified in case of an accident or emergency.
Organizations	Inquiry into applicant's membership in organizations which the applicant considers relevant to his or her ability to perform the job.	List all clubs, societies, and lodges to which you belong.
Photograph	None	Requirement or option that applicant affix a photograph to employment form at any time before hiring.
Relatives	Name of applicant's relatives already employed by the company.	Number, names, addresses, and ages of applicant's spouse, children, or relatives not employed by the company.

DISPARATE IMPACT INQUIRIES

Selection criteria which are facially neutral in their treatment of different groups but which impact more severely on one protected group and cannot be justified by business necessity are unlawful. Thus, inquiries which would otherwise be deemed lawful may, in certain circumstances, be deemed as evidence of unlawful discrimination when the inquiry seeks to elicit information about a selection criterion which has a disproportionately burdensome effect and the criterion is not job related. Such criteria may not be used as a basis for selecting employees, apprentices, or tenants or as a basis for deciding whether to make a real estate sale or lease. The inquirer may justify the making of such inquiry by the showing of a business necessity.

---

1. Polygraph testing: Inquiries which are unlawful when made by employers are also unlawful when made by polygraph testers as agents for employers. A federal law, effective 12/27/88, bans most employer use of polygraph tests. It bars pre-hiring polygraph screening and random testing and sets strict rules governing administration of polygraph tests to employees suspected of a particular wrongdoing. There are few exceptions from this ban in the law signed by the president on June 27, 1988.

2. Effective January 1, 1985, for public employers and January 1, 1986, for private employers, the maximum age limit for age discrimination purposes has been removed.

3. An applicant may not be denied employment because of a conviction record unless there is a direct relationship between the offense and the job or unless hiring would be an unreasonable risk. An ex-offender denied employment is entitled to a statement of the reason for such denial. Correction Law, Article 22-A, Sec. 754.

4. The Human Rights Law now extends coverage to those individuals who either have a record of a disabling condition or who are regarded by others as being disabled.

5. See Section 6, Disparate Impact Inquiries, infra.

6. Inquiries regarding military service should be accompanied by a statement that a dishonorable discharge is not an absolute bar to employment and that other factors will affect a final decision. This inquiry (as well as those related to age and marital status) may be asked after a person has been hired.

Other Legal Protections

Of course, there are laws that protect job applicants other than those relating to pre-employment inquiries. For example, the New York Human Rights Law prohibits employers from refusing to employ persons with disabilities that are unrelated to job performance. One woman who was five feet six inches tall and weighed 249 pounds was offered a job by Xerox subject to passing a pre-employment medical examination. The examining physician found her medically unacceptable because of her obesity, and she was refused employment. Xerox argued that obesity was not a present impairment but that it could refuse to hire the obese because of a statistical likelihood that obesity would produce impairment in the future and have an adverse impact on disability and life insurance programs. The woman was a widow and had raised five children after her husband died; she argued that her obesity constituted a disability but never prevented her from performing any task. The New York Court of Appeals held that her obesity constituted an impairment, and awarded her monetary damages for mental anguish and humiliation, plus back pay and a position at Xerox.

Age Discrimination

One extremely sensitive area involving unlawful pre-employment inquiries involves age. People forty years of age or older often have a difficult time finding jobs simply because of their age, even though the law specifically prohibits age discrimination. A job seeker who happens to be female, in addition to being forty or over, can feel as if she's starting out with two strikes against her. One forty-five-year-old woman attorney told me a story that epitomizes this problem and the way age discrimination can rear its ugly head when you least expect.

I was on my third interview with one of the largest firms in Sacramento. At that point I thought I was a shoo-in. I had to interview an older man who was on their management committee. We were talking about housing in Sacramento and where I would live. I mentioned that I'd like to live near my daughter because she would soon be moving to Germany with her husband.

He said, "Oh, you probably want to move up here so you can babysit your grandchildren." Then he paused and said, "Well, do you have any grandchildren?"

I did, but I smiled and said, "Well, I really don't think that's relevant," or something to that effect. It made me really uneasy because if I don't tell him, he's going to feel like I'm going to be uncooperative and secretive to work with. And if I do tell him, there's definitely a stigma attached to being a grandparent, and he's going to think I'll fall asleep in the afternoon, that I can't handle a regular fifty-hour workweek. Because I didn't answer the question, I felt I was being uncooperative.

Discriminatory questions in an interview are insidious, and this story shows how damaging they can be to an interviewee who is unprepared and/or does not know the law. Even if you know the law, as this woman did, being asked a question that probes prohibited areas can be devastating. The problem is that you're placed in a difficult position, as this woman so eloquently described. If you answer the question, you might be revealing information that could result in your losing an offer. If you don't answer it, you risk appearing uncooperative. If you challenge the question, you might appear argumentative.

How to Respond to an Unlawful Question

When you are asked a question that you feel must be challenged, you should deal with it head-on, immediately. That said, however, one point that I've hammered away at is that many selection interviewers are unsophisticated. They don't ask predetermined questions. They will ask you whatever pops into their heads. So they may ask you if you're religious because they are religious and wonder if you go to the same church or temple. In this event it would have nothing to do with whether or not they're going to hire you. Or you may be asked the derivation of your name because the interviewer (and for the balance of this chapter let's assume the interviewer is a woman) thinks you're nervous and this would be something you could talk about freely, not because you look Estonian and the interviewer hates all Estonians.

Remember, for the most part the interviewer is simply trying to find out what kind of person you are and whether she has a good feeling about you. So your best option in most cases, assuming your reply can't hurt you, is to answer the question, ignore the possibility of unlawful pre-employment inquiry, and go on with the interview.

But if the question bothers you, and you feel that the interviewer knows she's out of bounds, answer the question, but let the interviewer know that you know the law. One way to do it is to ask her if the question is an appropriate or lawful question to ask in a job interview. This puts the onus on the interviewer to defend the question. If you feel uncomfortable with the question and at the same time feel that your answer could hurt you, trust your feelings, decline to answer, and tell the interviewer of your feelings, in as nonthreatening a mode as possible, thereby putting her on notice that you are aware of the law and that she has entered a protected area. This is especially important if you feel your answer could cost you an offer, as the woman in the age discrimination story felt.

However, her method of handling it, by stating that she didn't think the question was "relevant," doesn't do the job. Far better to ask the interviewer if it's legal, which transfers the burden of defending the question to the interviewer and removes the onus of declining to answer from your shoulders. This also effectively challenges the legality of the question. "Relevance" and "legality" are two entirely different matters: There's nothing in the law that prohibits an interviewer from asking an irrelevant question. An easy way to challenge the legality of the question is to use a significant key word in asking the interviewer about the question. "Appropriate" is good. "Legal" is better. "Lawful" uses the terminology of most legislation.

In the end, if you can, you should give the interviewer the benefit of the doubt and go on with the interview as if nothing untoward has happened. If you're firm (but polite) in your position on not answering the prohibited inquiry, it's essential that you continue the interview in the same gracious tone that was present prior to the introduction of the discriminatory matter. By acting in such a professional manner, you accomplish one of two things. If the interviewer asked the question innocently, you will convey the impression that you don't hold any grudges, recognize that anyone can make a mistake, and are willing to accept her regardless of her mistake. If she asked it intentionally, this gives you the upper hand. Since you've shown that you know the law and that she's violated it, your interviewer has to worry about your making an issue out of it. If nothing else, from that point on in the interview, she should be reluctant to introduce any further discriminatory matter.

Handling an illegal pre-employment inquiry is never easy. But, as with other problems that can arise in an interview, if you're prepared for it, you will be in much better shape to handle it in the event it arises.

Filing Claims

If you really think that you've been treated unfairly and you don't get an offer you want, then you should feel free to file a claim with the state and the EEOC. But think about it and be sure that you really feel in your heart that you were discriminated against. Don't just file a charge on a whim or out of pique because you didn't get an offer. *The question must have been asked for the purpose of discriminating against you because of an illegal reason or have the effect of discriminating against you.* This may not be easy to determine, although an interviewer who asked such a question may have difficulty explaining why she asked it if not to make a hire/no hire decision based upon your answer. Still, the simplest thing to do is to chalk it all up to experience and go on to your next interview.

If you feel you were asked a prohibited pre-employment inquiry and as a result were discriminated against, and you want to pursue the matter, you should file a charge within the applicable filing period. You should file concurrently with both your state agency and the EEOC. The filing period in the various states varies, so you should contact your state agency to determine what it is. The filing period in California (and in approximately 75 percent of the states) is one year. The EEOC filing period is 180 days or the period allowed by the state in which the alleged violation occurred, whichever is longer. As a matter of procedure, the EEOC will defer until the state agency has investigated and taken action; the EEOC will investigate after the state agency deferral period has ended.

After the EEOC conducts an investigation, it will determine if there is reasonable cause to believe that your charge is true. Although the EEOC is currently making an effort to reduce its backlog of charges, it may take years to institute an investigation. If you wish to proceed against the employer sooner, you may request a notice to sue anytime after you file your charge with the EEOC. If the EEOC investigates, you will not take part in the investigation, and you do not need an attorney. All of the EEOC's investigation is confidential. All you'll find out is whether the EEOC has determined if there is reasonable cause to believe your charge is true. If the EEOC does not find such a reasonable cause, it will advise you of this and of your "right to sue" in court.

If the EEOC does find reasonable cause, it will attempt to conciliate the matter by meeting with the potential employer and reaching an agreement on the remedy. If no agreement is reached, the EEOC may file a suit or it may issue you a right-to-sue letter. You have ninety days after receipt of a right-to-sue letter from the EEOC to file your own suit.

If you don't have an attorney, the courts are authorized to appoint one for you and to start the action without payment of a filing fee. Just because the EEOC does not find reasonable cause does not mean that you can't file a suit yourself, and it doesn't mean that you won't recover.

If you can afford an attorney, you should retain your own. But if you can't, it has been held that all you have to do is file your right-to-sue letter in federal court and apply for the appointment of counsel. If you do these things within the ninety-day period after receipt of your right-to-sue letter, you should be safe in having preserved your cause of action.

However, according to EEOC counsel Steven Gaffin, "courts are not overly generous" in appointing attorneys for applicants. The United States District Court for the Central District of California requires that a lawsuit be filed and an application *in forma pauperis*, which describes permission given to a poor person to sue without liability for costs.

The remedies you can hope to receive if you get a favorable judgment from the court can include attorney's fees. So if you retain your own attorney and win, the employer may have to pay your attorney. Of course, you can also get damages. For example, perhaps you can prove that you were not hired because of discrimination. If the job for which you were interviewing paid $40,000 per year and you were out of work for a year thereafter and couldn't get a job despite diligent effort, the court could award you $40,000 in damages. State and local governments are *not* immune from paying salary and attorney's fees in cases of prohibited discrimination.

While you may be awarded your attorney's fees if you win, you might have to pay the other party's attorney's fees if you lose. Although this is very rare, and usually only occurs if the court determines that the case was frivolous, it has happened, and it is something of which you should be aware.

Now that you have a general idea of what your rights are, you must put this knowledge in the context of everything else you've learned in this book. Remember that the inquiry must have been asked for the purpose or impact of discriminating against you for an unlawful reason. Beyond that, the question is whether you have the energy and the time to follow through. Perhaps the better course would be to move on to the next interview—you wouldn't have been happy working under those circumstances anyway.

My final admonition is that litigation is hell. The feelings of the litigant are not relevant. Judges are all former lawyers, and they play the game. Discovery (the obtaining of information from you through depositions and subpoenas for documents and information) is its own special kind of hell, and all judges I've seen encourage it. I've never seen a judge limit discovery. If anything, they expand it. Even if you recover, and under our system of justice that can take years, even decades, you might find that it was not worth it, because litigation can take over your life. My advice is to avoid lawyers, judges, and litigation like the plague.

Job Applications

Reader Michael Rezendes of Ventura, California, expresses a frustration with the application part of the screening interview:

> During my job-hunting activities I have been continually confronted with and frustrated by job application forms. These pesky forms seem to continually be a stumbling block in my efforts to conduct effective interviews. They force you to reveal your liabilities, your limited experience, gaps in your job record, reasons for leaving jobs, references, and past earnings very early in the interview process.

The rules for pre-employment inquiries are equally pertinent to applications. (Refer to the questions listed as acceptable by the California Department of Fair Employment and Housing earlier in this chapter.) Filling out an application is much easier, however, because you have total control and time to think and plan.

Just because you are presented with a form to fill out does not mean that you have to answer all the questions on it. Take it from me, forms that contain questions or terms and conditions are not written in concrete. You can alter them before signing them, or decline to answer parts of them. What you must realize is that those forms have been drafted by highly paid lawyers. Each word is important or it wouldn't be in there. And you can bet that there isn't anything in there that is drafted with your interests in mind.

I know whereof I speak because, as an attorney for Litton Industries, I drafted the terms and conditions that were put on the back of our vendors' purchase order forms. I drafted the most onerous terms and conditions anyone's ever seen. They protected Litton from here to Timbuktu and back again. Still, 90 percent of the vendors would just sign off on them without questioning anything. If anyone questioned them, we would negotiate something that was acceptable to both sides.

So when you see an application that contains questions or terms and conditions, read it all and read it slowly and thoroughly. If you don't like something, don't answer the offending question, or alter the section you don't like. Remember, *everything is negotiable*. How negotiable depends upon your negotiating position, of course, and that's something only you can determine.

Following is a sample application taken from Matthew Bender's *Employment Law Deskbook*, which was written to advise lawyers who advise employers on how to comply with the law. Because it was prepared for use by attorneys, you can safely presume that nothing in it is prohibited by law. This is an excellent form for use by employers. It looks like something I might draft if I were the attorney for an employer, because it definitely protects my client. But that doesn't mean it would be in your best interests to answer all the questions and sign it. A form drafted for an employer is not one drafted with an employee's interests in mind. There's probably at least one provision that could easily redound to your disfavor. In fact, there are *many* areas of this application to which I would object.

XYZ COMPANY
EMPLOYMENT APPLICATION
An Equal Opportunity Employer

Name _____

S.S. No. _____

Present Address _____

Previous Address _____

Telephone Number _____

   (Home) _____

   (Business) _____

Positions applied for

1. _____

2. _____

3. _____

Full time _____ Part time _____ Temporary _____

Specify days and hours for which you are available: _____

Date available _____

Desired Salary _____

Are you willing to relocate? [Yes] [No] If yes, specify location(s). ___

How were you referred to the XYZ Company? _____
_____

Are you authorized to work in the United States? [Yes] [No]

(If you are a resident alien, please give your alien number on your
Resident Alien Card (Form 1-551). _____

Have you ever applied here before? [Yes] [No] If yes, specify the
date(s). _____

Have you been employed here before? [Yes] [No] If yes, specify the
date(s). _____

Give the names and relationships of any relatives you have working
for XYZ Company _____
_____

Describe any impairments, physical or mental, that would interfere
with your ability to perform the position(s) for which you are
applying. _____
_____

Have you ever been convicted of a criminal offense? [Yes] [No] If
yes, please explain. _____

Are you at least 18 years of age? [Yes] [No]

Employment history:

Start with your current or most recent employer.

1. Employer _____

    Address _____

    Phone Number _____

    Job Title _____

    Supervisor _____

    Salary _____

Duties Performed _____

Reason for Leaving _____

2. Employer _____

Address _____

Phone Number _____

Job Title _____

Supervisor _____

Salary _____

Duties Performed _____

Reason for Leaving _____

3. Employer _____

Address _____

Phone Number _____

Job Title _____

Supervisor _____

Salary _____

Duties Performed _____

Reason for Leaving _____

If you need additional space, please continue on a separate sheet of paper.

Have you worked under a different name for any of these employers? [Yes] [No] If yes, please identify the employer and state the name.

_____

U.S. Military Record:

Have you served in the United States Armed Forces? [Yes] [No] If yes, please give the dates of service. _____

Branch _____

If you have a disability or are a disabled veteran and would like to be considered under our Affirmative Action Program, please do so indicate. (You need not provide us with this information if you do not wish to do so. If you choose to provide the information, it will be kept confidential except that your supervisors may be informed regarding work restrictions or accommodations that may be appropriate, and first-aid people may be advised of possible emergency treatment.) [Yes] [No] If yes, describe any special skills you may have and any special adaptations needed because of the disability. _____

PLEASE READ CAREFULLY BEFORE SIGNING THIS APPLICATION.

I authorize the Company to investigate all statements in this application and to secure any necessary information from all my employers, references, and academic institutions. I hereby release all of those employers, references, academic institutions, and the Company from any and all liability arising from their giving or receiving information about my employment history, my academic credentials or qualifications, and my suitability for employment with the Company. I also authorize the Company to secure financial and credit information through an appropriate agency, and I understand that, upon my written request made within a reasonable period of time, the agency providing a consumer credit report to the Company will provide me with a complete description of the nature and scope of the credit report investigation.

I understand that any offer of employment is contingent upon receipt of a satisfactory report concerning my credit, academic credentials, and employment references. I further understand that any false or misleading statements will be sufficient cause for rejection of my application if the Company has not employed me and for immediate dismissal if the Company has employed me. I also authorize the Company to supply information about my employment record, in whole or in part, in confidence to any prospective employer, government agency, or any other party having a legal and proper interest, and I hereby release the Company for any and all liability for its providing this information.

In the event of my employment with the Company, I will comply with all rules, regulations, and policies set forth in the Company's policy manual or other communications distributed by the Company.

I understand that nothing in this employment application, in the Company's policy statements or personnel guidelines, or in my communications with any Company official is intended to create an employment contract between the Company and me. I also understand that the Company has the right to modify its policies without giving me any notice of any changes. No promises regarding employment have been made to me, and I understand that no such promise of guarantee is binding upon the Company unless it is made in writing and signed by a Company officer. I understand that if an employment relationship is established, I have the right to terminate my employment at any time for any reason. I also understand that the Company retains the right to terminate my employment for any reason.

I hereby acknowledge that I have read and understand the preceding statement.

Signature of Applicant _____

Date _____

Social Security number (SSN). There are probably two reasons why this is requested on the application. First, if you go to work for the employer, it will have legal entitlement to possession of your Social Security number. Second, it is on the application so the employer can do a credit check on you. I never give anybody my SSN unless there's a legal entitlement to it. And the only people who have a legal entitlement to your Social Security number are people who will be paying you, so they can file the necessary tax reports. Nobody else has a legal right to your Social Security number.

However, that said, you should know that by not providing my SSN I do miss out on some things. For example, at least once I was refused the right to apply for an apartment because I would not divulge the number. I felt that protecting the confidentiality of my SSN was more important than the apartment. You might not think it is more important than getting a job. It's a value judgment that each person must make.

Don't be misled into believing promises of confidentiality. The Federal Reserve, an agency of the United States government, requires the Social Security number of holders of Federal Reserve bills, notes, and bonds, and quotes the law as to confidentiality and promises confidentiality. Despite this, at one time the Federal Reserve put the recipient's SSN on the face of envelopes when it mailed interest checks. I protested and quoted the law to the Federal Reserve, but it denied that this was a breach of confidentiality and blithely continued to expose the Social Security numbers of all holders of Federal Reserve instruments for all the world to see on the face of the envelopes, a policy that was finally changed.

I would advise you to tell the interviewer that you'll supply your SSN if you accept an offer and become their employee. If they say that they won't process your application without it, you'll just have to make a judgment as to the importance of the confidentiality of your SSN. I'd estimate that more than 99 percent of the people disclose theirs with no worry and no problem. It is a lawful pre-employment inquiry in California.

Blanket release to your prior employers. I wouldn't agree to any language releasing a third party. That's the third party's problem. If the third party is worried about what they might reveal about you, then they can contact you for your release. If they do contact you, ask to see a copy of what they propose to reveal *before* you grant your release. If you don't like what they propose to reveal, you can deny your release. You may provide your consent to allow any prior employer to provide information to the company, but under no circumstances should you sign any language that purports to *release* your prior employer from liability. That's no legitimate concern of your interviewer. There's a big difference between *consenting to your prior employer's providing information* and *releasing your prior employer from liability* for any damages resulting from the release of false or defamatory information. You should recognize this difference and, if asked to sign such a statement, explain to your interviewer why you will sign the consent but not a release and why it's unfair for her to ask you to sign a release. Just hone in on the difference between a *consent* and a *release.* Maybe without your consent a former employer won't provide information, so you sign the consent. But a former employer who damages you should be liable for the damage done as a result of false or defamatory information, which is why you don't want to sign a release.

Arbitration agreement. Some employers will ask you, in your application, to agree to sign an arbitration agreement requiring arbitration of all employment-related legal claims. This is not a good idea, and I would resist signing such an agreement.

Arbitration is final. There is no appeal. And the arbitrators are generally "judge wannabes." My experience with them is that they are ignorant and biased. If you ever read the instructions for arbitrators promulgated by the American Arbitration Association, you'd see what I mean. They emphasize that an arbitrator should eschew putting much in writing so that nothing they do can be contested. There are very strict grounds for contesting an arbitration award, and factual or legal errors are not among them. So the arbitrator can be wrong and biased, but his award can't be challenged on either of those grounds, even if he is clearly factually wrong!

But California has held that its courts may refuse to enforce an unconscionable arbitration agreement, which has been defined as an absence of meaningful choice on the part of one of the parties when combined with contract terms that are unreasonably favorable to the other party.

A California case involving Circuit City held that Circuit City's arbitration agreement was unenforceable because "the agreement is a prerequisite to employment, and job applicants are not permitted to modify the agreement's terms." So, at least in California, if you see an arbitration agreement in your application, or anything else in the application to which you object, raise the issue and ask if you can delete or modify it.

I, personally, would not agree to any arbitration agreement in an employment environment unless I modified it so that questions of law were fully appealable as if the issue had been tried in a court of law. This at least protects you against the arbitrator deciding something that was contrary to what the law says.

Credit check authorization. If you are asked to authorize a credit check, you should ask for an exact copy of your credit report, not, as the application puts it, "a complete description of the nature and scope of the credit report investigation." The reason that this specific language is used is that the Federal Fair Credit Report Act only requires an employer to notify the applicant that such a report might be requested and to disclose information about its "nature and scope." So this consent only obligates the interviewer to comply with the *minimum* requirements of the law. There's no reason why you shouldn't be given an exact copy of the credit report. If you demand it as a condition to signing the consent, then the employer is required to provide you with it, regardless of the minimum requirements of the law. And the employer cannot correctly state that the law *prohibits* it from doing more simply because the law does not *require* it to do more. If you don't demand an exact copy in writing in your consent, you will have no enforceable right to receive it.

Please understand the difference between "prohibit" and "require." In this day and age, under the Gramm-Leach-Bliley Act relating to privacy, financial institutions blanket us with their "privacy notices." Generally, they say something hypocritical like, "Your privacy is important to us," then go on to state that they won't reveal information about you unless "permitted by law." Well, that's completely meaningless, and they know it. This is the scam of all scams because the law permits them to reveal just about anything. A very few institutions are honest about it and say they won't reveal anything unless "required by law." This is a statement that has teeth in it because the law does not *require* much to be revealed.

Similarly, if an employer tries to tell you that they can't provide you with the information because the law does not require it, that is meaningless. Just because the law doesn't *require* them to reveal it does not mean that the law *prohibits* them from revealing it. So, unless the law specifically *prohibits* them from providing you with information, you have the right to ask for it, and they really don't have any legal basis to refuse.

False information. I wouldn't agree to any stipulations that the company could dismiss me on the grounds of false information supplied by third parties. It's understandable that they might want you to agree to the right to dismiss you for false information *supplied by you*, but not for false information supplied by a third party beyond your control. I would not agree to the company's right to dismiss me for information that is "misleading." The term "misleading" is ambiguous and could mean anything. I would also delete the word "immediate" and request that in the event of any alleged false information I be given notice and the right to respond prior to any dismissal. You don't want to give your employer carte blanche to terminate you without being given a right to defend yourself.

Confidentiality. I wouldn't give the company authorization to supply information about me to anybody. That has nothing to do with your application for a job with them. It's important to your privacy that you control information disseminated about you to third parties. Nor would I agree to the release provision regarding the company providing information, for the same reasons enumerated above.

Finally, I'd modify the provision that the company can change its policies without notifying me by adding the proviso "so long as it doesn't affect me or my job." And I'd limit their right to terminate me "for any reason" to "for any reason allowed by law."

If you make changes in a document, do it in ink and initial each alteration. The example on the following page shows the sort of modifications to the fine print that I would make if this were my application:

PLEASE READ CAREFULLY BEFORE
SIGNING THIS APPLICATION

I authorize the Company to investigate all statements in this application and to secure any necessary information from all my employers, references, and academic institutions. ~~I hereby release all of those employers, references, academic institutions, and the Company from any and all liability arising from their giving or receiving information about my employment history, my academic credentials or qualifications, and my suitability for employment with the Company.~~ I also authorize the Company to secure financial and credit information through an appropriate agency, and I understand that, upon my written request made within a reasonable period of time, the agency providing a consumer credit report to the Company will provide me with a ~~complete description of the nature and scope~~ { *full and complete copy ĐEM* } of the credit report investigation.

I understand that any offer of employment is contingent upon receipt of a satisfactory report concerning my credit, academic credentials, and employment references. I further understand that any false ~~or misleading statements~~ { *of a material nature made by me ĐEM* } will be sufficient cause for rejection of my application if the Company has not employed me and for immediate dismissal if the Company has employed me. ~~I also authorize the Company to supply information about my employment record, in whole or in part, in confidence to any prospective employer, government agency, or any other party having a legal and proper interest, and I hereby release the Company from any and all liability for its providing this information.~~ { *after being given adequate and reasonable prior notice and the prior right to respond to all allegations made against me. ĐEM* }

In the event of my employment with the Company, I will comply with all rules, regulations, and policies set forth in the Company's policy manual or other communications distributed by the Company.

I understand that nothing in this employment application, in the Company's policy statements or personnel guidelines, or in my communications with any Company official is intended to create an employment contract between the Company and me. I also understand that the Company has the right to modify its policies without giving me any notice of the changes. { *that do not affect me or my job ĐEM* } No promises regarding employment have been made to me, and I understand that no such promise of guarantee is binding upon the Company unless it is made in writing and signed by a Company officer. I understand that if an employment relationship is established, I have the right to terminate my employment at any time for any reason. I also understand that the Company retains the right to terminate my employment for any reason_____ { *allowed by law ĐEM* }

I hereby acknowledge that I have read and understand the preceding statement.

_____   _____
Signature of Applicant   Date

Two final caveats: When you sign something, initial each page. That way pages can't be substituted without your knowledge. Finally, *always get, and keep, a complete copy of anything you sign!* Otherwise, you'll have no record of what you signed and won't know what your rights are in the event of a dispute.

Privacy and Confidentiality

Although there is not a specific right of privacy in the United States Constitution, many states have amended their constitutions to provide their citizens with a fundamental right of privacy. California amended its constitution in 1972 by vote of the people to provide:

> All people are by nature free and independent and have inalienable rights. Among these are the enjoying and defending life and liberty, acquiring, possessing, and protecting property, and pursuing and obtaining safety, happiness, and privacy.

Personnel records. The right to privacy has been interpreted by California courts to provide employees with the right to be free from intrusion into certain personal affairs and the right to have the contents of many records maintained on the employee kept secret. So a former employer would probably be prohibited from disclosing information from your personnel file without your prior permission.

Letters of reference. Many states have defined letters of reference broadly to protect them from inspection without your permission. The definition in California has been interpreted to include any confidential information concerning qualification for employment, promotion, additional compensation, termination, or other disciplinary action.

AIDS. Some states, including California, prohibit employers from using the results of an AIDS blood test or information relating to AIDS research in any way for the determination of the suitability of employment.

Pre-employment Testing

There are a number of conditions that may be attached to the screening phase of your job search. For instance, on the application form you may be asked to agree to submit to a physical exam or to sign a release for previous employment records. If you have reservations about any such conditions, you should either cross them out on the application form or alter the wording to protect yourself, as I discussed above. But if you do this, you need to be prepared to discuss your reasoning when you get into the interview situation.

DRUG AND ALCOHOL TESTS

Many employers will want to know if you use drugs, have used drugs, or are a potential drug user, and you might be asked in the interview or on the application if you would be willing to submit to testing.

The problem is that many of these tests for drugs are inaccurate. How can you protect against a false reading or a false conclusion? It would be a disaster if a urinalysis or a check of your hair (don't laugh, this is one of the tests) shows that you use drugs when, in fact, you don't.

So even if you don't use drugs or alcohol, you should be

wary of invasive tests because of their potential for inaccuracy. Any inaccurate test could have a profound influence on your reputation and ability to get a job. The problem is that it's not easy, when you are looking desperately for a job, to take a strong position against invasive testing, because your mere refusal to participate could result in your elimination. That's why it's so important for you to be cooperative, but why it's equally important for you to invest some money in protecting yourself.

If one of the conditions for employment is that you submit to a drug check, request the right to have the test run by a laboratory of your own choosing. This will probably be rejected because if testing is a standard procedure, the firm probably has arrangements with a particular lab. So if your request is rejected, ask why, just for the record, then ask if the firm will pay for an independent test to confirm their test. If the interviewer rejects that idea, make a record of it in your notes and, if it is important enough to you, go to an independent lab and have the same test performed that the interviewer required. Do this immediately after the interviewer's test or specimen is taken. The closer your test is performed to the interviewer's test, the better.

This has two desirable results. First, you have control of the test results. If they are not in your favor, you can do with them what you will. But second, and more important, if the interviewer's test comes out not in your favor but your test comes out in your favor, you are in an extremely strong position and can effectively and immediately counter any damage a negative report to your interviewer could have on your reputation.

You could also have a test done by your own lab *prior* to the interview, as close as possible to the time of your interview as is convenient. You wouldn't even have to reveal to the interviewer that you had the test done. Then you could submit to the same test with the confidence that you could rebut any unfavorable report with proof that you did not use drugs.

Noninvasive methods are being developed to check, not for drug or alcohol use, but whether or not you can safely do any potentially dangerous job. One consists of a software program in a computer operated by knobs. You use the knob to keep a swaying pointer in the center of the screen. The pointer swings faster and faster from left to right, and the test ends when the pointer swings too far, as it will always do. While this doesn't test specifically for drugs or alcohol, if you are drug- or alcohol-impaired, you will almost invariably fail the test.

Pre-employment Physical Examinations

In addition to a drug test, you might be faced with a pre-employment medical examination. Both the Americans with Disabilities Act and most state laws permit employers to use pre-employment medical examinations and to impose reasonable job standards for applicants. But there are three requirements. The medical examinations must be (1) job-related; (2) (in many states) conducted after an offer is extended; and (3) applied uniformly to all applicants. Additionally, California, for example, gives the applicant the right to submit the employer's medical examination results to an independent examination. Check your state's laws for a similar provision.

Many states prohibit employment discrimination on the basis of physical or mental disability, and federal law prohibits disability discrimination by federal government contractors, subcontractors, and grant recipients. The basic issue in such cases is whether or not the disability would affect job performance or pose a threat to others.

You may be requested to sign a consent and release form. I

would be very reluctant to sign a release. You should read it very carefully. The purpose of getting you to sign a release is to avoid your making tort claims relating to the physical examination, like invasion of privacy, assault, or battery. There's generally no problem with signing a simple consent form, but a release is another matter. The problem is that if you're presented with the form to sign and you don't sign it, either you could be eliminated from consideration or the inference could be drawn from your refusal to sign that you are a troublemaker.

This is a very sensitive issue. As a matter of course I never sign releases. But I'm an attorney, and I know the reason why people are asking me to sign a release. As I described earlier, I cross off any language I don't like, initial it, and then sign the form. Sometimes the person with whom you're dealing will take what you signed and go forward, accepting your changes. Others, however, may make an issue of it and say that they cannot proceed with processing your application unless you sign the form unchanged. That presents you with a question of whether or not you want to sign the release. Generally, nothing will happen and your signing the release will be okay. But what if something does happen? Then if you make a claim against the company, they'll pull out the release and take the position that you waived all your rights. I don't sign as a matter of principle. But, then, I don't need a job. It comes down to weighing of values between your needs and the potential for harm. Generally, there is very little potential for harm, so if you make a federal case out of it, you might disqualify yourself for a lot of jobs for which you might otherwise be considered. So my advice would be to question the release and tell them that you don't generally sign such all-encompassing forms and ask if you can sign only the consent and cross out the release. There's a fair chance that they'll say okay. If they don't, and you're not worried about anything happening for which you might want to make a claim, then you should go ahead and sign the release and proceed with the interview.

LIE DETECTOR TESTS

Polygraph, or lie detector, tests were once very popular among employers as a screening device. But almost half the states and the District of Columbia have passed laws severely limiting the use of polygraph testing. Federal law has prohibited the use of lie detector tests as a screening device since 1988. There are a few exceptions, and the federal law sometimes endorses more restrictive state law or bargaining agreements, so if the question arises, you should check your state laws if you don't want to submit. California, for example, has a specific prohibition against employers demanding or requiring an applicant to submit to a polygraph test as a condition of employment.

SCORED TESTING

A very controversial method of judging job applicants involves scored testing. The law at the time of the writing of this book is that if a test or battery of tests has a "significant disparate impact" on a protected class, its use is unlawful unless it is job-related. The flip side is that if the test does not have a disproportionate disparate impact on a protected class, it may be employed regardless of its validity or job relatedness. The tests for determining disparate impact are too complex to go into here. If you think you have been discriminated against because a test you took was unfairly tilted against your particular minority group, you should see an attorney who is familiar with this very complicated and litigious area of law, which is constantly changing.

Disability

Many state laws protect people with disabilities from discrimination in hiring. In California the Prudence K. Poppink Act makes the California law independent of the 1990 Americans with Disabilities Act (ADA) and affords broader protection than federal law. As an example, the ADA defines disability as "a physical or mental impairment that substantially limits one or more major life activities." Under California law, disability is defined as an impairment that only "limits one or more major life activities." You can see that California's law is far broader. It's much easier to show that something "limits" than showing that something "*substantially* limits" an activity.

Furthermore, in California "working" is a major life activity regardless of whether the actual or perceived working limitations implicate a specific position or broad class of employment, whereas under the ADA the mental or physical disability must affect a person's ability to obtain a broad class of employment. So in California if it affects your ability to "work," it's a limitation, even if it doesn't affect your ability to work in a broad class.

The important thing, for the purposes of an interview, is that you cannot be asked about your medical or psychological condition or disability except under certain circumstances.

California's definitions of mental and physical disability prevent discrimination based on a person's "record or history" of certain impairments. Moreover, California law protects those who are "perceived" as having a disability, even if they do not actually *have* a disability. Physical and mental disabilities include chronic or episodic conditions such as HIV/AIDS, hepatitis, epilepsy, seizure disorder, multiple sclerosis, and heart disease.

Specifically, California details the following as a medical condition entitled to "accommodation":

Physical disabilities: Having any physiological disease, disorder, condition, cosmetic disfigurement, or anatomical loss that affects one or more of several body systems and limits a major life activity. The body systems listed include the neurological, immunological, musculoskeletal, special sense organs, respiratory, including speech organs, cardiovascular, reproductive, digestive, genitourinary, hemic and lymphatic, skin and endocrine systems. A physiological disease, disorder, condition, cosmetic disfigurement, or anatomical loss limits a major life activity, such as working, if it makes the achievement of the major life activity difficult.

When determining whether a person has a disability, an employer cannot take into consideration any medication or assistive device, such as wheelchairs, eyeglasses, or hearing aids, that an employee uses to accommodate the disability. However, if these devices or mitigating measures "limit a major life activity," they should be taken into consideration.

Physical disability also includes any other health impairment that requires special education or related services; having a record or history of a disease, disorder, condition, cosmetic disfigurement, anatomical loss, or health impairment which is known to the employer; and being perceived or treated by the employer as having any of the aforementioned conditions.

The law covers not only physical disabilities but also mental. So you're protected if you have any mental or psychological disorder or condition, such as mental retardation, organic brain syndrome, emotional or mental illness, or specific learning disabilities, that limits a major life activity, or any other mental or psychological disorder or condition that requires special education or related services. An employee who has a record or history of a mental or psychological disorder or condition that is known to the employer, or who is regarded or treated by the employer as having a mental disorder or condition, is also protected.

However, under both physical and mental disability, sexual behavior disorders, compulsive gambling, kleptomania, pyromania, or psychoactive substance use disorders resulting from the current unlawful use of controlled substances or other drugs are specifically excluded and are not protected under the California Fair Employment and Housing Act (FEHA).

It goes further by protecting you if you have a "mental condition," which is defined as any health impairment related to or associated with a diagnosis of cancer or a record or history of cancer or a "genetic characteristic." The latter raises a catch-22 for an employer. You're protected if you have a genetic characteristic, which is a scientifically or medically identifiable gene or chromosome or an inherited characteristic that could statistically lead to increased development of a disease or disorder. But in California, Government Code Section 12940(o) makes it an unlawful employment practice for an employer to subject any applicant to a test for the presence of a genetic characteristic.

At-Will Employment Contracts

In 2000, the California Supreme Court came down with an extremely important decision of which people seeking jobs in California should be aware. It's *Guz v. Bechtel National, Inc.* In it, the Supreme Court made crystal clear how few rights an

employee has if he or she is working under an at-will agreement. After this case, most employers will be devising personnel policies that designate all employment as "at will," which
means that you may be fired at any time for any reason.

When you are negotiating for a position you should find out
about this. Generally it will be in the employment practices
material that are given to you, either during your interviewing
process or when you sign up to work for the company. You
should read all the information given you. If the material says
that your employment is "at will," you should ask about it.
Sometimes you can negotiate this.

If someone wanted to hire me and I saw an at-will provision
in the material, I'd red flag it and ask about it. It's not unreasonable for a company to want some sort of probationary
period during which they could terminate an employee for no
reason, but why would they want this to continue? Is it fair for
an employer to fire someone for no reason after twenty-two
years? You wouldn't think so, but that's what happened to Mr.
Guz, who was fired by Bechtel after twenty-two years of loyal
service and praiseworthy employee evaluations. And the law in
California says that this is perfectly okay because Bechtel had
established an at-will relationship in its employment manuals
and had communicated it to all employees.

Another issue that was raised in the Bechtel case was what's
called the implied covenant of good faith and fair dealing. This
says, basically, that it's unfair to fire someone at will, and that
Mr. Guz should be treated fairly with respect to other employees, and that Mr. Guz can't be discriminated against on the
basis of his age, because he wasn't offered other positions for
which he was qualified, but much younger people were. No
dice, said the Supreme Court. If you're working on an at-will
relationship, there is no covenant of good faith and fair dealing

that will save you. Bechtel had the right to fire Mr. Guz for no reason, so that's what they did, and he was out of luck.

I think it's definitely worthwhile to challenge your potential employer on this issue. If they want you, you could tell them that you're perfectly willing to agree to a probationary period during which you could be terminated at will, but after it is over you would like a provision stating that you can only be terminated for cause, and then only after notification and a chance to improve. Of course, you might jeopardize your chances of getting an offer if you are challenging company policy like this, but you also have to consider whether or not you want to devote years to a company while they retain the right to dump you for no reason. I wouldn't.

You have a couple things you can ask for:

(1) Sometimes a company will agree to an agreement that an employee will only be fired for cause. Many employers will go along with this because they want to say they won't terminate without cause anyway.

(2) Or you might be able to negotiate a severance package if the employer terminates you without cause. Maybe you can ask the employer to pay you three or six months' severance pay if you are terminated without cause.

Remember, this is a negotiating aspect. And it's pretty indefensible for an employer to want to be able to fire you for no reason, especially after you've been there awhile. If they want you they won't want to appear unfair or unrealistic. So if they say that the at-will provision is not negotiable, it would seem pretty unfair for them to refuse to discuss a severance provision. You can send a letter to the employer stating that after a certain amount of time you will not be terminated without cause, and ask for a written response. If you receive an at-will letter that states that the employer retains the right to terminate you at will, you can cross it out, initial it, and return it to the employer. However, if the at-will letter is part of an offer, your changing it operates as a rejection of the offer, so you might lose the job. It's probably better to call them and discuss it and try to reach an agreement verbally before responding in writing.

You should also check out the company's personnel policy because if it says that you may be terminated at will, it could be binding, even if you haven't discussed it or it's not a part of your written agreement.

Without a contractual right to be terminated for good cause, a covenant of good faith and fair dealing does not exist, so there's no duty for the employer to act with good faith or deal fairly. The California court specifically rejected an employer's duty to treat people fairly or equally. Courts won't impose terms beyond the contract between the parties of at-will employment, so there are no implied covenants of good faith and fair dealing.

Are stock options, deferred compensation, and bonuses compensation already earned? Be careful if you negotiate stock options if you have an at-will agreement because, if so, generally they vest only if you're still there after a certain period of time. They can terminate you the day before vesting and you're out of luck. If you do negotiate these, try to get into your agreement that they are awarded for work performed, not just for being there after a certain period of time. This might give you an argument that it was deferred compensation for services performed.

Checklist

- Pre-employment questions may not be asked for the purpose of discriminating on the basis of race, color, religion, sex, national origin, age, physical disability, or other protected class status.
- The EEOC views such inquiries with "extreme disfavor."
- State laws specifically prohibit bias.
- Most states have lists of lawful and unlawful questions.
- If you're asked an unlawful question, answer it if your reply can't hurt you, and then let the interviewer know that you know what may and may not be asked in an interview.
- Don't file a claim unless the purpose or impact of the question was to discriminate for an unlawful reason.
- You should file with both the state and the EEOC within the filing period.
- You can file a suit in court by filing your right-to-sue letter along with an application for appointment of counsel.
- Your remedies *might* include damages and attorneys' fees.
- State and local government employers are not immune from being ordered to pay damages because of illegal discrimination.
- You may have to pay the other party's attorney's fees if you lose, but only if it is found to be a frivolous case.
- Be wary of relinquishing control over employment or health records or required pre-employment tests such as drug tests or lie detector tests.
- Read every document thoroughly before you sign.
- If there's something you don't like or understand in a document you're asked to sign, discuss it with your interviewer before you sign, or cross it off and initial it.

- Obtain a complete copy of everything you sign.
- Initial each page of any document you sign.
- Protect yourself by having a laboratory of your choosing perform any required invasive test, either as a substitute for your interviewer's laboratory or as a backup to protect against a false result.
- Try not to agree to the employer's right to terminate you at will.

15

Decisions

Although those who write about how to conduct interviews would have us believe that hiring decisions are made empirically, the fact is that most such decisions are based on the interviewer's visceral reaction to the interviewee (and for this chapter let's assume the interviewer is a man). Sometimes this feeling is arrived at very quickly. Theodore Sorenson, who became President Kennedy's special counsel, was hired as a legislative assistant to the newly elected Senator Kennedy in 1953 after two five-minute interviews. Sometimes it comes after extensive contact.

Most Decisions Are Made Viscerally

How are decisions made? Selection decisions are no different from any other decision that we must all make. Much more often than not, decisions are made by choosing the path of least resistance. If you note the manner in which the following hundred-million-dollar decision was made, you'll be less impressed with the science involved in the decision-making process and less intimidated by how the decision on you is to be made.

In 1948 Henry Ford II put forth the idea of bringing out a new car. It was not until 1955, however, after exhaustive studies, that the Ford Motor Company made the big decision and put their final approval on the project.

A team was formed, and millions of dollars were spent in research relating to the design and marketing of the new car. One of the fundamental decisions that had to be made was what to call it. Very early it was suggested that the car be named after Henry Ford II's father, Edsel, but Ford and his brothers quickly scotched that idea, saying that they didn't believe their father would "care to have his name spinning on a million hubcaps."

So several research consultants were hired, and the entire nation was canvassed. People were asked their reactions to more than two thousand names. Ford also consulted poet Marianne Moore, who suggested such zingers as Intelligent Bullet and Utopian Turtletop. They next went to Madison Avenue and their advertising agency, Foote, Cone & Belding, which came up with eighteen thousand possibilities in the twinkling of an eye (including Drof). They cut this list down to six thousand and presented it to Ford. "There you are," an agency rep said proudly, "six thousand names, all alphabetized and cross-referenced."

"But," gasped a Ford executive, "we don't want six thousand names. We only want one." So Foote, Cone & Belding reduced the list of six thousand to ten and presented it to Ford's executive committee at a time when the three Ford brothers were away. The chairman of the committee looked at the ten suggestions and said, "I don't like any of them. Let's call it the Edsel." And that was that. After millions of dollars and months of research and work, the name chosen was the first one that had been suggested more than a year earlier. It was also the only one to have been categorically rejected by the top person.

And you think that the hire/no hire decision on you is going to be made scientifically? Don't kid yourself. Most decisions, regardless of the amount of money riding on them, are made viscerally.

The Halo Effect

The "halo effect," which Felix Lopez, in *Personnel Interviewing Theory and Practice*, defines as "the undue influence of an irrelevant trait on [the interviewer's] overall judgment," is probably the dominant factor in making a selection decision. The consequence of the halo effect can be devastating. I once made a terrible error that epitomizes the halo effect. I had been interviewing for a long time to fill a position in the law department for a client corporation. I simply could not find the right person for the job. Finally, I interviewed a candidate who seemed right only because of a short answer to one of my questions. He was an assistant counsel in a corporation, and I asked him what he did. "I don't know," he replied. "I can't tell you the specifics. All I know is that I'm always busy during the day and am always tired when I come home. I don't know why, but I just can't tell you specifically what I handle each day—but there are a lot of people who have problems who want to see me and they always return with more problems."

I made up my mind to hire him then and there. Why? Because as a young lawyer working for Litton Industries I had had the same problem. I was always terribly busy, people were always lining up at my door to see me, but when my friends asked me what I did, I couldn't tell them. He had expressed my feelings on the matter exactly.

Despite unanimous negative replies on my reference checks with ex-employers, I hired him. Unfortunately, it turned out that he had irreconcilable personality defects, which verified the reference checks. But the halo I put around his answer struck such a responsive chord in me that it superseded the empirical data I compiled of an unimpressive resumé and poor reference checks to such an extent that I offered him the job.

Lopez tells how an interviewer makes a decision. I offer his insights here with the caveat that he is talking of a screening interviewer who is a scientist in the interviewing process and not a selection interviewer. But the criteria he discusses may be relevant to both.

> If the interview has been conducted properly, a great many imperfections and weaknesses will have been discovered in the applicant. If not, there was something wrong with the interview or the selection program. This unfavorable information can be quite misleading and can create a halo effect in reverse when compared to the main specifications. . . .
>
> The shrewd evaluator weighs a man's weaknesses against his strengths to arrive at an overall appraisal. . . . He employs a system of checks and balances, to determine what asset of the interviewee will compensate for what weakness. In any occupation, despite the allegations of some job analysts and methods engineers, there is no set pattern of requisite human attributes. Lack of formal education can be more than offset by an unusually varied and broad life experience; deficiencies in intellectual depth can be compensated for by an abundance of persistency, dedication, and energy.
>
> Some defects, of course, cannot be compensated for. A lack of ambition or drive can never be offset by a high level of intelligence or by a scintillating personality; job knowledge and skill cannot overcome personal maladjustment.

Methods of Reaching a Decision

In *Principles of Selling* H. K. Nixon gives five methods of reaching a decision.

1. The method of logical reasoning
2. The method of reason followed by voluntary decision
3. The method of reason followed by emotional decision
4. The method of reason followed by suggestion
5. The method of suggestion

Most decisions are made by methods 3 and 4. Emotion is the most important factor in decisions made by emotional people. No matter how much logic is used, no matter how reasonable the person makes the decision, the deciding factor will almost invariably be emotion, a feeling.

The committee making its decision to name the car the Edsel rejected the advice of experts and made a final choice that belied both logic and common sense. They chose a name that had not been canvassed with the public, had no connotation of excitement or adventure (such as Corsair, which was the favored choice of Foote, Cone & Belding based upon their research), and had been rejected by the boss.

Why? The man who made the decision, the chairman, obviously reacted to some inner feeling he had about the other names and the one he chose. Could he define the feeling? Unlikely. Could he explain how he arrived at his decision? Doubtful. It was not arrived at through weighing empirical values. He looked at all the names and he had a feeling. "Let's call it the Edsel."

This is how you are going to be judged in your interview. The way an interviewer makes a decision on an applicant cannot be explained through logic. The interviewer will have some specific things for which he will be looking. And a candidate who does not measure up to this specification will be rejected. But the decision to make an offer will not be made simply because you fit the specification. There is something more. You must spark that feeling in him. If you do, you'll probably get an offer. If the interviewer is then asked why he made you an offer, he will most probably reply that you fit the specification for which he was looking. But that's not an accurate answer. Others fit the specification, too, but you hit that feeling and so you got the offer.

Follow-up Letters

Probably the first decision you'll have to make after an interview is whether or not to write a thank-you or follow-up letter to the interviewer. One of the main points you should have learned from *Sweaty Palms* is that the vast majority of selection interviewers don't want to be conducting interviews because it interferes with their job. So anything connected with filling the position is a royal pain, and the biggest part of that pain is having to interview prospects. They want to fill the job as quickly and easily as possible, while devoting the least amount of time to the chore as possible. After the interview is over, the last thing they want is to receive a letter from an interviewee.

Receiving a post-interview letter can have a negative effect on an interviewer for several reasons:

1. It's a piece of paper with which they must deal. What do they do? Answer it? File it? Throw it away? If they answer it, they are probably not going to be thinking kindly of you, as you've just imposed a further burden on their time.

2. If they're not interested in you, receiving a letter from you is going to be even more of an irritant. The standard and accepted protocol for rejection is for the interviewer not to make another contact. Your letter, breaching this protocol, may negate any possibility for a change of heart.

3. Sending a letter can look like you're begging or more in need of a job than the interviewer might have believed before receiving your letter.

4. Your letter might say something that negates a positive feeling the interviewer may have formed.

5. The letter reduces the control of the situation that the interviewer might feel he has. The interviewer has the control of when and how to make further contact. If the interviewee oversteps the bounds by making the first contact after the interview, it could make the interviewer feel he has to reply and he might not feel he's in a position to reply at that time. So if he has to make a decision before he wants to, the odds are that the decision will be negative.

An interviewer won't contact you unless he's interested in you, regardless of whether or not you write a letter, so, unless you know for certain you've been rejected, writing a letter subjects you to the risk of damaging your position. The interviewer knows that you are grateful for the interview, so you don't need to tell him that. He also knows that anything in a letter is probably insincere, with the ulterior motive of getting an offer or another interview. Because of that very real fact, a follow-up letter is a very difficult document to draft. There's not much you can say that doesn't sound hypocritical to the reader, who will be reading the letter with a far different perspective than the perspective from which you wrote it.

Finally, there is no question of courtesy involved here. You are in a business environment. The interviewer didn't do you any favors by granting you an interview. He was acting out of selfish motives because he has a position to fill, so you do not have an obligation to "thank" him for the interview.

There are three exceptions to this advice. The first is if the interviewer has asked you for additional information. That gives you an opening to provide the information and write a letter that could enhance your position. The second is when you know that you have been rejected in the interview. If you've been told that you won't be considered further, then you've got nothing to lose by making an additional contact. The employer might change his mind or refer you to another firm. The third exception is if the interview has been conducted over a meal. Then it might be appropriate to write a very short, polite note of thanks for the meal if the interviewer picked up the tab. It's not necessary to do so because the meal was part of the interview process, but this does give you the flexibility of making contact without breaching protocol and without looking insincere or hypocritical. If you do wish to write a note, limit it to a few words of thanks. Don't grovel about how much you'd like the job or how much you liked the interviewer's tie or what a terrific sense of humor the interviewer has. Don't mention the job or include the lamentable "I look forward to hearing from you." Just thank him for the meal and end it.

The effects of a follow-up letter in employment interviews was extensively researched for a 1996 master's thesis. This is, to my knowledge, the most detailed and professional analysis of the effects of a follow-up letter in interviewing for a job. The research was limited to professional recruiters whose main function is to interview, as opposed to selection interviewers, whose obligation to interview to hire someone is something for which they are not trained and for whom the interview is more often looked upon as an unpleasant but necessary chore. Since recruiting is a recruiter's occupation, one would anticipate that the professional recruiter's reactions would be more inclined to support the concept of a follow-up letter. Why? Because the pitfalls of a follow-up letter that I set forth above don't apply to a professional recruiter. A follow-up letter would not be something that interferes with his or her normal routine, since the recruiter's normal routine is to recruit. However, the research supported my position, even among professional recruiters! The research indicates that even among professional recruiters a follow-up letter will not help you if they have not otherwise decided that you will be offered a job.

To make certain that I had not misinterpreted the writer's thesis, I spoke with him, and he reiterated to me that his research fully supported my position. Reinforced by this research, my advice remains unchanged from when I first wrote about it in 1992.

However, when I asked him what *he* would do, he said he'd write a thank-you letter. But he had severe parameters. He said it should be short and sweet and should not include anything of substance. It should be written solely as an expression of courtesy and appreciation for having been given the opportunity for the interview. He said it becomes a negative if it reiterates what took place in the interview or adds something new. In short, it should contain nothing of substance. He said that his research indicated that the only time a thank-you letter might be of help is if the writer is one of the top two candidates. In that instance it's possible that it might be of slight advantage. But he said that his research never showed that a thank-you letter helped an interviewee who was not one of the top two candidates.

Here's what Brian Krueger, author of *College Grad Job Hunter*, advises: "Thank-you notes are not expected. However, they should always be sent. You have an opportunity to make a lasting good impression. Make the most of it."

And the *Los Angeles Times Career Builder* says, "Recruiters and managers who are undecided over their potential new employee often rely on a gut feeling about someone when making their decision—and your thank-you letter may be enough to put you over the top."

The *Times* is correct when it talks about the "gut feeling." However, the comments about the thank-you letter are dead wrong. In my opinion they are made by people who have no clue or experience in the job interview. It sounds good to say this, but in fact the truth is diametrically opposed to these opinions.

Here's what one reader, Canadian Athol Kelly, had to say about thank-you or follow-up letters:

I found your book a refreshing drink of water from other job interview books I have read. . . . Your book is the *only* place I've ever read that said not to follow up an interview with any sort of follow-up letter or communication. Every other book that has broached this subject has recommended follow-up letters to interviews and even rejections, which I always thought was odd. I've followed the conventional practices of sending thank-you letters after interviews and rejections, but I've felt that they really didn't do anything to help me achieve the goal of securing the job. Sending thank-you letters just seems to add an unnecessary irritation to harried interviewers and most likely will leave a negative impression as being desperate or pushy, and I believe coming off desperate or pushy isn't the way to go. Even if you are desperate, you shouldn't make it obvious and portray yourself as such.

I want to commend you on having the courage to buck the trend and affirm (at least for me) that while being polite is good, you don't have to overdo it and grovel with needless thank-you letters. My last job interview was a telephone interview, and I didn't send a thank-you letter afterwards. Although I wasn't offered that particular job, the interviewer did tell me to contact her in a month's time to see if they have other employment offerings. I figure if you give a good interview, then they will have a good impression of you, and if they have a good impression of you, then there is no need for thank-you letters.

Finally, here's what Sandor Feldman has to say in *Mannerisms of Speech:*

> Like many others, the two beautiful words, "Thank you," are often misused. . . . It is my personal conviction that the ideal situation would be one in which nobody should need either to expect thanks from or to express thanks to anybody. The stronger person should give help to the weaker for the reason that he is in a position to give help.

My final word on this subject is the way *I* react to a thank-you letter. I've conducted thousands of interviews, both screening and selection. As you've probably gathered, I don't like to have to hire someone, so don't like interviewing people, and I know what I'm doing! Receiving a thank-you letter is a real turnoff for me. It engenders several emotions:

1. The first is pity. I feel sorry for the person writing the letter because I know how it feels to need a job and not have one.

2. The second is a negative judgment resulting from my feeling that the letter is fawning and hypocritical.

3. The third is irritation. Either I've made a decision on the person or I haven't. In either case, I don't want to have to read an unsolicited letter from someone I've just had to take my time to interview. I didn't ask for the person to contact me. If I had wanted her to, I would have asked her. I didn't. So I'm not pleased that this person took an initiative I didn't invite.

4. The fourth is frustration. What do I do? Do I answer it? If so, what do I say? Do I file it? Do I throw it away?

5. The fifth is that the letter (ergo the writer) is insincere. The interviewee isn't really writing a thank-you note because she's polite or considerate. No, the letter is written for purely selfish reasons: to get a job. It can therefore reek of insincerity to the reader.

Believe me, I'm not alone in these feelings. Most interviewers won't be this frank. Who wants to sound like Simon Legree and put down someone who took the time to write a "nice" letter? Not many. So the people who give the advice to write a thank-you letter, most of whom have never actually conducted a selection interview, are relying on asking other people how they react. And whom do they ask? Counselors and employment professionals! I've gone through some of these books and there is virtually no personal experience relayed by the writer. And the people they quote aren't selection interviewers, they're screeners or consultants.

It would be well for you to understand why I feel that the opinions of consultants and recruiters on the advisability of writing a thank-you note—and other advice quoted by writers on the interview—are not reliable. How do consultants arrive at their conclusions? Generally a job search consultant sends prospective employees to prospective employers. After the interview the consultant contacts the prospective employer to find out how the interview went.

While the employer might be forthcoming, always lurking in the back of their minds is the possibility of litigation or other kinds of trouble. So they are circumspect in what they say to the consultant. The interviewer can't be completely honest because what they say might get back to the person about whom they are speaking, resulting in problems. The result is a sanitized version of how they reacted to the interviewee.

When I am quoting selection interviewers they have no such fear. In the first place they are not talking about anybody specific, so there is no threat of trouble from anybody. Second, if they don't want to be quoted they can request anonymity. So they can speak to me with candor. I don't get my information about selection interviewers secondhand from consultants; I get it directly from the selection interviewer.

The only reason to write a thank-you letter is to thank someone for a kindness that they performed through no obligation on their part and for no ulterior motive. Someone gives you a birthday present. You should write a thank-you note. Someone takes you out for a meal. You should write a thank-you note. Someone recommended you for something. You should write a thank-you note. Someone interviewed you for a job? You should *not* write a thank-you note. The interviewer did not do you a kindness, and he was not without an ulterior motive. In fact, his only motive was selfish!

That said, you will always find exceptions to the rule. I'm not denying that there are instances when someone has received a job offer based in large part on a thank-you letter. I'm sure that there's an interviewer out there who will read this and say, "I hired Peggy Sue because she was nice enough to write and thank me for granting an interview." That has happened and it will continue to happen. What I'm trying to do is to tell you how I feel and how many others feel. It's my opinion, based on talking to a lot of people who know that I'm not going to sue them over what they say, that in the majority of cases writing a thank-you letter is more of a risk than a help. You're risking more than you might receive. But in the final analysis everyone has to make up his or her own mind. If you want to write a thank-you letter, if that's what makes you feel right, then go ahead and do it. I just want you to be aware of the negatives. If you read this and still want to write the letter, go ahead and good luck. But if you do, keep it short, just a few lines thanking your interviewer for the interview. Period. End of letter. Don't flatter or fawn or add anything of substance.

The Final Decision

You must make a decision. Do you want to accept a position if it's offered? Often, interviewees use a halo principle in accepting or rejecting an offer. Perhaps the classic story epitomizing this was told to me by an executive of a major corporation. She had been interviewing for an employee and found someone she liked and offered her the job. The lady rejected it because of the "left turns." The executive asked what she meant, and the interviewee replied that in order to get to work, she would have to make a left turn, and she didn't want any job where she'd have to make a left turn every day because she wasn't good at making left turns.

You should be able to make a decision based on more relevant arguments (or be able to perceive obvious solutions like three right turns in lieu of the one offending left turn). You can use the principles set forth in this chapter, but basically, it comes down to two factors. The first is whether or not the job offered meets your requirements, which you determined in chapter 2. If it does, or if it meets them with reasonable variations, consider the second factor: What is your pathos? What kind of "feeling" do you have about the job? Do you like the person for whom you will be working? If not, can you at least get along with the person for whom you will be working? How intense is your feeling? Is it dislike, or is it ambivalence? If it's ambivalence, then there shouldn't be a problem working for him, and maybe the ambivalence will change to respect, if not affection. But if your feeling is a dislike of the person, you would be starting out with two strikes against your chances for success.

In evaluating your feelings for your potential employer, you must be honest with yourself as to how well you did in the interview, and this points up the importance of going into the interview feeling that you are also the interviewer. If you were able to probe the areas of your interviewer's personality that could affect your on-the-job relationship, then you should have a fairly confident opinion of how you feel about him. If you did not conduct a good interview, just went along with no control or confidence, then you're taking a crapshoot on your feelings.

If the interview was less than conclusive, you still have several alternatives. You could reject the offer and not take the chance of a personality conflict. You could take the job and hope that when you get better acquainted, things will work out. Or you could ask for another interview with the person, at which time you could probe on a more personal level to test your feelings.

One point in favor of accepting the position is that the mere fact of being offered the job signifies that the interviewer looks upon you with strong positive feelings. This could be an indication that any ambivalent or negative feelings you have might not be accurate and that the job could work out quite well for you.

I'll leave you with two philosophical suggestions to help you in making your decision. First is Double Approach Avoidance. This says, basically, that when you approach a fork in the road, you must take one branch or the other. What you cannot do is turn back because you can't make a decision.

The second is called Vain Regret, which might also be known as second-guessing. As Satchell Paige, the famed baseball pitcher, said, "Don't look back. Something may be gaining on you." Once you make a decision, go forward and forget it.

Checklist

- The halo effect, the undue influence of an irrelevant trait on the interviewer's overall judgment, is probably the dominant factor in making a selection decision.
- Emotion is the most important factor in decisions made by emotional people.
- Don't write a thank-you note unless you understand the pitfalls.
- If you have two choices, choose one and then forget it.

APPENDIX A

Commonly Asked Questions

This appendix consists of three sections of questions commonly asked in the selection interview. The first section contains questions reported by 242 companies surveyed for *The Northwestern Lindquist-Endicott Report*, by Victor R. Lindquist, published by the Placement Center, Northwestern University, Evanston, Illinois. Even though the *Northwestern Lindquist-Endicott Report* is no longer published, I think it is such a classic work that it still provides a good broad spectrum of questions to enable you to prepare for your interviews, and you can't get access to it anywhere but here. The second section contains questions suggested by Walter R. Mahler in his book *How Effective Executives Interview*. Questions in this section are usually used when interviewing people who are already in the job market. This is another book that has been out of print for a long time. I include the questions Mahler suggests here because they are as good a list as you will find and now that the book is no longer available, this is the only place where you can read them. The third section sets forth additional questions that can pop up in an interview and for which an interviewee should be prepared.

You can expect to be asked some of the questions in this appendix in an interview. Some are unlawful. I suggest that you go through a mock interview and have these questions shot at you at random in any order chosen by your mock interviewer. These questions present starting points. You should encourage your mock interviewer to ask follow-up questions not on this list, to press you, to impose stress, and to ask more difficult questions, if they pop into the interviewer's head, because that's the way your selection interviewer will operate. With preparation such as this, it is less likely that you'll be caught unaware in an actual interview.

Section 1: Assessment Questions Asked by Professional Interviewers

1. What goals have you set for yourself? How are you planning to achieve them?
2. Who or what has had the greatest influence on the development of your career interests?
3. What factors did you consider in choosing your major?
4. Why are you interested in our organization?
5. Tell me about yourself.
6. What two or three things are most important to you in a position?
7. What kind of work do you want to do?
8. Tell me about a project you initiated.
9. What are your expectations of your future employer?
10. What is your GPA? How do you feel about it? Does it reflect your ability?
11. How do you solve conflicts?
12. Tell me about how you perceive your strengths. Your weaknesses. How do you evaluate yourself?

13. What work experience has been the most valuable to you and why?
14. What was the most useful criticism you ever received, and who was it from?
15. Give an example of a problem you have solved and the process you used.
16. Describe the project or situation that best demonstrated your analytical skills.
17. What has been your greatest challenge?
18. Describe a situation where you had a conflict with another individual, and how you dealt with it.
19. What were the biggest problems you have encountered in college? How have you handled them? What did you learn from them?
20. What are your team-player qualities? Give examples.
21. Describe your leadership style.
22. What interests or concerns you about the position or the company?
23. In a particular leadership role you had, what was the greatest challenge?
24. What idea have you developed and implemented that was particularly creative or innovative?
25. What characteristics do you think are important for this position?
26. How have your educational and work experiences prepared you for this position?
27. Take me through a project where you demonstrated _____ skills.
28. How do you think you have changed personally since you started college?
29. Tell me about a team project of which you are particularly proud and your contribution.
30. How do you motivate people?

31. Why did you choose the extracurricular activities you did? What did you gain? What did you contribute?

32. What types of situations put you under pressure, and how do you deal with the pressure?

33. Tell me about a difficult decision you have made.

34. Give an example of a situation in which you failed, and how you handled it.

35. Tell me about a situation when you had to persuade another person to your point of view.

36. What frustrates you the most?

37. Knowing what you know now about your college experience, would you make the same decisions?

38. What can you contribute to this company?

39. How would you react to having your credibility questioned?

40. What characteristics are most important in a good manager? How have you displayed one of these characteristics?

41. What challenges are you looking for in a position?

42. Are you willing to relocate or travel as part of your career?

43. What two or three accomplishments have given you the most satisfaction?

44. Describe a leadership role of yours and tell why you committed your time to it.

45. How are you conducting your job search, and how will you make your decision?

46. What is the most important lesson you have learned in or out of school?

47. Describe a situation where you had to work with someone who was difficult. How was the person difficult, and how did you handle it?

48. We are looking at a lot of great candidates; why are you the best person for this position?
49. How would your friends describe you? Your professors?
50. What else should I know about you?

These questions reflect a significant movement away from standard directive questions toward more open-ended situational queries. Common themes include applications of analytical, problem-solving, and decision-making skills, leadership development, creativity, teamwork, and personal development.

Section 2

1. Beginning with your move into your first supervisory job, would you tell me briefly why each change was made?
2. Referring to your most recent position, what would you say are some of your more important accomplishments? I'd be interested in operating results and any other accomplishments you consider important. (Probe four or five accomplishments. Get specific data.)
3. Considering these accomplishments, what are some of the reasons for your success?
4. Were there any unusual difficulties you had to overcome in getting these accomplishments?
5. What two or three things do you feel you have learned on this job?
6. What did you particularly like about the position?
7. There are always a few negatives about a position. What would you say you liked least about the position?
8. What responsibilities or results have not come up to your expectations? I'd be interested in things you had

hoped and planned to accomplish which were not done. I sometimes call them disappointments. (Push for several specific answers.)

9. What are some of the reasons for this?

10. I'm interested in how you do your planning. What planning processes have you found useful, and how do you go about them?

11. In what way do you feel you have improved in your planning in the last few years?

12. What are some examples of important types of decisions or recommendations you are called upon to make?

13. Would you describe how you went about making these types of decisions or recommendations? With whom did you talk, and so forth?

14. What decisions are easiest for you to make and which ones are more difficult?

15. Most of us can think of an important decision which we would make quite differently if we made it again. Any examples from your experience? Probe: What's the biggest mistake you can recall?

16. Most of us improve in our decision-making ability as we get greater experience. In what respects do you feel you have improved in your decision making?

17. What has been your experience with major expansion or reduction of force? (Explore for details.)

18. How many immediate subordinates have you selected in the past two years? How did you go about it? Any surprises or disappointments?

19. How many immediate subordinates have you removed from their jobs in the last few years? Any contemplated? One example of how you went about it.

20. How do you feel your subordinates would describe you as a delegator? Any deliberate tactics you use?

21. Some managers keep a very close check on their organization. Others use a loose rein. What pattern do you follow? How has it changed in the last few years?

22. What has been the most important surprise you have received from something getting out of control? Why did it happen?

23. Let's talk about standards of performance. How would you describe your own? What would your subordinates say? What would your boss say?

24. Sometimes it is necessary to issue an edict to an individual or the entire staff. Do you have any recent examples of edicts you have issued? Probe: Reasons? Results?

25. What things do you think contribute to your effectiveness as a supervisor?

26. From an opposite viewpoint, what do you think might interfere with your effectiveness as a supervisor?

27. In what respects do you feel you have improved most as a supervisor during the last few years?

28. What kind of supervisor gets the best performance out of you?

29. Some managers are quite deliberate about such things as communications, development, and motivation. Do you have any examples of how you do this?

30. What have you done about your own development in the last few years?

31. Would you describe your relationship with your last three supervisors?

32. Considering your relationships both inside and outside the component, would you give me an example of how you have been particularly effective in relating with others?

33. Would you also give me an example of how you might not have been particularly effective in relating with others?

34. Some people are short-fused and impatient in their reactions. How would you describe yourself?

35. Have you encountered any health problems? What do you do about your health?

36. Most of us can look back upon a new idea, a new project, or an innovation we feel proud introducing. Would you describe one or two such innovations you are particularly proud of?

37. How do you feel about your progress (career-wise) to date?

38. What are your aspirations for the future? Have these changed?

39. We sometimes compare the assets and limitations of our products with competition. Let's do a related thing with your career. Thinking of your competition for jobs to which you aspire, what would you say are your limitations? (Get three or more assets and three or more limitations.)

40. Are there any conditions of personal business, health, or family which would limit your flexibility for taking on a new assignment?

Section 3: General Questions

Remember that a question may be more complicated than it appears on the surface. Before you respond, therefore, it is always a good idea to try to determine why the interviewer asked a particular question and the reason he or she would be interested in your answer.

1. Tell me about yourself.

2. What was your favorite subject in school? Why?

3. What was your least favorite subject in school? Why?

4. What were your grades/class standing?
5. Why did you go to the school you attended?
6. How did you choose your major/course of study?
7. What extracurricular activities did you participate in at school?
8. Did you have a favorite teacher?
9. Why did you like this teacher better than anyone else?
10. What have you accomplished so far in life?
11. What have you done of which you're most proud? Why?
12. What's your best asset?
13. What's your biggest weakness?
14. Have you ever been arrested?
15. Have you ever been convicted of a crime?
16. How do you get along with people?
17. What are your outside interests/activities?
18. Do they interfere with your job?
19. Have you ever told a lie? Explain.
20. Why do you want to work for us?
21. How would you handle an irate/irrational customer?
22. What is a good (whatever job you're applying for, e.g., secretary)?
23. What's the most difficult task you've ever undertaken? How did it work out?
24. What can you do for us?
25. Why should we hire you?
26. What can I do for you?
27. Why do you feel you are qualified for this job?
28. Does your present employer know you're interviewing for another job?
29. Why do you want to change jobs?
30. Did you have any problems in any of your previous jobs?

31. What do you think you'll be doing in ten years?
32. What would you like to be doing in ten years?
33. What do you want to accomplish in life?
34. If money were not a consideration, what would you want to do?
35. Do you consider yourself a professional? Why or why not?
36. Who/what has been the greatest influence in your life? Why?
37. How do you get along with your parents?
38. Do you prefer one of your parents over the other? Why?
39. Have you ever been fired?
40. Do you drink alcoholic beverages?
41. Have you ever used drugs?
42. Will you submit to a drug/blood test?
43. Do you think there's any correlation between grades in school and success on the job?
44. Who paid for your education?
45. If you were starting over again right now, what would you do?
46. Do you have a boy/girlfriend? Do you live together?
47. What's your sexual orientation?
48. Are you married?
49. How old are you?
50. Are you in good health?
51. Is there anything that you haven't revealed, either in this interview or on your resumé, that would affect our decision?
52. Have you had any other interviews? With whom?
53. What did you do to prepare for this interview?
54. Have you ever been rejected? How did you react/handle it?

55. Have you ever been passed over for promotion? How did you react/handle it?
56. How much money are you making now?
57. How much money do you want?
58. How much money do you think you'll be making in five years?
59. What did your father do?
60. Is your private life happy? Why or why not?
61. Are you a happy person?
62. Are you satisfied?
63. What makes you angry?
64. What's your net worth?
65. What's your Social Security number?
66. How well do you take criticism?
67. Have you ever supervised anyone? Explain.
68. Do you like to travel?
69. Do you have a family?
70. Do you plan on having any (more) children?
71. How do you feel about (any controversial issue, like the death penalty)?
72. Do you read? What? How often?
73. What magazines do you read regularly?
74. What's the last book you read?
75. Do you watch a lot of television/go to movies?
76. What's your favorite movie/book/TV show? Why?
77. How do you keep in shape?
78. What salary do you want?
79. Why do you think you're worth that?
80. Would you be willing to work for less?
81. Is money the most important aspect of a job for you?
82. Do you require close supervision?
83. Have you always been treated fairly?
84. Give me three references I can talk to about you.

85. Please sign this release so we can talk to your references about you.
86. What's the most important thing you're looking for in a job/employer?
87. Do you like people?
88. Have you ever done anything you regret?
89. Describe your character.
90. Have you ever done anything of which you're ashamed?
91. Have you ever been reprimanded?
92. Do you work better alone or with people?
93. Do you think you are unique? How?
94. Tell me about your present job.
95. How do you spend most of your time in your present job?
96. How do you feel about your job/employer?
97. Where do you rank your present job with others you've held? Why?
98. Is there anything about your present job/employer you'd change or of which you are critical?
99. How many hours a day do you think a person should spend on the job?
100. Do you devote any time or money to charity work?
101. What do you feel is an acceptable attendance record?
102. Do you arrive on time?
103. What do you think about your present supervisor/employer?
104. What do you think are your present supervisor's strengths and weaknesses?
105. How does your present supervisor treat others in your department?
106. What are your goals?
107. What have you done that indicates you are qualified for this job?

108. How do you think you should be judged on the job?
109. Do you go to church/synagogue/temple/mosque?
110. Are you tolerant of different people/opinions?
111. How long would you plan to work for us?
112. Do you like to travel?
113. Is there any section of the country in which you'd prefer to live/work? Why?
114. Have you always done your best?
115. Are you an overachiever or an underachiever? Explain.
116. Do you have any questions?

APPENDIX B

Why People Are Not Hired

Listed here are thirty-nine reasons interviewers give for not offering jobs to applicants. Notice that only one (number 25) has to do with technical ability.

1. Poor personal appearance
2. Overbearing know-it-all
3. Inability to express self clearly; poor voice, diction, grammar
4. Lack of planning for career; no purpose or goal
5. Lack of confidence and poise
6. Lack of interest and enthusiasm
7. Poor references, written or oral
8. Overemphasis on money
9. Poor scholastic record; just got by
10. Expects too much too soon
11. Makes excuses, evasive, hedges on unfavorable factors in background
12. Lack of tact
13. Lack of maturity
14. Lack of courtesy

15. Condemnation of past employers
16. Lack of social understanding
17. Lack of vitality
18. Fails to make eye contact
19. Limp, "fishy" handshake
20. Indecision
21. Sloppy application/resumé preparation
22. Merely shopping around
23. Only wants job for a short time
24. Little sense of humor
25. Lack of skills or experience for this position
26. No interest in company or industry
27. Excessive emphasis on who he/she knows
28. Unwillingness to relocate
29. Cynical
30. Low moral standards
31. Lazy
32. Intolerant, with strong prejudices
33. Narrow interests
34. Poor handling of personal finances
35. Inability to take criticism
36. Radical ideas
37. Late to interview without good reason
38. Asks no questions about job
39. Indefinite responses to questions

Questions Asked by Interviewers When They Check Your References

An interviewee should be aware that a reference check may be made at some time during the interview process. These are some of the questions that may be asked. Numbers 8 and 9 are catch-alls. They can elicit responses relating to the candidate's moral character or other sensitive areas that an interviewer may not wish to query specifically. Number 10 is a method to get references from people not suggested by the interviewee. Interviewers recognize that an interviewee is not going to suggest as a reference one who will not give a good one. Therefore, by having the reference name some other references, the interviewer is getting a more objective source—one who has not been preconditioned by the interviewee.

1. How long did the applicant work for you?
2. What was the quality of the work?
3. How much responsibility did the applicant have?

4. How did the applicant get along with people?
5. Did the applicant require close supervision?
6. Was the applicant prompt?
7. Why did the applicant leave your company?
8. Do you know of anything that would disqualify the applicant for the job we're considering hiring the applicant for?
9. Can you think of anything I should know about the applicant that I haven't asked about?
10. Do you know anyone else to whom I could speak about the applicant?

APPENDIX D

Questions to Ask the Interviewer

This appendix contains a list of questions suggested by William R. Nolan, founding director of the Institute for Executive Career Management in Toronto, Canada. Some of these questions will only be appropriate at later stages of the interview process and, if asked too soon, could be offensive to the interviewer. But you should review them prior to your first questions to ask if you are asked if you have any, a thorough review of them could help clarify your personal feelings about what you want in a job.

One caveat: In asking a question you should know why you want the answer. If you ask a question merely for the sake of asking the question and have no reason for wanting the knowledge, you risk looking foolish. A smart interviewer will spot an idle question right away. For instance, if you ask, "How long has present management been in control?" the interviewer might ask you why you want to know that and what possible difference that makes to whether or not you take the job. If you don't have a good reason, you will be in a very difficult position, and the pain you feel will be you kicking yourself for having asked the question. So for each question you ask, be sure you have a reason for asking in case you're challenged.

Job Specifications

1. What are the duties and responsibilities for this position?
2. How can the job be altered and upgraded?

Job History

1. How long has the position been in existence?
2. How long has the position been open?
3. Who had the job until now?
4. Did he or she succeed or fail?
5. What led to the success or failure?
6. How many preceded?
7. What happened to them? Why?

Personnel

1. Who are the people—immediate superior, subordinates, associates in related departments—with whom I will be working?
2. What are their titles, history with the company, background, education, etc.?
3. Any helpful suggestions?

The Organization

1. Where does this position fit into the company's organization plan?
2. What are the reporting channels?
3. To whom will I be accountable (more than one boss?)?

Orientation Training

1. Does the company have an orientation program for new employees?

2. How do I become familiar with company policies, practice, and etiquette?
3. Does the company have an executive development program?
4. Other training programs?
5. What are its facilities?
6. What resources does it utilize?
7. Does the company sponsor courses at universities? At management associations or industry conferences?
8. Are suggestions welcomed?

The Company

1. How long has the company been in existence?
2. Who owns it? Family-dominated?
3. How long has its present management been in control?
4. What is its management/operating style?
5. What has been its gross sales and profit (or loss) pattern during the past ten years? Five years? Two years? Now?
6. Does the company have a growth plan?
7. (See annual report.) What do the company's annual report and the Dunn & Bradstreet report show about its credit rating and financial history?
8. If the company is public, what do recent stockbroker's reports say about its management and its prospects? How does the company rate in the industry? What is the economic trend of the industry?

The Community

1. Where can I get information on housing, cost of living, religious and social organizations, shopping, schools, libraries, educational and recreational facilities, etc.?
2. Does the company dominate the community? Social life?

Compensation, Advancement

1. Does the company offer stock options or deferred payment plans? Bonus arrangements?
2. What is the executive package at top levels?
3. Does the company reimburse moving expenses? Losses incurred in selling one's house? Living and travel expenses while employee is commuting and finding permanent housing for his/her family?
4. Does the company arrange employment contacts?
5. What is the company's policy regarding vacation and sick leave?
6. What is the company's policy regarding international tax matters?
7. Is tax and legal advice available where "international" payments are involved?
8. When and how is the salary usually paid?
9. What is the company's policy regarding agency fees?
10. Does the company have a periodic employee appraisal or performance review?
11. What are the prospects for salary increase? Promotions?
12. Will there be opportunities for greater responsibility and broader experience?

APPENDIX E

Self-Discovery Exercises

Exercise 1: Talents

Write down what you believe your best talents are, what you like to do most, what you like to do least, and what you would most like to do (your dream job). Be honest with your assessment—concentrate on you, not what you had to do at your last job. Do not read ahead. You will get more out of the exercises by taking them in sequence.

Talents are things that you do best. They are usually not skills, which are learned; they are characteristics (e.g., I work well with people, I can sing, etc.) that define you and what you can do best. When you are finished, review the list. Make sure you were honest before moving to the next exercise.

My talents are:

_____

_____

_____

_____

_____

I most like to do:

_____

_____

_____

_____

_____

I like least to do:

_____

_____

_____

_____

_____

My dream is:

_____

_____

_____

_____

_____

Exercise 2: Work Values

This exercise contains a list of work values. Please read all work values carefully before beginning the exercise. Use a pencil so you can make changes. Beside each work value description, place the number that best describes how important you feel the value is in your life. Choose one of the following numbers:

1 = Very important
2 = Somewhat important
3 = Not very important
4 = Not important at all

RANK

_____ Help society: do something to contribute to the betterment of the world.

_____ Help others: be involved in helping other people in a direct way, either individually or in small groups.

_____ Public contact: have a lot of day-to-day contact with people.

_____ Work with others: have close working relationships with a group; work as a team toward common goals.

_____ Affiliation: be recognized as a member of a particular organization.

_____ Friendships: develop close personal relationships with people as a result of my work activities.

_____ Competition: engage in activities that pit my abilities against others' where there are clear win-and-lose outcomes.

_____ Make decisions: have the power to decide courses of action, policies.

_____ Work under pressure: work in situations where time pressure is prevalent or the quality of my work is judged critically by supervisors, customers, or others.

_____ Power and authority: control or partially control the work activities and destinies of other people.

_____ Influence people: be in a position to change attitudes or opinions of other people.

_____ Work alone: do projects by myself without any significant amount of contact with others.

_____ Knowledge: engage myself in the pursuit of knowledge, truth, and understanding.

_____ Intellectual status: be regarded as a person of high intellectual prowess or as one who is an acknowledged "expert" in a given field.

_____ Artistic creativity: engage in creative work in any of several art forms.

_____ Creativity (general): create new ideas, programs, organizational structures, or anything else not following a format previously developed by others.

_____ Aesthetics: be involved in studying or appreciating the beauty of things, ideas.

_____ Supervision: have a job in which I am directly responsible for the work done by others.

_____ Change and variety: have work responsibilities that frequently change in their content, setting, or responsibilities.

_____ Precision work: work in situations where there is little tolerance for error.

_____ Stability: have a work routine and job duties that are largely predictable and not likely to change over time.

_____ Security: be assured of keeping my job and maintain a reasonable financial reward.

_____ Fast pace: work in circumstances where there is a high pace of activity and work must be done rapidly.

_____ Recognition: be recognized for the quality of my work in some visible or public way.

_____ Excitement: experience a high degree of (or frequent) excitement in the course of my work.

_____ Adventure: have work duties that involve frequent risk-taking.

_____ Profit, gain: have a strong likelihood of accumulating large amounts of money or other material gain.

_____ Independence: be able to determine the nature of my work without significant direction from others; not have to do as I'm told.

_____ Moral fulfillment: feel that my work contributes to a set of moral standards that I feel are very important.

_____ Location: find a place to live (town, geographical area) that is conducive to my lifestyle and affords me the opportunity to do the things I enjoy.

_____ Community: live in a place where I can get involved in the community.

_____ Physical challenge: have a job that makes physical demands that I would find rewarding.

_____ Time freedom: have work responsibilities that I can perform according to my own time schedule; no specific working hours.

_____ Travel 0–10%: have minimal need to travel away overnight.

_____ Travel 50–100%: willing to travel often.

MY FIVE MOST IMPORTANT WORK VALUES

From the work values you have given a 1, choose the five most important. List these below in order of importance, with the most important value first. Surprised? These are the work values you consider most important in your life.

1. _____

2. _____

3. _____

4. _____

5. _____

Exercise 3: Skills List

Using the number and letter values, rank your skills by two factors: first, how much you enjoy utilizing the skill; and second, how proficient you are in that skill.

1 = Totally delight in using   A = Highly proficient
2 = Enjoy using very much   B = Competent
3 = Like using   C = Little or no skill
4 = Prefer not to use
5 = Strongly dislike using

1–5   A,B,C

_____ _____ Academic: read, study, and understand instructions, and underlying principles; use knowledge meaningfully and apply it to other principles to create ideas.

_____ _____ Act as liaison: represent, serve as a link between individuals or groups.

_____ _____ Analyze: break down, figure out problems logically.

_____ _____ Artistic: draw, sketch, paint; recognize similarities in colors or contrasting shapes; perceive forms, pictorial detail, shapes; decorate and coordinate fashions.

_____ _____ Budget: economize, save, stretch money or other resources.

_____ _____ Classify: group, categorize, systematize data, people, or things.

_____ _____ Compose music: write and arrange music for voice or instruments.

_____ _____ Counsel: facilitate insight and personal growth; guide, advise, coach students, employees, or clients.

_____ _____ Count: tally, calculate, compute quantities.

_____ _____ Deal with feelings: draw out, listen, accept, empathize, express sensitivity, defuse anger, calm down, inject humor, and appreciate.

_____ _____ Design: structure new or innovative practices, programs, products, or environments.

_____ _____ Entertain, perform: amuse, sing, dance, act, play music for, give a demonstration to, speak to an audience.

_____ _____ Estimate: appraise value or cost.

_____ _____ Evaluate: assess, review, critique feasibility or quality.

_____ _____ Expedite: speed up production or services, troubleshoot problems, streamline procedures.

_____ _____ Generate ideas: reflect upon, conceive of, dream up, brainstorm ideas.

_____ _____ Host/Hostess: make welcome; put at ease; provide comfort and pleasure; serve visitors, guests, or customers.

_____ _____ Implement: provide detailed follow-through of policies and plans.

_____ _____ Initiate change: exert influence on changing the status quo; exercise leadership in bringing about new directions.

_____ _____ Interview for information: draw out subjects through incisive questioning to elicit information.

_____ _____ Maintain records: keep accurate and up-to-date records; log, record, itemize, collate, tabulate data.

_____ _____ Make arrangements: coordinate events; handle logistics.

_____ _____ Make decisions: make major, complex, or frequent decisions.

_____ _____ Manual dexterity: work with one's hands, machines, or tools with speed and accuracy in arm/hand/eye movement, and operate machinery skillfully.

_____ _____ Mechanical: assemble, repair, and maintain machinery and appliances.

_____ _____ Mediate: manage and resolve conflict.

_____ _____ Monitor: keep track of the movement of data or frequent decisions.

_____ _____ Motivate: recruit involvement, mobilize energy, stimulate peak performance.

_____ _____ Negotiate: bargain for rights or business advantages.

_____ _____ Numerical: comprehend, compute, and analyze mathematical operations with accuracy.

_____ _____ Observe: study, scrutinize, examine data, people, or things scientifically.

_____ _____ Perceive: intuitively sense, show insight and foresight.

_____ _____ Plan, organize: define goals and objectives, schedule and develop projects or programs.

_____ _____ Plant, cultivate: grow food, flowers, trees, or lawns, prepare soil, plant, water, fertilize, weed, harvest, trim, prune, mow.

_____ _____ Portray images: sketch, draw, illustrate, paint, photograph.

_____ _____ Prepare food: wash, cut, blend, bake, and arrange for nutrition, taste, and aesthetics.

_____ _____ Produce skilled crafts: shape, weave, attach, etch, or carve ornamental gift or display items.

_____ _____ Proofread, edit: check writings for proper usage and stylistic flair; make improvements.

_____ _____ Read for information: research written resources efficiently and exhaustively.

_____ _____ Sell: promote a person, company, goods, or services; convince of merits; raise money.

_____ _____ Spatial reasoning: understand forms of space and visualize the relationships of space and objects in two and three dimensions.

_____ _____ Stage shows: produce theatrical, art, fashion, or trade shows and other events for public performance or display.

_____ _____ Supervise: oversee, direct the work of others.

_____ _____ Synthesize: integrate ideas and information; combine diverse elements into a coherent whole.

_____ _____ Teach, train: inform, explain, give instruction to students, employees, or customers.

_____ _____ Tend animals: feed, shelter, breed, train, or show domestic pets, farm animals, or ranch animals.

_____ _____ Test: measure proficiency, quality, or validity; check and double-check.

_____ _____ Transport: drive, lift, carry, or haul.

_____ _____ Treat, nurse: heal, cure patients or clients.

_____ _____ Use carpentry abilities: construct, maintain, or restore buildings, fittings, or furnishings.

_____ _____ Use physical coordination and agility: walk, run, climb, jump, balance, aim, throw, catch, or hit.

_____ _____ Visualize: imagine possibilities; see in mind's eye.

_____ _____ Write: compose reports, letters, articles, ads, stories, or educational materials.

ANALYZING YOUR RESULTS

You have just completed an exhaustive analysis of your primary values, your skills, and how much you enjoy using them. This may be the first time you have been through such an analysis, so what have you discovered about yourself?

Take the information from your Skills List and enter it in the appropriate boxes on the Self-Discovery Motivated Skills Matrix. If you find that you have a lot of skills in any one box, prioritize them to establish what your top five skills are.

The job that you don't want to have will require skills that show up in the C4 and C5 area. The job that you do want to have will require the skills that show up in the A1 or A2 area. Your challenge is to seek out the type of job that requires these skills.

Remember! The objective of the exercise is to find out what *you* want. You may have discovered that you like performing, want to use physical coordination, and want excitement. Maybe you would rather be a trapeze artist than a bookkeeper!!

Self-Discovery Motivated Skills Matrix

	A Highly proficient	B Competent	C Little or no skill
1 Totally delight in using			

	A Highly proficient	B Competent	C Little or no skill
2 Enjoy using very much	_____ _____ _____ _____ _____	_____ _____ _____ _____ _____	_____ _____ _____ _____ _____
3 Like using	_____ _____ _____ _____ _____	_____ _____ _____ _____ _____	_____ _____ _____ _____ _____
4 Prefer not to use	_____ _____ _____ _____ _____	_____ _____ _____ _____ _____	_____ _____ _____ _____ _____

A Highly proficient	B Competent	C Little or no skill

5 Strongly dislike using	_____	_____	_____
	_____	_____	_____
	_____	_____	_____
	_____	_____	_____
	_____	_____	_____

Bibliography

Alvarez, Walter C. *Nervousness & Indigestion*. 3rd ed. Collier Books, 1967.

Ambrose, Stephen E. *The Supreme Commander*. Doubleday & Co., 1970.

Andrews, Colman. *Los Angeles Times*, July 19, 1987, "The waiting game may be only a state of mind."

Aristotle. *Rhetoric* (translated by W. Rhys Roberts).

Armstrong, Howard. *High Impact Telephone Networking for Job Hunters*. Bob Adams, Inc. Publishers, 1992.

Atkins, Dr. Robert. *Dr. Atkins' New Diet Revolution*. Avon Books, 1992.

Bach, George R., & Deutsch, Ronald M. *Pairing*. Avon Books, 1971.

Baker, Carlos. *Ernest Hemingway: A Life Story*. Charles Scribner's Sons, 1969.

Baldridge, Letitia. *The Amy Vanderbilt Complete Book of Etiquette*. Doubleday & Co., 1978.

Bellows, Roger M. *Employment Psychology: The Interview*. Rinehart & Company, 1954.

Bernstein, Harry. *Los Angeles Times*, December 25, 1990, "Performance Tests vs Drug Tests."

423

Brooks, John. "The Fate of the Edsel." In *Great Business Disasters*, edited by Isadora Barmash. Ballantine Books, 1973.

California Lawyer, April 1982, "All About Sleep."

Capra, Frank. *The Name Above the Title*. Macmillan, 1971.

Carnegie, Dale. *How to Win Friends and Influence People*. Simon & Schuster, 1936.

Confucius. *The Analects* (translated by Arthur Waley). Alfred A. Knopf, 2000.

Davies, Hunter. *The Beatles*. Dell, 1968.

Fast, Julius. *Body Language*. Pocket Books, 1971.

Feldman, Sandor S. *Mannerisms of Speech and Gestures in Every Day Life*. International Universities Press, 1959.

Fenlason, Anne F. *Essentials in Interviewing*. Harper & Bros., 1952.

Fraser, John Munro. *A Handbook of Employment Interviewing*. 3rd ed. Macdonald & Evans, 1954.

———. *Employment Interviewing*. 4th ed. Macdonald & Evans, 1966.

Freeman, Michael. *ESPN: The Uncensored History*. The Rowman & Littlefield Publishing Group, 2000.

Gallwey, W. Timothy. *The Inner Game*. Random House, 1974.

Glaser, Connie Brown, and Smalley, Barbara Steinberg. *More Power to You*. Warner Books, 1992.

Goldman, William. *Adventures in the Screen Trade*. Warner Books, 1983.

Griffith, Thomas. "Newswatch." *Time*. November 8, 1976.

Halberstam, David. *The Best and the Brightest*. Random House, 1969.

Harriman, W. Averell, and Abel, Ellie. *Special Envoy to Churchill & Stalin*. Random House, 1975.

Hepburn, Katherine. *Me: Stories of My Life*. Alfred A. Knopf, 1991.

Honig, Donald H. *Baseball: When the Grass Was Real*. Coward, McCann & Geaghegan, 1975.

Ivey, Paul W. *Successful Salesmanship*. 6th ed. Prentice-Hall, 1942.

Jameson, Robert. *The Professional Job Changing System*. 4th ed., rev. Performance Dynamics, 1976.

Jones, A., and Crandall, R. "Validation of a short index of self-actualization." *Personality and Social Psychology Bulletin* 12 (1986), 63–73.

Lay, Beirne, Jr. *Someone Has to Make It Happen.* Prentice-Hall, 1969.

Lindquist, Victor R. *Northwestern Lindquist-Endicott Report.* The Placement Center, Northwestern University.

Lopez, Felix M., Jr. *Personnel Interviewing Theory and Practice.* McGraw-Hill Book Company, 1965.

Los Angeles Magazine, December, 1986, "Insider."

Los Angeles Times Careerbuilder, "Interview Tips," November 28, 2004.

Lundgren, Hal. "Injury Effects Still Plague Greene," *The Sporting News.* November 13, 1976.

Mahler, Walter R. *How Effective Executives Interview.* Dow-Jones-Irwin, 1976.

Maltz, Maxwell. *Psycho-Cybernetics.* Pocket Books, 1966.

Martin, Judith. *Miss Manners' Guide to Excruciatingly Correct Behavior.* Atheneum, 1982.

Maslow, Abraham H. *Motivation and Personality.* New York, Harper, 1954.

McMartin, Jim. *Personality Psychology.* Sage Publications, 1995.

McQuaid, Peter. "Job Security," *Los Angeles Times Magazine,* September 12, 2004.

Medley, H. Anthony. *UCLA Basketball: The Real Story.* Galant Press, 1972.

Nierenberg, Gerard I. *The Art of Negotiating.* Pocket Books, 1984.

Nixon, H. K. *Principles of Selling.* McGraw-Hill Co., 1931.

Oldfield, R. C. *The Psychology of the Interview.* 4th ed. Methuen & Co., 1951.

Peale, Norman Vincent. *The Power of Positive Thinking.* Prentice-Hall, 1952.

Pogue, Forrest C. *George C. Marshall: Ordeal and Hope.* Viking Press, 1966.

Rancho News, February 14, 1991, "Salaries for Office Help Low."

Rapaport, Ron. "A Man Has to Fear What's Down the Road." *Los Angeles Times*. November 2, 1976.

Rahula, Walpola. *What the Buddha Taught*. Grove Press, 1959.

Rickenbacker, Edward V. *Rickenbacker*. Prentice-Hall, 1967.

Schuller, Robert H. *Move Ahead with Possibility Thinking*. Fleming H. Revell, 1975.

Shawe and Rosenthal. *Employment Law Deskbook*. Matthew Bender, 1991.

Shirer, William L. *20th Century Journey*. Simon & Schuster, 1977.

Smith, Sam. *The Jordan Rules*. Simon & Schuster, 1992.

Somers, Suzanne. *Suzanne Somers' Get Skinny on Fabulous Food*. Three Rivers Press, 1999.

Sorensen, Theodore C. *Kennedy*. Harper & Row, 1965.

Sun Tzu. *The Art of War*. Oxford University Press, 1963.

Thomas, Bob. *Thalberg*. Doubleday, 1969.

Time magazine, May 9, 1983, "Embellishment Yes, Lying No."

Turnbull, Andrew (editor). *The Letters of F. Scott Fitzgerald*. Charles Scribner's Sons, 1963.

Walters, Barbara. *How to Talk with Practically Anybody about Practically Anything*. Doubleday, 1970.

Weinland, James D., and Gross, Margaret V. *Personnel Interviewing*. Ronald Press Company, 1952.

Woolf, Bob. *Friendly Persuasion*. G. P. Putnam's Sons, 1990.

Zunin, Leonard, with Zunin, Natalie. *Contact—The First Four Minutes*. Nash Publishing Company, 1972.

Index

A

ABC, 201
acceptance:
   decisions and, 386–87
   preparation and, 45–46
activities, questions on, 330, 332
Adler, Felix, 303
Adventures in the Screen Trade
   (Goldman), 18–19
advice, confidence and, 218–19, 247
African Americans, 89–90, 264–66,
   275
aftershaves, 254
age:
   discrimination and, 182, 184,
     339–42, 368
   honesty and, 182, 184
   questions on, 326, 332–33, 335,
     339–42, 349, 371
agreeing, assumptions and, 156–57
AIDS, 360, 365
Ailes, Roger, 112
Albeck, Stan, 248–49
alcohol, 261, 263

assumptions and, 162
energy and, 232
questions and, 398
sleep and, 225–26
stress management and, 243
tests for, 360–62
Alibrandi, Joseph F., 72–73,
223–24
Allen, Fred, 310
Allen, Tim, 42
Ally McBeal, 256
Alvarez, Walter, 225
ambiguity:
   and mannerisms of speech, 201
   questions and, 117–18, 149
American Arbitration Association,
   355
Americans with Disabilities Act
   (ADA), 362, 365
AmeriMed, 137
"am I right?," 202
Amy Vanderbilt's Everday Etiquette
   (Vanderbilt), 162
". . . and, uh . . . ," 208
Andrews, Colman, 129–30

About the Author

H. Anthony Medley invented, developed, and pioneered the videotape interview, conducting and videotaping thousands of interviews at major law schools nationwide for law firms around the country. As an attorney and businessman he conducted countless selection interviews to hire employees and retain consultants.

He is an attorney, businessman, and writer who received his B.S. in business from UCLA, where he was sports editor of the *UCLA Daily Bruin*, and received his J.D. from the University of Virginia School of Law. His other books include *UCLA Basketball: The Real Story* (1972) and *The Complete Idiot's Guide to Bridge* (Alpha Books, 1997, 2004). His articles have been published in numerous newspapers and magazines, such as the *Hollywood Reporter*, *Los Angeles Magazine*, *Good Housekeeping*, among others. He is a film critic accredited by the Motion Picture Association of America, and his cri-

tiques appear in several newspapers and on the Internet on the Movie Review Query Engine (www.mrqe.com) and Rotten Tomatoes (www.rottentomatoes.com).

As an attorney, he was a member of the Litton Industries law department and negotiated and signed the largest contract the United States Navy had ever signed up to that time, the $2 billion contract for the design and construction of the Spruance Class destroyer. In private practice he represented major corporations. Among many varied and interesting transactions with which he was involved, he negotiated the last agreement Aristotle Onassis entered into before his death, for the design and construction of a 100,000 barrel a day oil refinery in Canada. As a businessman, he owned and operated agricultural businesses that produced oranges, lemons, avocadoes, grapefruit, and field crops, and developed and managed residential and commercial real estate.